The New Technological Condition

Architecture and Design in the Age of Cybernetics

T0335316

Georg Vrachliotis

The New Technological Condition

Architecture and Design in the Age of Cybernetics

Birkhäuser
Basel

Georg Vrachliotis
Professor for Theory of Architecture and Digital Culture
Faculty of Architecture and the Built Environment
TU Delft

Acquisitions Editor: David Marold, Birkhäuser Verlag, A-Vienna
Content & Production Editor: Bettina R. Algieri, Birkhäuser Verlag, A-Vienna
Translation from German into English: Alisa Kotmair, D-Berlin
Cover design: Floyd Schulze
Layout: Ekke Wolf, A-Vienna
Typography: Sven Schrape, D-Berlin
Printing: Beltz Grafische Betriebe GmbH, D-Bad Langensalza
Paper: Werkdruck 90 g/m²
Typeface: Adobe Caslon Pro, Univers

The author has made every effort to clarify all image rights. In the event of any omissions,
we ask for your understanding and request that you notify the publisher.

Library of Congress Control Number: 2021949124

Bibliographic information published by the German National Library
The German National Library lists this publication in the Deutsche Nationalbibliografie;
detailed bibliographic data are available on the Internet at http://dnb.dnb.de.

ISBN 978-3-0356-2477-9
e-ISBN (PDF) 978-3-0356-2481-6
German edition: ISBN 978-3-0356-1561-6

© 2022 Birkhäuser Verlag GmbH, Basel
P.O. Box 44, 4009 Basel, Switzerland
Part of Walter de Gruyter GmbH, Berlin/Boston

9 8 7 6 5 4 3 2 1   www.birkhauser.com

Contents

Preface to the English Edition (2022)

Books sometimes have a long way to go before seeing the light of day. Such is the case with this one. Originally written between 2006 and 2009 at the Department of Architecture at ETH Zurich, it was first published by Springer Verlag New York/Vienna (2011), then included in a second and slightly revised version in the venerable Bauwelt Fundamente series (2020). The fact that this book is now finally available in an English translation is due to the encouragement and infinite patience of the editors at Birkhäuser Verlag, David Marold and Bettina R. Algieri, and the support of Dick van Gameren, Dean of the Faculty for Architecture and the Built Environment at TU Delft. Alisa Kotmair has provided an excellent translation, for which I thank her as well.

What started out as a project on "digital unrest" has grown into a long-term, ongoing examination of the role of design and architecture in a globally operating data society, from the mid-20th century to the present day. Since the publication of the first edition of my book, a number of seminal books and exhibitions on the architectural history of digital culture have been published, of which I can only mention a few here: Orit Halper's *Beautiful Data* (2014), Peter Weibel's exhibition *Infosphere* at ZKM (2015), Benjamin Bratton's *The Stack* (2016), Molly Steenson's *Architectural Intelligence: How Designers and Architects Created the Digital Landscape* (2017), Roberto Bottazzi's *Digital Architecture Beyond Computers: Fragments of a Cultural History of Computational Design* (2018), Theodora Vardouli and Olga Touloumi's *Computer Architectures: Constructing the Common Ground* (2020), and Teresa Fankhänel and Andres Lepik's catalogue for the exhibition *The Architecture Machine* (2020) at the Architecture Museum of the TU Munich.

Over the past 15 years, I have been able to develop, correct, and repeatedly test individual theses from this book in lectures, colloquia, and personal discussions. A long list of wonderful friends and colleagues have proven to be patient and inspiring interlocutors, whom I would like to thank here in alphabetical order: Elisabeth Walther-Bense (1922–2018), Roberto Bottazzi, Mario Carpo, Beatriz Colomina, Clemens Finkelstein, Yona Friedman (1923–2020), Sokratis Georgiadis, Andrea Gleiniger, Fabio Gramazio, Gabriele Gramelsberger, Michael Hagner, Dirk van der Heuvel, Nikolaus Hirsch, Ludger Hovestadt, Erich Hörl, Kees Kaan, Alexandre Kapellos, Evangelos Kotsioris, Nikolaus Kuhnert, Armin Linke, Joaquin Medina-Warmburg, Anna-Maria Meister, Achim Menges, Frieder Nake, Anh-Linh Ngo, Tobias Nolte, Eeva-Liisa Pelkonen, Monika Platzert, Bart-Jan Pohlman, Dennis Pohl, Margit Rosen, Fabian Scheurer, Laurent Stalder, Peter Weibel, Jan Wenzel, Mark Wigley, Andrew Witt. I would also like to thank Susan von Salis of the Harvard Art Museum Archive, Albert Müller of the Institute of Contemporary History in Vienna, and Tanja Morgenstern of the Archives of the Academy of Arts in Berlin.

The architectural history of digitization has long since grown into a broad and vibrant field of research. The sight of black-and-white photos of computers has given way to the challenge of coming to terms with the enormous potential but also the impacts of artificial intelligence in society, which cannot yet be properly assessed. It may come as a surprise, but I still draw on various aspects of this work to anchor current developments of our increasingly data-based society in history. Several lectures in recent years have provided me with valuable opportunities to do so, in particular the symposium of the Princeton-Mellon Initiative in Architecture, Urbanism, and the Humanities and the Program in Latin American Studies at Princeton University (2017); the Program in Media and Modernity of the

School of Architecture at Princeton University (2018); the B-Pro program of the Bartlett School of Architecture (2018); the international Datatopia Summer School in cooperation with ARCH+ and projekt bauhaus (2018); the Datapolis design studio of the Complex Projects group at TU Delft; the symposium *Algorithmic Controversies: Dialogues Towards an Unveiling of Architectural Agency*, organized by the AA PhD program (2021); and the Jaap Bakema Study Centre at Het Nieuwe Instituut in Rotterdam, with whose team I had the pleasure of organizing the two symposia *Re-Positioning Architecture in the Digital* (2020) and *Building Data: Architecture, Memory and New Imaginaries* (2022).

Rotterdam, May 2022

Introduction

"Introductory Remarks on Cybernetics for Future Architects and Urbanists" was the title of a lecture given in 1973 at the Architecture Department of the Swiss Federal Institute of Technology Zurich (ETH).[1] It would be one of the last attempts to make cybernetics appealing to aspiring architects—like then students Jacques Herzog and Pierre de Meuron—as a "general, formal science of the structure, relations, and behavior of dynamic systems."[2] However, some two decades after its rapid rise, there was barely a sign of the enthusiasm with which cybernetics had once been embraced in architecture. The mid-1970s saw a fundamental reversal in its nearly 25-year-old history. Gone was the time when architects dreamed aloud of automated design processes, intelligent calculating machines, the design of space capsules, thoughtful technology, technical developments, and a more humane world after the Second World War. The spirit of optimism that cybernetics sparked for many architects at the start of the 1960s had waned. The intellectual glamor of computer graphic experimentation and philosophizing about information, communication, and complexity had faded. In the architectural journals, where the wind of progress and future had been swirling around cybernetics just a few years earlier, one searches in vain for its traces after 1975. The academic debates about how to harness thinking in terms of control loops and communication structures as a scientific design and planning method in architectural education also fell silent. In the mid-1950s, the architecture world welcomed cybernetics with euphoria and transformed it into something productive—until it visibly lost its influence just a short time later and completely disappeared from view after barely two decades. Nevertheless, as the architectural historian Antoine Picon recently put it—thus underscoring the relevance of a reappraisal of this period for architectural history—our world today is "the inheritor of the universe that cybernetics and electronic art were opening up in the 1950s and 1960s. However, who would have predicted that digital life would become so close to the individual skin and experience?"[3] Today, inquiries regarding this short-lived chapter in the history of architecture are often met with murmured responses (if the antiquated term "cybernetics" rings a bell at all) about fantasies of control, faith in science, and technological utopias. Given the seemingly unimpeded penetration of information technology into every conceivable area of everyday life, Picon's image of digitalization almost getting under the skin may well be accurate. That Picon looks back into the mirror of architectural history onto a metaphorical heritage reflects the topicality of cybernetics as a historical object of investigation.

Cybernetics, like a once banished and now rediscovered specter of the postwar period, has long since been a subject of investigation in the histories of art, media, and science—but in terms of architectural history, it seems to have been utterly overlooked.[4] But it was not only artists who were fascinated by cybernetics and information theory—such as Nicolas Schöffer, who worked on adaptive kinetic sculptures, or Frieder Nake, whose generative computer drawings laid the foundation for contemporary media art. As this book aims to show, it was especially architects who explored the wealth of design possibilities that cybernetics and information theory could offer society in the future. Among these architects were Nicholas Negroponte and Yona Friedman, whose ideas about the habitability of the cybernetic universe sketched the first contours of today's so-called digital life.

The Intellectual Rigor of Cybernetic Thinking

In the mid-20th century, architecture underwent "the communication age's first wave of demythologization, which unfolded under the auspices of an exact knowledge of information."[5] From the beginning, the question of the usability of cybernetic concepts for architectural practice was therefore linked to the question of the architect's cultural role in a society that was becoming increasingly enmeshed with communication structures and networks. Architects were confronted with technical systems, procedures, and processes in a new operational realm of possibility. Architectural journals printed photographs of scientists sitting in front of mainframes; the colossal calculating machines exuded an aura of exoticism and mystery, exerting tremendous fascination. And caught in the crosshairs of cybernetics and the computer was the traditional image of the architect as an intuitive designer, creator, and demiurge. What was at stake was nothing less than the preservation of the architect as author in an advanced, technoscientific world. Design processes were stripped of their creative essence and reduced to scientific problem-solving procedures. Buildings were no longer crafted with the sweeping power of poetry but calculated by a tightly woven methodology of circuit diagrams and feedback loops. Floor plans and blueprints were no longer sketched by hand but produced on an intelligent computing machine. Even aesthetics were no longer a matter of emotion or expression, but relegated to the realm of communication technology. The importance of creativity, fantasy, and social imagination was pitted against the technical intelligence of electronic brains and thinking machines.

In contrast to the broad field of cybernetic art, the hope in architecture and urban planning was that cybernetics could solve concrete methodological problems. Underlying the methodological impact and enormous diversity of the cybernetic theoretical models that emerged was the confidence that, in the words of Claude Lévi-Strauss, it was possible to "develop a rigorous approach to problems which do not admit of a metric solution."[6]

In this book, the mentality underlying the transformation processes outlined above is interpreted as an expression of the technical thinking that was particular to the era of cybernetics. The rigorous approach taken in addressing certain related issues implied an intellectual rigor that operated exclusively with technical models of reality: the "circuit diagram" of the world was interesting, not its materiality. But even this did not necessarily lead to the rigorous approach mentioned above, which was based on a much subtler and simultaneously more radical aspect of cybernetics: the idea of finally being able to transcend the boundaries between object and subject, nature and culture—to arrive at a new theoretical model, an all-encompassing instrument of knowledge, and ultimately, a superior method of analyzing the world. In many ways, this rigor was rooted in the ambition of cybernetics to become a universal science. What was the promise of these communication structures and control circuits that made countless architects want to abandon the traditional humanist foundations of their discipline and replace the materiality of architecture with an abstract world of symbolic machines? What was the methodological appeal of this technical thinking for architecture?

Niklas Luhmann attributed this fascination with cybernetics to two promises that captivated many architects with their seductive luster. In a world that was apparently in a state of constant flux, cybernetics seemed to technically manifest a sense of "constancy" and to "explain invariant states of variables (i.e., not things!) through communication processes."[7] For Luhmann, the ability of cybernetics

Information circuit with a design sketch pad, computer, telephone, light pen, and television.

Charles Jencks, *Architecture 2000: Predictions and Methods* (London: Studio Vista, 1971), 56 © Charles Jencks

to guarantee some sort of stability in an unstable environment took on a concrete sociopsychological nuance: technical stability became a synonym for social stability. The concept of feedback, understood as the basic regulation of any self-controlling system, gained new status as a sociological metaphor. The basis for this new sociotechnical imagery and the scientific self-understanding that supported it can be found in the proceedings of the so-called Macy Conferences, which are considered the "modern foundational document" of cybernetics.[8] Held in New York between 1943 and 1953, the conference series was organized by the scientific elite of the United States and financed by the Josiah Macy, Jr. Foundation. Taking a uniquely interdisciplinary approach, it addressed aspects of neurophysiology, anthropology, psychology, and sociology in relation to early computer technologies, forming a conceptual fabric that wrapped itself around notions of

15

communication, information, system, and feedback, giving them a functionalist bent. In the wake of the politicization of science during the Second World War, bringing together perspectives from multiple disciplines was elevated to a criterion of successful knowledge production. The participants in this exclusive and equally illustrious scientific circle included representatives from more mathematically oriented disciplines, such as the neurophysiologist Warren McCulloch, the physicist Heinz von Foerster, and the mathematician John von Neumann, as well as the anthropologists Gregory Bateson and Margaret Mead, and the psychologist Kurt Lewin.

Another prominent Macy participant was Norbert Wiener, an American mathematician of above-average intelligence since his youth, who had studied with Bertrand Russell in Cambridge and David Hilbert in Göttingen. With his book *Cybernetics: Or Control and Communication in the Animal and the Machine*, published in 1948, Wiener presented a summary of his decade-long research on the topic.[9] It ranged from basic investigations into mathematical, intelligence, and neuroscientific aspects, to concrete, though unsuccessful, applications in military science. Behind the term "cybernetics,"[10] which Wiener adapted from the Greek κυβερνήτης (kybernētēs; meaning "steersman"),[11] lay his attempt to "find common elements in the functioning of automatic machines and the human nervous system and to develop a theory that covers the entire field of control and communication in machines and living organisms."[12] Shaped by his ideas on control, regulation, and feedback, Wiener's focus was on abstract control processes, system properties, and functional mechanisms instead of individual characteristics. Whether these involved biological organisms, machine automation processes, or human perception was of secondary importance.

Wiener's book was groundbreaking and became a "scientific bestseller."[13] Communication and control were elevated to principles of a

Book cover, Norbert Wiener, *Cybernetics: Or Control and Communication in the Animal and the Machine* (1948), 2nd edition (Cambridge, MA: The MIT Press, 1961).

© The MIT Press

universally valid system, whether at the level of people or machines. In his second book, *The Human Use of Human Beings: Cybernetics and Society*, published just a few years later,[14] Wiener showed that he wanted his theory to transcend the boundaries of mathematics and technology. "Society can only be understood through a study of the messages and the communication facilities which belong to it,"[15] he explained, making it clear that cybernetics should not only strive for scientific but also societal relevance. As a general explanatory model, cybernetics did not offer the definitional coherence of an academic discipline, but the far more sophisticated gesture of an epistemology. Cybernetics was to be understood as a heterogeneous "conglomerate of models, figures of thought, and concepts" implying "a different order of knowledge in the sciences, which, under the sign of this new epistemology, saw themselves challenged to a critical and productive revision of their concepts and foundations."[16] The productivity of these revisionary processes was largely due to the conceptual fuzziness of this conglomerate. Although Wiener's description of cybernetics as the study of control and communication in living beings and machines served as a foundational definition of the field, numerous conceptual modifications emerged in the years that followed, which should be viewed against the backdrop of different, often national, scientific traditions. Cybernetics, one might say, functioned as a "buzzword that challenged modern intellectuals or socially critical intelligentsia to express certain thoughts about society."[17] This book therefore approaches cybernetics as a historical complex, which appeared mainly under the term coined by Wiener, but actually encompassed a heterogeneous, branching, and productive spectrum of conceptual models with a variety of leanings.

In this respect, cybernetics was an international phenomenon. In the Soviet Union and East Germany, for example, Wiener's principle of communication and control was initially rejected as a product of the class enemy. Later, it was placed in the service of socialism and Marxism and transformed into a state regulator controlling the whole of society.[18] In England, three scientists in particular shaped the concept of cybernetics: the psychiatrist W. Ross Ashby, who wrote two key works on the science of self-organizing systems, *Design for a Brain* (1952)[19] and *Introduction to Cybernetics* (1956)[20]; the psychologist Gordon Pask, who, as described in the chapter "Swinging Cybernetics" in this book, played a major role in developing the concept of the Fun Palace designed by Cedric Price; and the psychologist Stafford Beer, who, besides his management theories that are still cited today, also developed a cybernetic model of government for socialist Chile under President Salvador Allende in the early 1970s.[21] Compared to Ashby and Beer, Pask had the most significant influence on British architecture with his experimental, and in many ways, playful interpretation of cybernetics. With his ideas on interactive technology, Pask provided the Architecture Machine Group—which was founded by Nicholas Negroponte in 1967 and later became the MIT Media Lab—with key conceptual building blocks to challenge the role of the architect as designer and sole decision-maker with the computer as an intelligent planning machine. Underpinning this was an understanding of people as users of technology and science who should have the greatest possible freedom in making decisions and actions related to technical objects and tools. There was an emphasis on practical issues: architecture should not be strictly scientific but repeatedly explored through new tools in a technically advanced experimental realm. Driving ideas behind this could also be found, albeit under a different guise, in the Buckminster Fuller-inspired concepts championed by California counterculture and its manual for alternative living, the *Whole Earth Catalog*.[22]

West German cybernetics contrasted in many ways with the American approach. While the United States was busy building mainframes and developing user interfaces suitable for the masses, people in postwar Germany were theorizing about cybernetic concepts in art, aesthetics, and education. The Stuttgart-based philosopher Max Bense quickly took the intellectual lead. Arguing with concepts from cybernetics, information theory, and semiotics, he became the central figure of a counterculture that distanced itself from the apparent monotony of the German postwar period. Bense drafted the comprehensive philosophical program of existential

Book covers, from left to right: Norbert Wiener, *Kybernetik: Regelung und Nachrichtenübertragung in Lebewesen und Maschine* (Dusseldorf: Econ, 1968). English edition: *Cybernetics: Or Control and Communication in the Animal and the Machine*, 2nd edition (Cambridge, MA: The MIT Press, 1965); Max Bense, *Einführung in die informationstheoretische Ästhetik: Grundlegung und Anwendung in der Texttheorie* [Introduction to information aesthetics: foundations and application in text theory] (Reinbek: Rowohlt, 1969); Jürgen Claus, *Expansion der Kunst: Action, Environment, Kybernetik, Technik, Urbanistik* [Expansion of art: action, environment, cybernetics, technology, urbanism] (Reinbek: Rowohlt, 1970).

rationalism, whose principles were well received, mainly in the sparse rooms of the Ulm School of Design [Hochschule für Gestaltung Ulm]. Committed to preparing budding designers and architects for a technical world driven by automation and cybernetics, Bense played a vital role at the Ulm School, especially in shaping the philosophical foundations of the curricula. In this way, Wiener's cybernetics became a cornerstone of the university's institutional identity.

Thanks to several scientific research institutions, cybernetics became a highly regarded project on the social and political playing field in German-speaking Europe.[23] At the same time, from the late 1960s onwards, there was increasingly open talk of a crisis in architectural education across the region. The assumed practicality of scientific conceptual models moved to the epicenter of swelling political debates about higher education. Industry and business demanded a more streamlined academic program for architects. During this time of upheaval, cybernetics briefly emerged from the chaos at the universities as a leading scientific ideology, establishing itself in academic discourse. Especially at the architecture departments of the technical universities, the impression prevailed that they were lagging behind progress. At a seminar in Zurich in 1971 on "Higher Education Didactics and Political Reality," architecture was declared to be in an "underdeveloped state" in terms of methodology and reflection.[24] "Behind the persistent facade of high social prestige" supposedly lay an "extraordinarily desolate state of practice and education in architecture and planning."[25] Such statements were symptomatic of the mood of upheaval in higher education, where many succumbed to the appeal of economic downsizing in their displeasure over the inadequate education at the universities. The conceptual contours of restructuring projects demanded by protagonists of the so-called socially critical intelligentsia were often drawn in the glaring light of a belief in technology and science: "Architectural education must become mobile, the architect must redefine his tasks—or the profession of master builder will disappear, as so many other professions have disappeared […] like clog makers and lamplighters."[26] Cybernetics promised to fill an important gap in the reform efforts at the universities. With its stringent systems thinking, it incorporated decisive operational attributes that were repeatedly called for in the often heated debates on education: efficient organization and control on the one hand, and methodological integration and interdisciplinarity on the other.[27]

Of course, there were also vehement critics of these developments. Many resisted the idea of being squeezed by the industry
into a regulated corset of effectiveness on an academic stage illuminated by science and technology. Yet, despite its universal scientific claim, many initially found the idea of cybernetics promising.
Only a few years after hosting the seminar on university education,
the ETH Zurich established a guest professorship in cybernetics,
hoping to save its architecture department from missing the boat
on technological and scientific progress in the field. The role of the
"cyberneticist" was not fully understood, but it was a specialization
that would certainly be needed to solve problems in the future.
In a world perceived as increasingly complex, cybernetics wore—
at least for a moment—a technoscientific garb of hope. At the
ETH, "Cybernetics for Architects" was part of an academic focus
whose seminars and lecture series had programmatic, often very
similar-sounding titles, such as "Systems Thinking" and "Systems
Engineering." Architecture students in those classes were familiar-
ized with the idea that tasks in architecture "can be characterized by
properties that can be represented with cybernetic categories and
whose laws can be investigated using cybernetic methods."[28] However, before gaining insight into the fundamentals of cybernetics,
the students learned how cybernetic and architectural thinking
were related. To this end, a schematic and still popular distinction
was made: architecture was divided into two gravitational fields,
the first of which was assigned to so-called humanistic and artistic issues, the second to more technological, scientific issues.
Cybernetics, students were told, was not dedicated to only one or
the other sub-area but encompassed the entire field of architecture—addressing the "interdisciplinary, the all-embracing, which
is already present in the systems thinking of the architect."[29] The
assumption that cybernetics should apply to existing aspects of

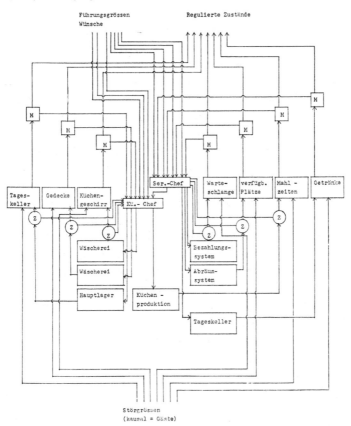

Gesamtsystem der Regelung :

Cybernetic circuit diagram representing the organization of a spatial program for a cafeteria building. Student project at the Department of Architecture, ETH Zurich, 1974.

Systemdenken. Semesterübungen über dessen Anwendung [Systems thinking: Semester exercises for its application], ed. Departement für Architektur der ETH Zürich, Dokumentation ORL II (Baubibliothek des Dept. Architektur, 1974), 34
© Departement für Architektur, ETH Zürich

architectural thinking reveals its aim to be recognized as a holisti-cally arguing, yet precisely operating science.

Some students may have wondered why it was necessary for ar-chitects to deal with the rigorous conceptual models of cybernet-ics. An answer can be found in the introductory note to a seminar transcript: "Since the circumstances to be investigated or influenced by the planner generally exhibit a diversity of relationships that is no longer manageable for the individual, and since planning tasks cannot be mastered by individual disciplines alone due to their complexity and scope, we will attempt to present conceptual and methodological tools for thought, work, and research that have a distinctly interdisciplinary character, in order to demonstrate their applicability and to implement them using concrete examples."[30] A glance at the exercises from the various cybernetics classes at that time provides a good impression of what this attempt looked like: pages and pages of mathematical formulas and technical circuit di-agrams. What emerges from the tangle of endless feedback loops are the contours of cybernetically represented planning processes; one must look closely to realize that they are not notes from a class on electrical engineering.

The processes that could be represented by a cybernetic model varied in their complexity. For example, one task for the architecture students was to develop an optimally functioning infrastructure and supply system for a trade fair, and to design a spatial program based on the associated cybernetic control loop. But it was much more spectacular to develop a complete planning simulation. Taking a cue from the study *Urban Dynamics* by the systems theorist Jay Wright Forrester,[31] published only a few years earlier, one cybernetics assign-ment at the ETH Architecture Department was to link numerous feedback processes into an urban planning simulation model. The first task involved an analysis at the level of individual buildings.

The second task was to develop a multilayered system of social, economic, and ecological parameters on a nearly global scale. In both tasks, the final product was an abstract circuit diagram, which revealed little of the specific characteristics and features that had been developed over the course of the project. The differences, as well as any heterogeneity were to be resolved both visually and conceptually in a technical system. What remained in each case was the abstract schematic of a general model, which suggested that it was verifiable down to the detail. Norbert Wiener had created not only a very specific view of society but also a new technoscientific perspective on architecture, which radically transformed architectural thinking in both theory and practice.

This book is divided into seven chapters, which are not strictly chronological, but function as thematic fields for a new perspective and detailed historical analysis of an era.[32] The first chapter outlines the characteristics of the cybernetic machine, and in doing so, illuminates the foundations of cybernetic thinking. The second chapter presents a cybernetic urban model developed by Norbert Wiener during the Cold War. This urban model can be understood as a spatialization of the cybernetic machine, and in this sense can also be found a short time later in architecture and urban planning, for example in the work of the Metabolists in Japan. The third chapter examines the interplay of architecture, industrial construction, and automation and their role in the history of the Ulm School of Design. The fourth chapter discusses the attempt in architecture to use cybernetics to define an objective aesthetic theory, known as information aesthetics. The idea that architectural criticism could be objectified and formalized so that it could be automated (calculated by a computer), clearly shows how reductionist cybernetic thinking was for architecture. The fifth chapter looks at the relationship between architecture, cybernetics, and performative aesthetic concepts.

The focus is not on the West German postwar period, but on "Swinging London" and the beginnings of Pop Art. The action-oriented and subjective understanding of aesthetics that emerged there, which starkly contrasts with that of information aesthetics, illustrates the broad spectrum of how cybernetics was applied to the field of architecture. The sixth chapter follows with the fundamental question of how the computer, given its increasing use in architecture, could be used in practice—via invisible program code or a graphical user interface. Behind this seemingly trivial question are two opposing ideas about how the interplay of computer and architectural drawing should be approached in architectural practice. Whether the computer is primarily a calculating machine or a drawing machine is discussed with regard to the emerging field of artistic computer graphics. This chapter also looks at the first architectural conferences on computer-aided design (CAD), such as the debates during the 1964 "Architecture and the Computer" conference in Boston, which included participants like Walter Gropius and Christopher Alexander. They reveal how the idea of the architectural tool played an increasingly important, but by no means uncontroversial, role in popularizing the computer in architecture. The seventh and final chapter builds on the previous discussion of tools, expanding on considerations about the interaction between "man and machine"[33] to include the aspect of participation. It examines cybernetic answers to the general question of how the computer could become a planning tool for use by a building's future occupants. The aim of breaking up the rigid hierarchy in the planning process to favor the occupants and weaken the architect's role as the sole decision-maker, assumed an increasingly technical tone under the influence of cybernetics and information theory. Ultimately, this was accompanied by the hope that the architectural design and planning process could be democratized to a certain extent by the computer.

Following Antoine Picon's assumption, quoted at the beginning of this introduction—that today's world is heir to the universe opened up by cybernetics in the 1950s and 1960s—a considerable part of this legacy for current architectural practice lies in the fact that some of the conceptual vanishing points and coordinates laid out by Norbert Wiener have remained intact, though the perspectives have shifted over time. Today, some 80 years after Wiener's *Cybernetics*, architects sit in front of computer screens daily. They experiment with novel algorithms, develop powerful tools, and are again discussing the automation of the design process and the programming of communication structures. The era of cybernetics is therefore interpreted in this book as a Janus head, whose one face provides a historical view of a rather neglected chapter in postwar architectural history. The other face shows aspects that make it clear that—given the increasingly dominant role that information technologies play in shaping architectural production today—a critical contextualization of cybernetic conceptual models in the history of architecture is both unavoidable and urgent.

Universalization of the Machine

The design theorist Tomás Maldonado saw in it the foundation for a scientific theory of design. The architect Yona Friedman transferred its operative functional logic to the architectural planning process, with the intention of weakening the architect's traditionally dominant role as decision-maker. And for the architect and computer scientist Nicholas Negroponte, it formed the basis for his theory of the "architecture machine" in a world of interactive computing and drawing machines.[1] Norbert Wiener's machine theory of cybernetics uniquely managed to not only question how the concept of the machine could be redefined for architecture, but also how this concept itself could be fundamentally rethought.

"The machines of which we are now speaking are not the dreams of the sensationalists nor the hope of some future time," declared Norbert Wiener at the end of the first chapter of his book *Cybernetics: Or Control and Communication in the Animal and the Machine.*[2] In terms of the history of technology, he was not entirely wrong, although his notion of the machine elegantly and radically departed from the familiar image of the machine known from photographs of mass production or mechanical engineering.[3] That sense of familiarity, which was disrupted by cybernetics, was based on the general view of a machine as a technical object that could be precisely defined by its physical enclosure, basic principles of force and energy, and its purpose. Wiener, however, did not speak of energy but of "information." In doing so, he laid the foundation for a world of machines in which the characteristics of a machine were not its mechanics, but mathematical control and, above all, self-control through abstract input and target variables. To embed his scientific views in a larger social and cultural context, Wiener juxtaposed the image of cybernetics as a young mathematical machine with popular metaphors from the age of technology—such as the clock for the 18th century and the steam engine for the 19th century.[4] Although cybernetics was only at the beginning of its short-lived heyday, Wiener gave epochal status to his conceptual models of computing machines, nervous systems, and control loops, speaking confidently of the "age of communication and control."[5] It was the proclamation of a worldview that replaced the model of the mechanical machine with that of the cybernetic machine.

Abstraction

In November 1947, when Sigfried Giedion completed the final chapter of his extensive study, *Mechanization Takes Command*,[6] a milestone in the cultural history of technology, he could not have known that in November of that same year, Norbert Wiener would also finish work on his own book. Giedion's *Mechanization Takes Command* as well as Wiener's *Cybernetics* were published in the following year and one could almost be inclined to read the latter as a mathematical appendix to Giedion's historical machine narratives, despite being formulated under a difference premise and as an outlook to the future. The coincidence of these two publications marks a turning point that clearly shows how rapidly the notion of the cybernetic machine was expanding the discourse. While Giedion drew the final contours of a machine age based on power and energy, Wiener sketched the mathematical foundation of a playing field of computing machines, technical control circuits, and information and communication systems.

In architecture, this playing field was explored in different ways and with various intentions. At first, Wiener's machine theory seemed to have neither conceptual nor technological points of contact with architecture. The cybernetic machine was not a machine tool with a dedicated area of application for use in construction. Nor did it embody an aesthetic exterior, a concise form, or a specific materiality, which could have been metaphorically referenced in architectural design. It is therefore all the more astonishing that the cybernetic machine was so incredibly appealing to architects.

With the shift from the resource of energy to that of information propagated by Wiener, the everyday concept of the machine was stripped not only of its corporeality, but also its expressiveness—the latter being of fundamental relevance to architecture and art.[7] This new degree of abstraction was reflected in the images of the cybernetic machine and how it was described. The loss of the figurative and the representational became a distinguishing feature of the iconography of cybernetics.[8] In the visual language of cybernetics, man and machine merged into a functional diagram in which "it is indifferent, in which substrate certain functions are articulated."[9] In cybernetics, the construction of a universal functional logic was more important than an emphasis on the specific and concrete. Organisms could be viewed as cybernetic machines, and vice versa.[10] The broad applicability of this reversible machine logic triggered both intra-disciplinary and interdisciplinary dynamics in a wide range of fields in the human sciences. The scientific landscape saw the spread of an "ontological unrest," which "consisted in the blurring of or confusion about what was previously distinct from artifacts under the concept of human beings."[11] As Wiener tellingly wrote in *Cybernetics*, "The newer study of automata, whether in the metal or in the flesh, is a branch of communication engineering, and its cardinal notions are those of message."[12] Man and machine were no longer aligned, no

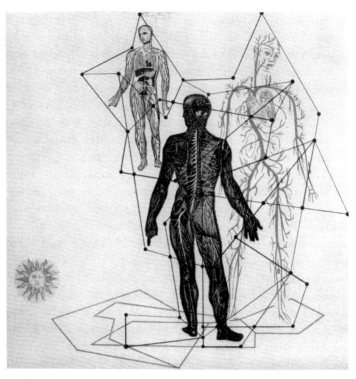

The human body a network and structure.
Konrad Wachsmann, *Wendepunkt im Bauen* (Dresden: Verlag der Künste, 1989),
87. English edition: *Turning Point in Building: Structure and Design* (New York, NY:
Reinhold Publishing Corporation, 1961).

UMSCHAU VERLAG

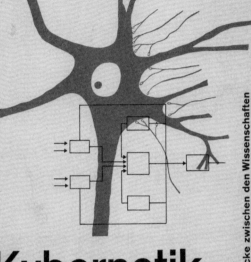

Brücke zwischen den Wissenschaften

Kybernetik -

B. Hassenstein - K. Küpfmüller - W.D. Keidel - D. Trincker
H. Meves - M. Spreng - M. Lindauer - W. Reichardt
W. Heiligenberg - G. Schramm - H. Schaefer - H. Kretz
F. Jenik - E. Zwicker - H. Kazmierczak - W. Endres
H. Wettstein - E. Krochmann - K. Steinbuch - W. Fucks
H. Henkel - A. Hoppe - H. Schnelle - R. Gunzenhäuser
Herausgeber H. Frank

Image of a neuron superimposed on a circuit diagram. Cover of the book *Kybernetik: Brücke zwischen den Wissenschaften* [Cybernetics: bridge between the sciences], ed. Helmar Frank, 5th edition (Frankfurt am Main: Umschau, 1965).

matter which side they were viewed from, neither by anthropomorphizing the machine nor by mechanizing man. Rather, both were abstracted to such a high degree that they became operative components of a common technical communication model.

Construction

Similar considerations had already been taking place in the field of architecture. Konrad Wachsmann's frequently printed graphic, for example—depicting a schematic image of the human body and blood circulation system superimposed by a web-like construction diagram of interconnected nodes—is a poetic and striking illustration of the effort to create an abstract alloy of architecture, nature, and machine. A similar idea is conveyed by Kisho Kurokawa's prefabricated high-rise structure shaped like a gigantic double helix.[13] Both Wachsmann's diagram and Kurokawa's architectural vision are artistic architectural transformations of scientific images. Machine and nature were not seen as two separate elements, but as connected through the principle of construction and were metaphorically declared to be the basis of a common technical dimension.

Despite this abstraction, the range of cultural implications for architecture remained bound to its inherent functions and concrete areas of application. A machine concretized its cultural meaning only through its existence as a technical artifact for a specific purpose and a determinable function. There are countless examples of this in 20th-century architecture. The notion of construction used in this context, often rhetorically loaded with metaphors from nature and the world of machines, became a favorite argumentation and

Yakov Chernikhov, machine architecture: "Constructive Union of Bodies with Rounded Edges. Calm Static State."

Jakow Tschernichow, *Konstruktion der Architektur und Maschinenformen* (1931), trans. from Russian into German by N.A. Jepantschin (Basel: Birkhäuser, 1991), 136 © Jakow Tschernichow

legitimation template for architects and artists alike when it came to contextualizing their design concepts.[14] For example, the machines Yakov Chernikhov included in his manifesto *Construction of Architectures and Machine Forms*, published in 1931, feature prominent rotational joints.[15] Their bulky, oversized hinges make the weight of the material and the tremendous power of the machines tangible. "The very nature of a machine necessitates its movement because a machine without functional movement is not a machine," argued Chernikhov, revealing how important the notion of movement was for him.[16] However, the movement mechanics of a technical object

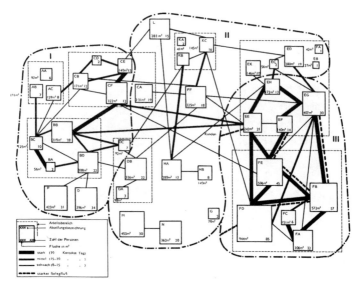

Ottomar Gottschalk, architectural space as a communication network.
Ottomar Gottschalk, *Flexible Verwaltungsbauten* (Quickborn: Schnelle, 1968), 45 © Quickborner Team

cannot be transferred to a building without further ado. Although a building's form might lend aesthetic expression to the transience of movement, for Chernikhov it remained static and "monolithic" on a constructive level, a condition he described as "frozen movement."[17] In Chernikhov's work, the rhythmic rotational movements of machines were in the foreground, which distinguished him from the speed fetishism of the Futurists. An artistic confrontation with this movement of the constructive is necessary, "because otherwise no machine could emerge from it—in any case no perfect machine that serves its purpose, i.e., that precisely fulfills its function."[18] The purposefulness that Chernikhov demanded was missing in cybernetic machine theory, as were materiality, corporeality, or even a precise outer form. While Giedion's *Mechanization Takes Command* includes countless technical apparatuses along with scientific and artistic images of movement,[19] Wiener's *Cybernetics* contains mathematical formulas, hinting that they can be used to describe the physiology of a nervous system as well as the functional logic of an automaton. From an architectural point of view, what kind of machine was the cybernetic machine?

Behavior

The psychiatrist W. Ross Ashby, who, along with the two psychologists Stafford Beer and Gordon Pask, was considered the most prominent figure of the British cybernetics movement, gave an insightful answer to this question in his highly regarded *Introduction to Cybernetics*. Ashby took up the intention described by Wiener but emphasized a particular aspect of the cybernetic concept of machines: "Many a book has borne the title 'Theory of Machines,' but it usually contains information about *mechanical* things, about levers and cogs. Cybernetics, too, is a 'theory of machines,' but it treats, not things but *ways of behaving*. It does not ask 'what *is* this thing?' but '*what does it do?*'"[20] With this comparison, Ashby underscored the behaviorist principles of the new machine theory and touched upon an essential idea in Wiener's project: developing an operative machine model that would unite two levels: the description of biological behavior in mathematic terms, and the functional logic of a system that could be implemented technically. Creating the necessary conditions for linking these two levels was achieved by declaring that "materiality is irrelevant."[21] This liberated the machine from its status as a technical artefact and material object. Mechanics were replaced by mathematical modeling using feedback loops. The calculated recursion this entailed, and the associated ability of an operation to function in both a forward and backward manner, were considered a basic mathematic building block of cybernetics.[22] Cybernetics transformed the previous notion of the machine as a physical, functional, concrete object into an operative conceptual model detached from specific functions: a symbolic behavioral machine.

A vivid example of how the cybernetic machine was transformed into architecture can be found in the work of Team Quickborn. In the late 1950s, this planning collective of designers and organizational consultants developed one of the most innovative workspace concepts of the German postwar period with their concept of "office landscapes."[23] An underlying assumption was that it was only with the help of "conceptual means provided by the theories gathered under the name of cybernetics"[24] that new architectural concepts could emerge. Cybernetics was approached as the combination of a magnifying glass and an X-ray machine: it was said that "the essence of office work" could be "illuminated" thanks to cybernetics.[25] Through cybernetics, it was possible "to make information, communication, control, and regulation of processes of all kinds partly visible, partly measurable, and in any case more manageable with mathematical scientific methods."[26]

From this architectural-cybernetic point of view, planning administrative and office buildings was a rewarding design task, in which several different levels of process regulation overlapped. Office work was considered, in the sense of Wiener, not only as "information processing in humans as preparation for an action," but also always in a "sociological system, which can be described as a group, department, company, or national or world economy."[27] This complex nesting of communication structures was intensified by factoring into the model the heightened administrative use of electronic data processing (EDP). Information processing could be extended from the social processes taking place inside the building, through the man–machine interaction, to the machine itself. An office building could therefore be treated as an enormous information processing system, a structure described as a "symbiosis between man, machine, and method"[28] in conjunction with Pierre Bertaux's book *Mutation der Menschheit* [Mutation of humanity].[29] Cybernetics promised not only to make all processes circulating in a building visible and controllable, but also, as advocated by Niklas Luhmann, to explain them in a general model with the help of communication structures. By extension, the architect became an organizer of exact communication. In such a world, the architectural concept of scale was no longer relevant. A sociological system could be understood as a small group, a firm, but also the entire economy of a country. The cybernetic concept of communication thus held an important key for architecture, a tool that could be used to open up each of the above-mentioned processes, allowing their inner structure to become an operative model in the form of circuit diagrams and functional diagrams.

City Plan, Escape Plan

Hiroshima is a dark chapter in 20th-century American politics, science, and technology, and can also be seen as the earliest encounter between cybernetics and urban planning. In the autumn of 1946, when the Japanese government invited Kenzo Tange to visit Hiroshima on the country's southwestern coast, the young architect looked upon a city that was no longer a city. On the morning of August 6, 1945, the United States government dropped an atomic bomb on Hiroshima and its more than 250,000 inhabitants. The intention was maximum destruction. At an altitude of half a kilometer, it exploded directly above the bustling urban center. With its blinding light, tremendous shock wave, and subsequent radioactive wind, the bomb hit the city with unimaginable force and decimated everything within a radius of several kilometers. Aerial photographs taken from the rear of the plane that had released the massive bomb show a barren, ghostly surface, where just a short time before entire city districts had stood.[1] Barely a minute after the explosion, an apocalyptic mushroom cloud formed above the area, the images of which burned deeply into the memory of an entire generation. In view of the uncontrollable consequences of nuclear technology, the philosopher Günther Anders wrote of the self-destructive third industrial revolution in his two-volume work, *Die Antiquiertheit des Menschen* [The obsolescence of human beings].[2] Anders's basic assumption was that technological developments would increasingly widen the gap between humans and their tools, and that, compared to the constantly growing perfection, expertise, and power of the technological world, human beings were outdated and becoming increasingly obsolete as a life form. The development and use of the

41

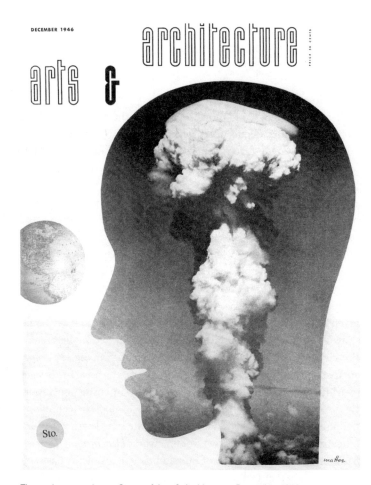

DECEMBER 1946

arts & architecture

PRICE 50 CENTS

Sto.

matter

The nuclear apocalypse. Cover *of Arts & Architecture*, December 1946.

atomic bomb provided Anders with the definitive proof that humans were no longer in control of the technology they were inventing and surrounding themselves with.

Norbert Wiener and the Atomic Bomb

The images from Hiroshima and Nagasaki also shook Norbert Wiener. Upon learning of the horrendous extent of the destruction, he gave up his previously military-oriented research goals for a more pacifist approach. In his biography, he devoted an entire chapter to this turning point.[3] Given the seemingly uncontrollable power of the bomb, Wiener wrote that it was the first time in the history of mankind that the technical "power of destruction" had caught up with the human "will for destruction"[4]—and, one might well add, in the sense of Anders, overtaken it. In 1950, the same year that construction began on Kenzo Tange's Hiroshima Peace Memorial Park, Wiener published not only his second book, *The Human Use of Human Beings*, but also an article for the December issue of the popular *Life* magazine under the forthright title, "How U.S. Cities Can Prepare for Atomic War."[5] In it, Wiener laid out his proposal for a technical, functional model of the city that was, in its logic, an urban communication machine—an aspect that makes it relevant not only for the history of cybernetics but also for the history of architecture and urban planning.[6]

In the mid-1950s, the United States was experiencing a time of national insecurity. The trauma of Hiroshima and Nagasaki lingered on, while the increasingly surreal menace of the Cold War and the arms race was in full swing. One year before Wiener published his

Photograph of crowded downtown New York City.
"How U.S. Cities Can Prepare for Atomic War," *Life,* December 18, 1950, 76–77 © Life Magazine

article in *Life*, the Soviet Union conducted a successful nuclear test, proving it was technically capable of ending America's nuclear supremacy. This was the particular historical context surrounding the scientific discourse that Wiener was part of at the time.

It was a somewhat controversial discourse, permeated by the personal fears of individual scientists, mostly physicists. A glance through issues of the respected scientific magazine *Bulletin of Atomic Scientists* from that time reveals the prevailing opinion that an active defense strategy for American cities, such as a targeted missile defense, would not be adequate in the event of a Soviet atomic bomb attack.[7] For the American public as well, the images of the tragedy in Japan had long since become a political boomerang. People openly

Norbert Wiener's civil defense plan for the American city (1950).
"How U.S. Cities Can Prepare for Atomic War," *Life*, December 18, 1950, 78–79 © Life Magazine

questioned whether, and if so, to what extent, American cities could be hit by Soviet atomic bombs and what measures should be taken in case of an attack. Wiener strictly rejected the notion of rearmament, not only for reasons of feasibility.

He considered the entire situation of the arms race to be a dangerous undertaking, in which any further armament would have uncontrollable consequences for the existence of humanity. "There is no end to this vast apocalyptic spiral,"[8] Wiener proclaimed, describing an aspect of technological progress that would also lead Anders a few years later to attest to mankind's "apocalypse blindness" due to its inability to think about the other side.[9] Later, Wiener criticized that "we are the slaves to our technical improvement," pointing out

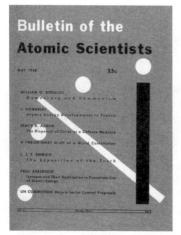

Covers of the *Bulletin of the Atomic Scientists* with the imposing "doomsday clock," issues from May 1948 and March 1950.

that "[we] have modified our environment so radically that we must now modify ourselves in order to exist in this new environment."[10] Wiener placed particular emphasis on the process of the existential modification of the self. From a spatial perspective, he was proposing an urban planning solution to serve as a defensive, protective measure in the event of an atomic war. The central question for him was: "What if the target for the bomb had been an American city?"[11]

This is precisely where Wiener's article came in. Together with his two co-authors, the political scientist Karl Deutsch and the philosopher Giorgio de Santillana, Wiener proposed the spatial decentralization of American cities. After his book *Cybernetics*, which was originally intended for a small circle of specialists, now he was trying

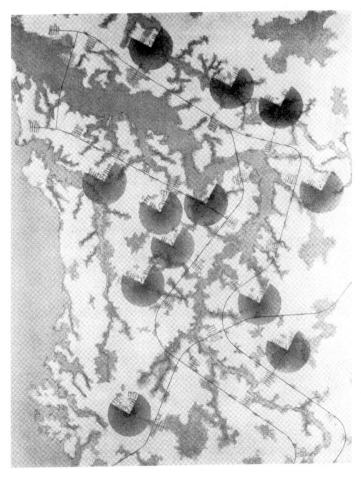

Design of decentralized urban structures.

Ludwig Hilberseimer, *The Nature of Cities: Origin, Growth, and Decline, Pattern and Form, Planning Problems* (Chicago, IL: Paul Theobald & Co., 1955), 267 © Ryerson and Burnham Libraries, Art and Architecture Research Collection of the Art Institute of Chicago not only to popularize his cybernetic worldview, but also to put it at the service of society as a humanitarian program. Added to this was the fact that the concept of urban decentralization as a passive defense strategy was becoming widely popular.

A few years after Wiener's article appeared in *Life*, the diagnosis offered up by the architect, urban planner, and former Bauhaus teacher Ludwig Hilberseimer in *The Nature of Cities* was that, "Decentralization already exists as a trend, not to say as an established fact. It is gaining more and more momentum, especially now that the trend is reinforced by the new concept of defence and security. Defence necessity forced the concentration of cities of the past; defence necessity may force the dispersal of the present city. Incredible as it may seem, we may be on the way to realizing our human aims in an effort to save ourselves from military destruction! It is strange, but true, that the very developments which would solve some of our greatest social problems—decentralization, diversification of production, the creation of self-sustaining regions—are also the developments required by defense necessity in this Atomic Age."[12]

The City as a Brain

Hilberseimer, who was known for his rationalized approaches to architecture and urban planning, considered the concept of decentralization the only possible answer to the question of how to protect against the devastating effects of an atomic bomb. In addition to countless decentralized city models, he developed a series of "wind diagrams" that could be used to graphically calculate how far radioactive wind would spread around the drop site.[13] The *Bulletin of the*

Atomic Scientists, which Hilberseimer also cited in his chapter on decentralization as a means of defense, had published a special issue in August 1950, three months before Wiener's *Life* article, dealing with spatial defense strategies in the event of an atomic bombing. The journal's editor stated that in view of the obvious threat, it was necessary to prepare a "master plan, analogous to the industrial mobilization plan for war emergency."[14] A central concern was preserving urban transportation networks and infrastructure.[15] One might speculate whether Wiener had read the article, or whether he later became aware of Hilberseimer's diagrams and calculations. One thing is certain, however: that he indeed had come up with a "master plan" for American cities. Going beyond the usual notions of urban decentralization, it can be interpreted as a spatial rendering of the cybernetic machine.

"Defense-by-communications" is how Wiener referred to his urban concept.[16] It involved the spatial modification of major American cities, such as New York or Boston, in which the existing infrastructure would be reinforced by a second layer of infrastructure, called "life belts."[17] This transportation network took the form of interconnected radial supply belts that wrapped around the city like giant life preservers. Wiener envisaged a dual function for these rings. On the one hand, they would secure all vital transportation and traffic systems and keep them functioning in the event of an attack. On the other hand, they would provide the population with a widely ramified network of escape routes, leading them away from the immediate vicinity of the impact site. The damage that had to be avoided would not only be caused directly by the explosive power of the bomb, but also indirectly by the ensuing panic among the population and the collapse of information and communication systems. Like a large circular template superimposed on the inner cities of all major metropolitan areas, a nationwide decentralized infrastructure network of sufficient functional stability should be built, according to Wiener. This would spatially absorb selective destruction of the city caused by bombing. Communication had become the equivalent of mobility.

In the history of urban planning, Wiener's approach of defining the structure of a city mainly through its transportation system is nothing new. As for the design's geometric form, his concept fits almost seamlessly into the history of concentrically organized ideal cities going back to the Renaissance.[18] The formal analogy to Tommaso Campanella's "City of the Sun," perhaps one of the most famous state utopias of the 17th century, is immediately apparent. Likewise, Thomas More's dialogue *Utopia*, from the 16th century, may have provided him with inspiration on the structure of an ideal society. Such literary derivations, however, would distract from the brutality of the war setting from which Wiener's cybernetic urban machine emerged. In the sense of "defense-by-communications," his model can be seen as an abstract fortress city in the age of communication.

Wiener's design differed conceptually in two essential ways from other decentralized city models, which (as previously mentioned in regard to Hilberseimer), were a widespread topic in urban planning and scientific discourses in the early 1950s. First, he did not propose to establish entirely new cities, but saw his proposal as a complement to existing city structures. As he put it: "Let us reorganize our cities where they stand."[19] This situated Wiener's position in between planned and evolved city models. Second, he went beyond the level of geometry or topography in his argumentation to consider the city model in terms of intelligence criteria, i.e., the regulation and control of information in the urban space. For Wiener, a city functioned like a cybernetic machine. Its purpose was, on the one hand, to unite a mathematical description of biological behavior with the functional logic of a technically implementable system, and, on the other hand, to declare the materiality of the machine "irrelevant."[20] The extent to which Wiener was committed to cybernetic thinking and the associated universality of mechanical thinking in questions of urban planning can be seen in his design of the city as a technical system, even while describing it in analogy to a natural system, specifically, the brain: "We have conceived the city as a net of communication and of traffic. The danger of blocked communication in a city subject to emergency conditions is closely analogous to the danger of blocked communication in the human body. [...] when an artery in the brain is blocked, the part of the brain which it feeds dies, and we have an apoplectic stroke; minor disasters may be our salvation under the blast of an atomic bomb; they cause us to improve our channels of traffic, and in fact, to produce the extra channels to save us when the day of reckoning comes."[21]

The city as both machine and brain—this was the conceptual triad of Wiener's abstract metaphor. Yet, it is noteworthy that Wiener did not mention the brain's neuronal complexity or structural adaptability to changing environments as examples in his city analogy. One could assume that these aspects were much too connected to a representational and physical image of the brain. Instead, he was concerned with the logic of abstract functional circuits. Only in this way was it possible to look not only at a machine and a brain but also at a city in equal measure. Wiener's proposal could be seen as a complement to Ashby's book *Design for a Brain*, in the form of a "design for a city." However, this triad of machine, brain, and city only gets its dramatic portent from the fact that Wiener wrote in terms of "blocked communications" and an "apoplectic stroke."[22] According to Wiener, blocking the flow of information could have "gravest" consequences.[23] The conceptual accent of his urban model was thus on the flow of information, or more precisely, on the moment in which this vital process threatened to be interrupted. Wiener saw the city as a natural system, whose functional logic could be equated with that of an information-processing machine. In the same breath, he spoke of the technical weaknesses and the human vulnerability of this urban organism. The death of the brain was also the death of the city—it was in this radical line of argument that Wiener proved his conceptual skill. While adhering to the apocalyptic rhetoric used at the time to express fears of a Soviet nuclear bomb attack, he also created an image of decentralization that was much more effective in its message than other urban models put forth in this context. Wiener could hardly have explained more vividly how serious the destruction of an American city by an atomic bomb would be, and how indispensable and existential the humane manifestation of his cybernetic motto of "communication and control" would be for modern society in the 20th century.

Metabolist Thinking

An early obvious reference to cybernetics can be found in Japanese Metabolism, a movement that included the architects Kiyonori Kikutake, Kisho Kurokawa, Masato Otaka, Fumihiko Maki, and the critic and theorist Noboru Kawazoe.[24] Although they did not belong to the group's original core, Kenzo Tange and Arata Isozaki are also considered representatives of this movement. In the word "metabolism," which they adopted from the field of physiology, they saw the expression of a new Japanese identity. While feeling obliged to uphold the Japanese building tradition, such as prefabricated timber construction, they also confronted a highly technological,

Kisho Kurokawa, collage of different capsule structures.

Kisho Kurokawa, "Capsule Declaration," *Space Design*, no. 3 (March 1969): 18 © Kisho Kurokawa

increasingly mobile society. The two conceptual pillars of Metabolism emerged from this field of tension: an organic aesthetics, predominantly circumscribed by biological metaphors, and a building technology characterized by movable, exchangeable elements.

It is hardly surprising that the shock of the atomic bomb was deeply inscribed in the programmatic texts of the Metabolists. Despite the dark shadow of nuclear war, Noboru Kawazoe, the group's theoretical head, remained positive. In his essay "Material and Man" published in 1960,[25] Kawazoe nevertheless took a critical view of those he saw as contributing to its advancement. "If all mankind really came to believe that there will be no war, I think a new epoch would begin at the moment, and it will be an epoch of construction which aims at bringing happiness to everyone. […] If all the people in the world try to do this, there will be no excuse for the big countries to make nuclear weapons. Who will be, then, the leaders of optimism? It has become clear that the politicians and thinkers are incapable. The established artists must also be excluded, since they are participating in the preparation of the war. Those who fear the destruction of mankind have no courage to fight against the A-bombs and H-bombs. Only optimists who do not worry about our destiny can fight against them. Those optimists, I believe can be found only among architects and designers, by which I mean the people who give hope and form to all the things men make."[26]

In the face of widespread societal disorientation, architecture offered a way out, Kawazoe maintained, trusting it with nothing less than the fate of civilization as a whole. Although a touch of amusement might be detected in Kawazoe's metaphor of the "leaders of optimism," the heightened pathos in this gesture is hard to ignore. His insistence that audacity and a decidedly optimistic outlook were needed to avert the "destruction of mankind" might seem almost grotesque given the devastating events in Hiroshima and Nagasaki. However, it is also clear here how much trust in politics had been lost through the controversial debates on the atomic bomb, and how strong the will was to understand architecture as a modernizing design instrument on a global scale. Metabolism provided the theoretical underpinnings for the latter. While Kawazoe did not mention Wiener by name in his essay, the guiding figure he invoked alongside that of the optimistic architect was the dedicated scientist—an image that in many respects was attributed to Norbert Wiener at that time.

Max Bense was also widely considered to be the prime example of a critical contemporary who, in his role as a bold and fearless

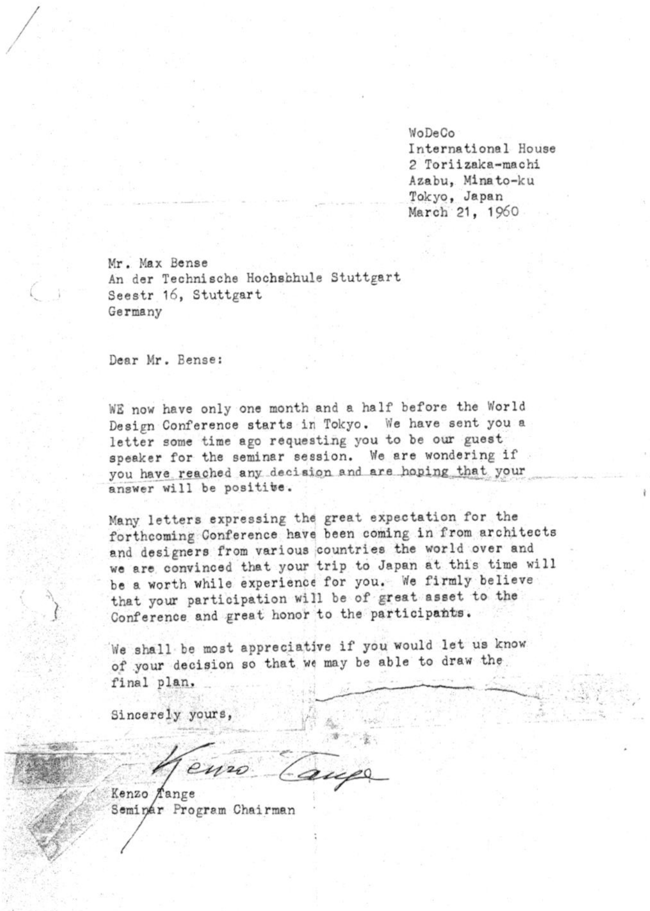

WoDeCo
International House
2 Toriizaka-machi
Azabu, Minato-ku
Tokyo, Japan
March 21, 1960

Mr. Max Bense
An der Technische Hochschule Stuttgart
Seestr 16, Stuttgart
Germany

Dear Mr. Bense:

WE now have only one month and a half before the World Design Conference starts in Tokyo. We have sent you a letter some time ago requesting you to be our guest speaker for the seminar session. We are wondering if you have reached any decision and are hoping that your answer will be positive.

Many letters expressing the great expectation for the forthcoming Conference have been coming in from architects and designers from various countries the world over and we are convinced that your trip to Japan at this time will be a worth while experience for you. We firmly believe that your participation will be of great asset to the Conference and great honor to the participants.

We shall be most appreciative if you would let us know of your decision so that we may be able to draw the final plan.

Sincerely yours,

Kenzo Tange

Kenzo Tange
Seminar Program Chairman

Kenzo Tange's invitation to Max Bense to the World Design Conference in Tokyo, March 1960.

Max Bense Nachlass, Handschriftensammlung, Deutsches Literatur Archiv Marbach

philosopher of technology, had long since been recognized even in faraway Japan, at the latest through his work at the Ulm School of Design. Bense argued that "the decisive technical event of our era is not the invention of the atomic bomb, but the construction of the great mathematical machines, which, perhaps with some exaggeration, have occasionally also been called thinking machines."[27] He justified his provocative point of view with the assertion "that technology [with the thinking machines] has gained a new area of responsibility, one might almost say: a new meaning."[28] Despite the devastating and destructive power of the atomic bomb, Bense emphasized that falling into a pessimistic technological lethargy was not an option. He represented a view that can be seen in contrast to Anders's metaphor of antiquity, which is critical of civilization. For Bense, the task of an intellectual—whether philosopher, artist, or architect—was to sound out the conceptual spectrum of an advanced technoscientific world, and to approach it with optimism. It is therefore not surprising that Kenzo Tange made several efforts, albeit in vain, to win Bense as a speaker for the 1960 World Design Conference in Tokyo, where the Japanese architect presented not only his groundbreaking Plan for Tokyo but also the founding manifesto of Metabolism.

In the spirit of Wiener's cybernetic machine, technology's new task consisted of the operationalization of information. With his defense plan for cities, Wiener had shown what this could mean for architecture and urban development. Urban inhabitants became elements of a cybernetic unity, in which space, man, and machine were understood on the level of information as belonging together in a single communication system. Communication also played a central role for Kawazoe. The regulation of communication offered a way to regard humans as part of a natural whole: "The metabolism of our life will be operated in such a way as to follow the order of Nature, while Nature will be developed at the hands of men. Men and Nature will be unified into one."[29] In contrast to Wiener's man–machine hybrid, Kawazoe proposed a man–nature unity. In the 1960s, nature, as developed "at the hands of men," was no longer about agriculture or the steam engine, but the spatialization of communication. From a theoretical perspective, nature remained the model, but only the information technologies were able to make this principle of nature usable, thus eliminating the difference between nature and culture.

Communication Networks

Even more obviously cybernetic were the considerations of Kenzo Tange, who went on to design the Osaka World Expo a few years later. "Creating an architecture and a city may be called a process of making the communication network visible in a space," Tange explained, making direct reference to Wiener.[30] Tange was so fascinated by Wiener's universe of information, feedback, and communication that he believed he could see a "sharp reflection of this phenomenon on spatial organization."[31] And further: "Architecture or urban space has a spatial organization containing various sorts of elements. […] Then it becomes necessary to see these elements in their relation to each other in time and space. This approach might be called a structural approach. […] If we ask what the thing is that gives structure to space we can answer that it is communication."[32] For Tange it was clear: "In modern civilized society, space is a communication field."[33] Coupling the concept of communication with that of space, he did not see a symmetrical relationship between them but an asymmetrical one. Space acquired its structure only through communication, and therefore space without communication was space without structure. Tange grounded his argument in what he saw as a paradigm shift in 20th-century architecture. This shift progressed from functionalism, which Tange dated between 1920 and 1960, to structuralism (which he also referred to as "structurism").[34] His critique of functionalism was that the relationship between space and function was too static and rigid. In contrast, a structuralist way of thinking considered the relationship between space and function on a dynamic level. While Tange used the term "function" to refer only to the requirement that architectural space be open to functional change, flexibility, and changeability, the term "structure" played a special role for him. Given a certain number of different "functional units," for example, our desire is to connect them to create a whole. Tange was interested in the idea of networked organization, a process he called "structuring." Since this process of structuring was dependent on communication, the communication network should be made visible in the space. With his use of the word "symbol," Tange was reacting to what he saw as a general lack of symbols in cities, which was sorely needed: "I venture to say we need a symbolic approach to architecture and urban space in order to secure humanity."[35] His underlying view was that space was not merely a three-dimensional container for people, but is shaped and deformed by their actions and, to a certain extent, charged with meaning. At the end of his essay, Tange formulates the most general and at the same time likely the most personal position in his argumentation: "Architects and urban designers are men who have the responsibility of creating the channel between the physical environment and the metaphysical world, of building a bridge between technology and humanity, and of restoring human significance to man's environment."[36] Tange thus described the ideal of the optimistic architect in the service of humanity that Kawazoe had propagated a few years earlier in the name of Metabolism. At the same time, his statement reveals how much the idea of cybernetic communication networks was permeated by a mythologization of the technical.

Tange's Plan for Tokyo in particular reads like a transfer of Wiener's thoughts onto a city with ten million inhabitants at the time. Like many other utopian urban models developed during this period, Tange's concept was based on a vision of the future shaped by the triad of economic growth, faith in science, and predictions of an uncontrolled world population growth. While in Brazil, an entire city could be designed on the drawing board and planned on an open plain, Japan was confronted with the looming lack of living space on a geographical level, not least due to the mountainous topography of the archipelago. It was assumed that the small and densely populated country would be defenseless against the anticipated population explosion.

At the same time, the uncontrolled growth of the Tokyo metropolis, which already had a population of over one million in the 19th century, was threatening to consume the entire island with no end in sight. Due to its topography, the water seemed to be the only possible space for Tokyo to gain land. With this scenario in mind, Tange proposed to build on top of Tokyo Bay. A giant, well organized floating belt structure, nearly one kilometer wide, would provide space for more than five million inhabitants. At the heart of this linear city would be an infrastructure axis containing all supply and administrative units, linking the two coastal sections like a monumental highway. The new residential districts were oriented perpendicular to this axis. Like two arms growing from either side, they were intended to transform the entire bay into a single urban matrix. On a formal level, Tange's design reveals parallels to the linear city designed by the traffic engineer and urban planner Arturo Soria y Mata. In the late 19th century, Soria y Mata developed a model for a city whose

Kenzo Tange, design of an urban megastructure for Tokyo Bay (bird's eye view of general plan).

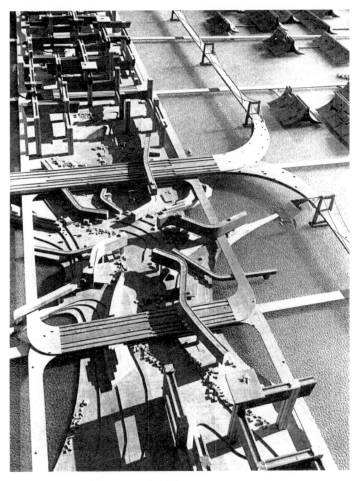

Kenzo Tange, design of an urban megastructure for Tokyo Bay (detail).

entire urban structure was based on the spatial structure of a rapid transportation system—at that time still the railway.[37] Tange, however, went beyond the idea of a local transportation system, speaking of a "communication network."[38] While the "transportation system is the basic physical foundation for the functional operation of the city,"[39] the urban structure, transportation system, and architecture were to be combined into an organic whole. The ground plan and city map merged in the light of Metabolism and cybernetics to form the circuit diagram of a gigantic communication field.

In cybernetics—the "general, formal science of the structure, relations, and behavior of dynamic systems,"[40] Tange found suitable instruments for approaching the complex questions of an increasingly globalized world—conceptually, technically, and aesthetically. Communication was understood as "essentially a social affair"[41] that should be investigated, explained, and solved with the exact methods of communications technology. A system's connections and relationships were given greater importance than its individual elements. No longer was it only about the single individual, but about the group; not about the object, but about the ensemble. The question of individuality increasingly became one of community and the collective.

Tange was by no means alone in this view. Many architects responded to the widespread perception of a changing and technically more mobile world by conceptualizing process characteristics, such as adaptivity, organization, and regulation. Eckhard Schulze-Fielitz's *Raumstadt* [Spatial city] (1959), Yona Friedmann's *La Ville Spatiale* [Spatial city] (1960), and Nicolas Schöffer's *La Ville Cybernétique* [Cybernetic city] (1969) are early testimonies of this thinking, and exemplary of a slew of utopian projects that saw the human represented in huge residential structures.[42] For architecture and urban planning, the appropriation of key cybernetic concepts such as communication, system, and feedback, opened up promising perspectives.

Book cover, Nicolas Schöffer, *Die kybernetische Stadt* [The cybernetic city] (Munich: Heinz Moos, 1970).

A project by Arata Isozaki, for example, shows in all clarity the strong adherence to the belief that the ambiguities of social space could be precisely regulated and controlled with cybernetic conceptual models. The concept of the "Computer-Aided City," the programmatic title of the project Isozaki developed in 1972, envisaged a vast city complex resembling an oversized antenna. The basic structure of the symmetrically organized complex consisted of two long, monumental blocks, with numerous branches attached orthogonally along the edges. A two-pole fiber optic network, in which every receiver could also be a transmitter, would serve as the city's infrastructure system. "If information is limited to one-way messages like television and radio, then the system is no different from cable tv. Since coaxial cables are able to transmit easily large volumes of

Arata Isozaki, design of a computer-aided urban structure (1970–1972).

Arata Isozaki, "Computer-Aided City," *Kenchiku Bunka*, no. 310 (August 1972): 99 © Arata Isozaki

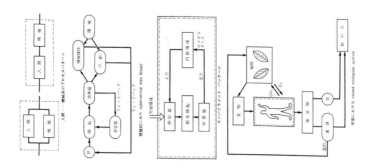

Arata Isozaki, "Cybernetical Man Model," detail of a circuit diagram for the computer-controlled urban structure (1970–1972).

Arata Isozaki, "Computer-Aided City," *Kenchiku Bunka*, no. 310 (August 1972): 147 © Arata Isozaki

Fritz Haller, urban
infrastructure nodes
(scale 1:8000).

Fritz Haller, *totale stadt: ein globales
modell/integral urban: a global model*
(Olten: Walter Verlag, 1975), 73 ©
gta Archive, ETH Zürich: Fritz Haller
Nachlass

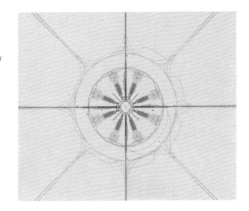

information both ways, super-computers, if used to exchange, process, and store information, can begin to serve as 'the brain' of the
city."[43] What initially sounds like a purely technical description of
space reveals itself to be a concept for an urban space that is completely controlled and managed by machines.

Studies on Swiss architect Fritz Haller's *totale stadt* [literally:
"total city," published in English in 1975 as "integral urban"] oc-
cupy a special place in this context, although his first study was not
published until 1968 and the second in 1975.[44] The urban concept
he developed was in no way inferior in its radicalism to those by
Wiener, Tange, and Isozaki. Similar to Wiener, Haller saw the ideal
functioning of a city organized in the geometry of circular structures.
As in a computer network, he started from individual nodes in a decentralized communication system, which—due to their high degree
of abstraction—could not only be thought of on an urban scale, but
also on a global scale. Haller's focus was not on the individuality
and uniqueness of a space, but rather on its potential for integration

65

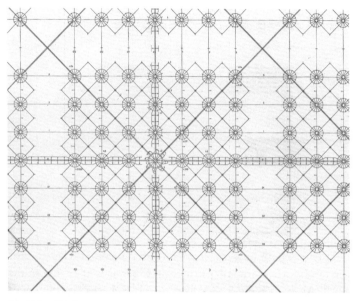

Fritz Haller, kinetic system with network of infrastructure nodes (scale 1:100,000).

Fritz Haller, *totale stadt: ein globales modell/integral urban: a global model* (Olten: Walter Verlag, 1975), 56
© gta Archive, ETH Zürich: Fritz Haller Nachlass

into a functional matrix that was organized in an interference-free manner.

Although Haller's concept of the city can be read as a purely technical model, cybernetics functioned in this case as merely one of several scientific building blocks. The organization of a city was approached as a collective work by different scientists: "specialists in cybernetics, mathematics, electronics, physics, biology, geography, technology, psychology, sociology."[45] For Haller, Wiener's machine theory had the function of an avant-garde cultural cipher, which

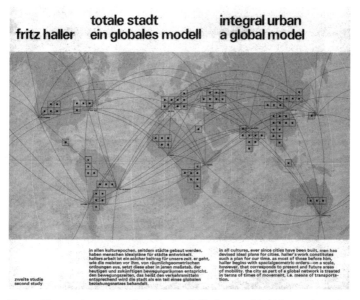

fritz haller · **totale stadt** · **integral urban**
ein globales modell · **a global model**

in allen kulturepochen, seitdem städte gebaut werden, haben menschen idealpläne für städte entwickelt. hallers arbeit ist ein solcher beitrag für unsere zeit. er geht, wie die meisten vor ihm, von räumlichgeometrischen ordnungen aus. setzt diese aber in jenen maßstab, der heutigen und zukünftigen bewegungsräumen entspricht. den bewegungszeiten, das heißt den verkehrsmitteln entsprechend wird die stadt als ein teil eines globalen beziehungsnetzes behandelt.

in all cultures, ever since cities have been built, man has devised ideal plans for cities. haller's work constitutes such a plan for our time. as most of those before him, haller begins with spacialgeometric orders—on a scale, however, that corresponds to present and future areas of mobility. the city as part of a global network is treated in terms of times of movement, i.e. means of transportation.

zweite studie
second study

The world as an urban communication network. Book cover, Fritz Haller, *totale stadt: ein globales modell / integral urban: a global model* (Olten: Walter Verlag, 1968).

could be used to describe the future image of a highly technologized society that replaced the architectural object with systems of limitless networks, applicable at all scales. Although Haller did not elaborate on his thoughts on cybernetics, it is clear that Wiener was the silent godfather of his two studies and his concept of the total city. Ultimately, the dream was to spatially organize social communication processes, and thereby do justice to the longstanding utopian urban planning ambition to create structures for a more humane society. Widespread forecasts about the growth of the global population conjured up the threat of a society coming apart at the seams, and fed the idea of finding a way out in the technical controllability of abstract model worlds.

A common approach shared by these urban planning projects was to combine the dynamics of social intimacy and community with the technical logic of industrial construction. It was thus a matter of systematizing the "socializing function of space."[46] This was certainly radical thinking, but it was part of a broader current. In his famous manifesto, *Perspektiven einer Architektur* [Perspectives of an architecture], Wolfgang Döring even declared the complete irrelevance of the single-family home: "It is no longer a matter of individual things, of separate, isolated results, but of overall structures, network-like structures, which are open to future changes that we cannot possibly fathom."[47] The systematic consideration of the unknown called for the greatest possible flexibility in planning, and this unknown was above all the "constant change of our environment through communication media and technologies."[48] By elevating communication to an "organizational tool for programming an architecture" of the future,[49] Döring touched (albeit in a somewhat more optimistic way) on one of Wiener's central theses: that the life and survival of a city depends first and foremost on the extent of its communication channels.

Conceptual Confusion

The social change that was being loudly proclaimed at the time was reflected in the international architectural discourse. Reyner Banham, for example, wrote of the "psychological and aesthetic break necessary to free themselves from architecture's time-honoured roots in the ground."[50] Sigfried Giedion was also aware of the radical nature of such projects. This is evident not least from his seminal work, *Space, Time and Architecture*.[51] In the fifth revised edition from 1967 in the section on "Space–Time in City Planning: Continuity and Change," Giedion wrote: "It is now clear to everyone that this unparalleled population growth and the traffic chaos within the city organism indicate a completely different way of life and demand radical changes. [...] What is needed is a completely new attitude toward the structure of the city. The contemporary planner must be fully aware that he must simultaneously satisfy the most heterogenous needs and create a 'dynamic field' in which these forces are related to each other. In place of the rigid master plan proposed in the early years of the century, a flexible 'master program' is now being put forward, one that allows for changes and that leaves open-ended possibilities for the future."[52] Giedion's notion of a dynamic field struck a chord with the times. Freestanding buildings were replaced by interconnected spatial structures, and the idea of a system replaced thinking in terms of isolated structures. Even the headings Giedion chose for various sub-chapters in his book appear in a new light when viewed from a cybernetic standpoint: "Spatial Organization," "Individual and Collective Spheres," "Signs of Change." Cybernetics functioned like an undercoat applied in the background, which sometimes shone more clearly, sometimes less so. A fabric of structuralist and cybernetic views of space emerged, which the architectural historian Jürgen Joedicke—with a view to the overlaps between Metabolist and structuralist thought—described as cybernetically influenced structuralism.[53]

In May 1967, Joedicke edited a special issue of the magazine *Bauen + Wohnen* [Building + Living] on this topic. His introduction to that issue reveals the ambivalence with which Banham's proclaimed "break" with the usual architecture was perceived. In a way that was almost symptomatic of the combination of skepticism and curiosity that this architectural concept provoked, Joedicke pointedly informed readers that the special issue would "deviate from the familiar framework of *Bauen + Wohnen*."[54] Joedicke's editorial reads like a cautiously formulated warning to the unknowing architects about to discover the projects under the sober heading of "Urban Planning." This title makes two things clear: not only was Joedicke concerned with the attempt to classify these new architectural concepts, but also, given the radical nature of their underlying ideas about society, he was still somewhat uncertain about them as a whole. The simple subtitle, "Experiments and Utopias," is accordingly relativizing and distanced. But the usual framework had long since been overturned by others. Cybernetically influenced terms such as "system" and "structure" became the buzzwords of a new generation of architects who believed in bearing future responsibility for a global communication space that was yet to be designed. The idea of being able to do even more than only technically design and control the dynamics of social space led to a search for the smallest spatial unit of human dwelling. The smaller, more universal, and technically autonomous this habitable unit was conceived, the more precisely it was hoped to be able to react architecturally to spatial changes in society.

For Joedicke, however, talk of a humane architecture had become too subordinate to the technical concepts of communication and mobility. He soberly derived one of his key questions from this prognosis: "It is striking how much importance is attached to technology, transportation, residential mobility, and densification. However, the question that has not been asked is what kind of person must live in these superstructures, indeed, whether people with all their predispositions are prepared to identify with such forms of living."[55] Joedicke was well aware that with this remark he was testing the technological playfulness and spirit of experimentation of many of these architectural concepts, which were regarded as utopian, at their most sensitive point: their suitability for reality. Although he conceded a certain technical feasibility to this new type of systems thinking—for instance, in the prefabrication of individual housing modules—he found the danger of "falling into fantasy or banality,"[56] on the social level to be immensely greater. Joedicke attempted to classify systems thinking in already familiar and established conceptual fields and, in doing so, downgraded it in terms of feasibility. In essence, his skepticism was "not directed against the thing, against the fantasy, without which great architecture cannot be and never has been, but against the way in which one becomes intoxicated with concepts and misses the point."[57]

Cybernetic Path to Humanity

In *The Human Use of Human Beings,* Norbert Wiener explained "that society can only be understood through the study of messages and the communication facilities which belong to it."[58] For architecture, such a statement initially seemed rather abstract. Giedion, for example, wrote of architecture and community,[59] not of communication and information. In the notion of community, he saw an appropriate recipe for closing the rift between the "highly developed powers of thinking of the 19th century and its debased powers of feeling," which industrialization had released into the psyche of modern society.[60] For Giedion, the path to unifying thinking and feeling was through the elevating platform of art. He hoped that art would provide the key to a reality in which there would be a balance between technical progress and its impact on the "general organization of society that we call its culture."[61]

Tange also sensed this rift.[62] He did not speak of art as a solution, however, but of communication. For him, the path to humanity did not lead through the sublimeness of the artistic spirit, but through the new realm of possibilities offered by technology and science. Giedion's question of reconciling thinking and feeling was posed differently by Tange: "Can modern technology restore humanity? Can modern civilization find the channel linking itself and a human being?"[63] Although Tange was not uncritical of technological developments, this optimism about technology is somewhat surprising in the wake of the events in Hiroshima and Nagasaki. In "Function, Structure and Symbol" he affirmed these two fundamental questions as central to a deeper understanding of his architectural approach. Cybernetics marked out a new realm of possibilities that modern civilization would have to enter in order to connect with every individual. Instead of ignoring technical progress, the architect must consciously look to the latest developments in technology and science. Tange saw this as the only way to achieve an adaptable architecture aimed at building a new foundation for a more humane society. Wiener's assumption, that society could only be deciphered through communication, not only takes on new meaning through Tange, but also a concrete function. For Tange, communication was more than just an instrument for deciphering social structures. If space only acquires structure through communication, this changes the modus operandi: from scientific analysis to architectural synthesis. In projects such as the Communications Center in Kofu (1964–67),[64] the Tokaido Megalopolis (1968–71),[65] and the Plan for Tokyo (1960),[66] Tange manifested what this change meant for architecture. Communication was no longer only about a sense of community and collective feeling, as Giedion emphasized, but also information theory, communications technology, and cybernetics. Whether for a few hundred residents or, as in the Plan for Tokyo, for 10 million residents, it seemed as if architecture could move unhindered in the all-connecting scalelessness of communication.

Max Bense seems to have had some thoughts in this direction when he wrote: "The technical reality of our civilization, which is hierarchically structured in layers of primary, secondary, and tertiary machine spheres, makes refined, selectable, and manipulable mobile means serving information and communication appear necessary in its outermost layer."[67] Wachsmann, who was on friendly terms with both Bense and Tange, put it succinctly with a nod to Tange's cybernetic planning rhetoric: "The vocabulary is well known: communication, mobility, humanity."[68] With this, Wachsmann articulated nothing less than the signature of an entire epoch.

Between Automation and Metatechnology

Norbert Wiener published his book on cybernetics during a period marked by the end and the new beginning of the two most influential art academies of the 20th century in Germany and West Germany, respectively. For architecture, this meant that the era of cybernetics began at a time of institutional transition: a decade and a half after the Bauhaus had been shut down by the Nazis in 1933, and a few years before the Ulm School of Design was founded by Inge Scholl, Otl Aicher, and Max Bill in 1953.

In the run-up to its foundation, there was hopeful talk of a "university for civic and democratic education" and the emergence of "social and political sciences,"[1] and the creation of a "crystallization point" for the "intellectual youth, which today is without a precise goal or knows neither the way nor the means to realize its goals."[2] In the city of Ulm, which had been bombed heavily during the Second World War, there was a spirit of intellectual optimism. Max Bill, a Bauhaus student and the academy's first president from 1953 to 1956, took up pedagogical concepts by Walter Gropius and made them the basis of the Ulm curricula. The founding of the new university, which Bill initially wanted to call "Bauhaus Ulm,"[3] not only represented the continuation but also the institutionalization of the Bauhaus heritage. As such, it was an opportunity to reformulate the foundations of a political approach to art in general. "It wasn't about extending art into the everyday, into application," recalled Aicher, whose abstract orientation systems made him the personification of this politicization effort, far beyond the confines of the university. "It was about a counter-art, about work on society, about the culture of society. We discovered architecture particularly in the construction of factories, we found form in the construction of machines, and shape in the making of tools."[4] Especially with the new potential applications offered by automation, there was a hope to create "free space for a genuine culture," as Max Bill put it.[5] The central aim was training the "man of tomorrow"[6] and a future type of architect who would know how to deal creatively and sensibly with this new freedom gained through automation. Amid this atmosphere of new beginnings and the strategic effort to distance themselves as quickly as possible from the skewed worldview of Nazi mysticism, the importance of critical thinking was supported by several young, predominantly mathematical areas of science. Cybernetics, information theory, and semiotics were taught to the students in Ulm as a mathematical antiserum against the intellectual aberrations of the past. It did not take much to make an impact. A few key figures, such as Max Bense, and later the psychologist Abraham A. Moles, were enough to emerge as charismatic proponents of this new cure. They established thinking in terms of control circuits and communication structures as the basis not only of a scientific methodology for design and planning, but also of a quantifiable approach to art and architecture criticism. Bense spoke like a philosopher and wrote about aesthetics, but thought like a physicist and engaged in passionate debates, equipped with small handwritten notes and self-made, matchbox-sized notebooks. He taught philosophy, philosophy of science, and semiotics at Ulm from 1956 to 1960, initially alone, and later, together with Elisabeth Walther. Bense was one of the first to understand cybernetics and information theory as both a conceptual and technical enrichment, not only of mathematics, philosophy, and anthropology, but later also art and architecture. His 1951 essay "Kybernetik oder die Metatechnik einer Maschine" [Cybernetics or the metatechnology of a machine],"[7] is a key philosophical document for the history of cybernetics in postwar Germany.

View of the Ulm School of Design [Hochschule für Gestaltung Ulm] building complex (1952–1955), designed by Max Bill.

Herbert Lindinger, ed., *Hochschule für Gestaltung Ulm: Die Moral der Gegenstände* (Berlin: Ernst & Sohn, 1987), 75
© HfG-Archiv Ulm, Photo: Hans Conrad

With its goal of epitomizing a model progressive artistic institution, the Ulm School of Design was initially a continuation of the Bauhaus. And like the Bauhaus, it was closed after only 15 years of operation. While the Bauhaus played a decisive role in the early years of its existence, the Ulm School emancipated itself almost completely from the artistic leanings of its institutional and intellectual predecessor. Nevertheless, the enormous success of the Ulm model, together with the failure of its ambitious academic program and its aspiration to function as the moral nucleus of a new society, should be seen as interrelated chapters in the academy's controversial history.

Visit by the Anti-Metaphysical Scientist

During the early postwar years, Ulm quickly developed into an international hub of critical thought. Reyner Banham, whom Tomás Maldonado invited to give a lecture on "Consumption and Product Design" in 1959, believed that this was due to "the skeptical rigor of the thinking—which was largely derived from the Frankfurt School and was still very unknown in England."[8] Besides Banham and a series of international heavyweights—such as Buckminster Fuller, Charles Eames, and Martin Heidegger—Norbert Wiener was also invited to Ulm. Wiener, whose invitation was organized by Bense, visited the newly built rooms of the academy in July 1955. His visit was an event for the students and faculty alike. Here was the American professor of mathematics who had written the highly discussed book that Bense had recently praised as the "fundamental book of modern natural and technological philosophy."[9] Wiener also represented a way of thinking that coincided with the functionalist and moralist foundations of Ulm in a crucial way: he embodied what one might call an "intellectual scientist,"[10] someone who was not only an expert in his discipline, but who also understood how to embed and reflect on the discipline itself in a wider cultural and political context. This is likely what led Maldonado to describe Wiener as an "anti-metaphysical scientist."[11] What united the father of cybernetics with the architects and designers in Ulm was his rhetoric of the

Reyner Banham and Martin Heidegger at the Ulm School of Design, March 14, 1959.

abstract, his passionate lecturing on precision, reason, and rationality, and his belief that he was not only surrounded by a world of abstract machines but could also design and shape it himself.

One year after Wiener's visit to Ulm, Max Bill's resignation as rector marked a conceptual turning point at the academy. "The machine, designed with a particular end product in mind, will be replaced by the machine for basic operations,"[12] Maldonado proclaimed, just one year after Bill left the school. The penetration of cybernetic machine theory into design thinking at Ulm could not have been captured more clearly, and the break with Bill and the design principles he represented could not have been expressed more hochschule für gestaltung ulm

<u>einladung</u>

an die förderer der hochschule für gestaltung ulm
und an die freunde der geschwister-scholl-stiftung

<u>zu einer gastvorlesung von professor dr.norbert wiener</u>

am donnerstag, den 14.juli, punkt 17 uhr
in der hochschule für gestaltung ulm

das thema der in deutscher sprache gehaltenen vorlesung von prof.
wiener bewegt sich im rahmen seiner neuesten forschungen auf dem
gebiet "künstlicher grammatiken" für universell anwendbare
"sprachen".

norbert wiener ist professor der mathematik am MIT massachusetts
institute of technology und gastforscher am instituto nacional de
cardiologia in mexiko. seine gedanken und forschungen gehören zu
den wichtigsten beiträgen zur entwicklung des wissenschaftlichen
denkens der nachkriegszeit. er gilt als gründer der kybernetik,
der von ihm so benannten wissenschaft der information und kommunikation. gegenstand der kybernetik ist das studium von nachrichten-
übermittlungsmethoden bei lebewesen und maschinen. unter den prak-
tischen arbeiten, die prof.wiener und einige seiner kollegen mit
hilfe der kybernetik durchgeführt haben, befindet sich ein tropis-
musgerät, das der beobachtung der parkinsonschen krankheit dient,
sowie eine sinnesprothese für taube und blinde, mit deren hilfe
die umwandlung von nachrichten von einem sinnesgebiet auf ein an-
deres gelingt. ein wichtiges anwendungsgebiet der kybernetik sind
die elektronischen hochgeschwindigkeitsrechenmaschinen und die
voraussagemaschinen.

in deutscher sprache ist von norbert wiener das populär gehaltene
buch "mensch und menschmaschine" im verlag alfred metzner, frankfurt a.m.und berlin, erschienen. es ist eine sehr gute einführung
in die problematik der welt der elektronischen maschinen und ihre
anwendungen.

es ist das ziel der hochschule für gestaltung, eine einheit des
gestalterischen schaffens zu erreichen, deshalb verfolgt sie mit
grossem interesse die entwicklung der kybernetik und lehrt ihre
grundlagen in vorlesungen innerhalb der "kulturellen integration".
die kybernetik ist besonders als wissenschaft der information und
kommunikation auch eine der grundlagen der abteilung "information"
der hochschule.

mit freundlichem gruss

max bill, rektor

Invitation by Max Bill to Ulm School of Design faculty to the guest lecture
by Norbert Wiener held on July 14, 1955.

Tour of the classrooms of the Ulm School of Design. Left: Max Bense; middle: Norbert Wiener; right: Max Bill, July 14, 1955.

René Spitz, *HfG Ulm. Der Blick hinter den Vordergrund. Die politische Geschichte der Hochschule für Gestaltung (1953–1968)* (Stuttgart: Edition Axel Menges, 2002), 173 © HfG-Archiv Ulm, Photo: Hans Conrad

radically. The so-called "machine for basic operations" had become the epitome of a technical worldview. The unity of art and technology, which had been championed mainly by Gropius at the Bauhaus and by Bill in Ulm, was replaced by an increasingly analytical and methodically scientific concept of art and architecture, which found its aesthetic expression in the abstraction of diagrams and circuits.

Automation and Enlightenment

Tomás Maldonado succeeded Bill in 1956, joining a collective rectorship together with Otl Aicher, Hans Gugelot, and Friedrich Vordemberge-Gildewart. In this position, he became a key figure who was jointly responsible for the theoretical shift in the academy's institutional orientation. Looking back, Maldonado recalled that in Ulm there was a "feverish, insatiable curiosity directed [...] towards some disciplines that were then in a phase of ascendancy: cybernetics, information theory, systems theory, semiotics, ergonomics [...]; disciplines such as the philosophical philosophy of science and mathematical logic. The driving force behind our curiosity, our studies, and our theoretical endeavors was our will to provide the work of designing with a solid methodological foundation."[13] In short, Ulm was a discursive space where architecture oscillated between automation and cybernetics. Amid this excitement and fascination with the new and supposedly better, but also in an atmosphere charged by recent German history, Maldonado embodied an attitude towards technology that can best be described as the amalgamation of a playful spirit of invention and a heightened spirit of enlightenment.

Another protagonist at the Ulm School who personified this amalgamation in a unique way was Konrad Wachsmann. Known for his signature white tie and cigarette dangling from the corner of his mouth, he did not want to be a typical architect, but a "technologist."[14] With his original research, he was deeply involved in the mechanical logic of mass production and the automation industry. Wachsmann's focus was not on the individual building but the system, not the object but the series, not craftsmanship but automation. His experimental thinking revolved around variants and prototypes.

More than a decade after Albert Einstein commissioned him to oversee the design and construction of his home in Caputh, Germany, Wachsmann emigrated to the United States in 1941 with Einstein's help.[15] Just a few years later, he and Gropius developed one of the world's first fully automatic factories for prefabricated building elements.[16] Wachsmann went on to achieve great renown with his innovative and no less spectacular architectural models. His graceful model for the United States Air Force aircraft hangar he designed even made it into the Museum of Modern Art in New York in 1946.[17] It was hoped that his appointment to the Ulm School of Design, where he lectured on industrial construction from 1953 to 1957, would capture a bit of the cosmopolitan flair that surrounded Wachsmann. With him, the school was sure to have found a committed teacher who, with industrial construction, represented a field that differed fundamentally from traditional architectural ideas. At the same time, Wachsmann embodied an attitude towards technology that he was skillfully able to integrate into the school's rebellious stance and enlightened design aspirations.

Industrial construction was considered a marginal field in the international architectural discourse. As a discipline of the technological avant-garde, however, it represented a passionate belief in progress that would become a significant component of the Ulm institution. Since the school's founding, its architecture department had undergone a constant process of reorientation in terms of its curriculum.[18] While fields such as visual communication and industrial design were genuinely new subjects and able to establish themselves quickly, it was more difficult for the traditional discipline of architecture to develop a new profile that would distinguish it from other technical colleges and art institutes. Wachsmann's belief that the focus should not be on designing a new kind of architecture, but a "new interpretation of architecture, which does not arise from our wishes, but from our possibilities,"[19] served as a guideline for the architecture department.

Konrad Wachsmann at the drawing table with a model (seated) and Claude Schnaidt (standing behind Wachsmann), Department of Construction, Ulm School of Design, October/ November 1956.

René Spitz, *HfG Ulm. Der Blick hinter den Vordergrund. Die politische Geschichte der Hochschule für Gestaltung (1953–1968)* (Stuttgart: Edition Axel Menges, 2002), 173
© HfG-Archiv

In 1959, for the launch of his book *Wendepunkt im Bauen* [The Turning Point of Building],[20] Konrad Wachsmann vividly described society's increasing orientation around the economy of the machine: "Only recently [...] the concept of automation [...] has penetrated more into the consciousness of the general public and taught us that a machine is not something that works with brutal energy, but is also something very sensitive from time to time, similar to man himself, whereby I do not yet want to make the machine a human being. And these machines have already been so refined in their empathy and responsiveness that they have almost reached that point of being a controllable work instrument, which allows us to respect the machine as a tool directly connected to the will of man."[21]

Wachsmann liked to use big words. He could talk about space, time, and energy, about the "development of the civilization of mankind" and "the limits of the sources of power"—and then suddenly turn to detailed processes for producing machine parts.[22] The image of the "sensitive" machine he described, his talk of machine "sensitivity" and "responsiveness," and his suggestion of the fusion of man and machine, should be understood in light of Wiener's cybernetics. Wachsmann, however, was not interested in the fusion of man and machine, but rather the economic organization of production and manufacturing processes in the construction industry.

Technical Transparency

In the 1960s, many architects dreamed of the liberating potential of automation, of release from the tiring confines of repetitive activities, and the dawn of a world where mankind could realize true values with the help of technology and science. The goals were similar: architecture should adapt to technological developments, orient itself to their speed, and exploit the production capacity of the machine.[23] However, no one understood as well as Wachsmann how to speculate on the complex effects of automation on architectural thinking, and how to make the cultural power of the machine perceptible in detail. In his book *The Turning Point of Building*, whose transformative title became synonymous with the fascination for technology and belief in progress, Wachsmann outlined his vision of architecture in which automation would transform not only design but also aesthetics,

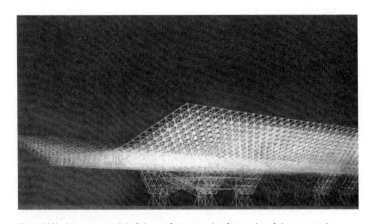

Konrad Wachsmann, model of the roof construction for an aircraft hangar made
of prefabricated elements, commissioned by the United States Air Force, 1951.

Konrad Wachsmann, *Wendepunkt im Bauen* (1959), reprint (Dresden: Verlag der Kunst, 1989), 186 © Judith Wachs-
mann/Konrad-Wachsmann-Archiv, Akademie der Künste Berlin

construction, and even language: "Modular coordination systems,
scientific testing methods, automation laws, and precision all influence creative thinking. [...] The terms of traditional architecture are
no longer precise enough to interpret the thought of this time. [...]
Every statement will therefore have to be limited to point, line, area,
volume. [...] Thus stripped of mystery, the building will expose itself
to undisguised critical scrutiny."[24]

This last sentence reveals the radicality of Wachsmann's considerations and gives a foretaste of what Bense attempted a short
time later in the context of architecture and urban planning using
the analytical precision of information aesthetics. Similar to Bense,
Wachsmann operated with the rhetorical instruments of demythologization. What united them both was the steadfast will to conduct

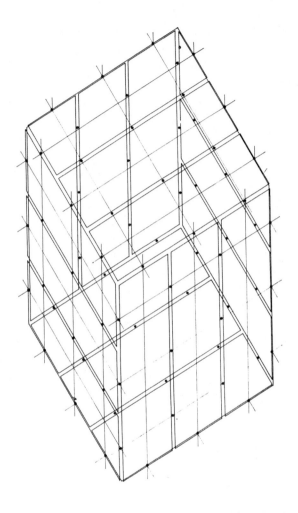

Konrad Wachsmann, diagram of a modular building structure with drawn connection points.

experimental research in the spirit of enlightenment—one with the tools of construction, the other with the tools of theory.

The idea that a building could be "stripped" of its secrets is an impressive illustration of Wachsmann's understanding of the potential of automation in building production and beyond. Looking at a building that has been metaphorically stripped bare, one discovers its inner structure. It follows that "critical scrutiny" of architecture is only possible when a building has been freed of all veiling ornamentation and enveloping facades. The idea that a building can be designed and produced entirely through machine logic not only challenges the idea of the architect in the traditional role of intuitive demiurge. It also reveals a concept of aesthetics whose criteria are based entirely on the assumed flawlessness of technical transparency. Each view into the deep space of Wachsmann's spatial frameworks advances to become a symbol of automation, whose spectrum of meaning encompasses both the production of a building and an aesthetic, corresponding criteria of observation. "The machine is the tool of our time. It is the cause of those effects through which the social order makes itself manifest."[25] Technical transparency, as a characteristic of demythologization and enlightenment, Wachsmann and Bense would have agreed, was also considered a basic condition for social transparency.

Industrialization of Knowledge

"Automation is nothing more than the work process brought under perfect control," Wachsmann explained in *The Turning Point of Building*.[26] A corresponding photograph shows the interior of a machine hall where countless machines are connected as modules in a line. They form a seemingly endless chain of automata, a monstrous production apparatus, which Wachsmann called a "transfer line," in reference to its function.[27] He mentions the synchronization of "any number of special machines," each of which controls itself through "self-control and feedback."[28] The machine modules formed a self-synchronized machine organism. Wachsmann was so fascinated by this idea that he briefly elevated the transfer line to a "symbol of the concept of automation."[29]

The new realm of possibilities offered by automation, whose potential Wachsmann constantly pointed out, was inseparably linked to the possibilities opened up by modularity. In this coupling, the methodological narrowness and the moralizing connotation inherent in the ambitious project of industrial construction become clear. Technology and science became a playing field of possibilities, liberated from the complexity of society. Despite the close interaction between society and automation, they could be considered on different scales. While automation was a phenomenon with profound implications for society, the acts of tinkering with the machine, handling tools, and solving concrete, detailed geometric problems initially had little in common with thinking about automation in its social dimension. A look at the history of industrial construction reveals that the idea of being able to link one element directly to the other was the charm, but also the dogma, of its generalizing approach.

Wachsmann was fully aware of this ambiguity. He differentiated between the nuances of "automation as a social philosophy of production" and "automation as a method of production."[30] That he was more interested in the synchronization of these areas than in their separation becomes apparent in his attempts to transfer the process of group-based work to the technical sphere of automation. For Wachsmann, the organization of teamwork resembled the modular

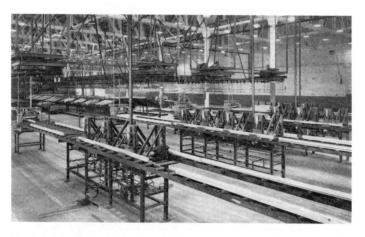

View into the automated construction factory.

Konrad Wachsmann, *Wendepunkt im Bauen* (1959), reprint (Dresden: Verlag der Kunst, 1989), 149 © Judith Wachsmann/Konrad-Wachsmann-Archiv, Akademie der Künste Berlin

structure of the transfer lines, in which independently operating machines were joined to form a large apparatus. Automation was an entirely controlled work process, he formulated soberly in *The Turning Point of Building*—regardless, one might add, of whether it was a machine or a human work process: "Following the conditions of industrialization, the building should develop indirectly through the multiplication of cell and element."[31] The modularization of the building went hand in hand with the modularization of knowledge. Like in a factory, work processes were increasingly broken down into individual tasks.

Wachsmann first experimented with group work at the Institute for Design at the Illinois Institute of Technology in Chicago[32] in the

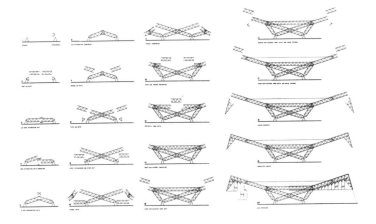

Konrad Wachsmann, assembly sequence for the roof construction of the United States Air Force aircraft hangar.

Konrad Wachsmann, *Wendepunkt im Bauen* (1959), reprint (Dresden: Verlag der Kunst, 1989), 183 © Judith Wachsmann/Konrad-Wachsmann-Archiv, Akademie der Künste Berlin

early 1950s. This was followed by seminars he taught at the Technical University of Karlsruhe with Egon Eiermann (1954), in Tokyo with Kenzo Tange (1955), and then at the Summer Academy in Salzburg (1956–1959). From the experience he gained there, Wachsmann concluded that the number of students in a seminar should not exceed the ideal number of 21 participants. As if at the drawing board, he sketched out every single step of the group's work, which was also reflected in the language he used. Wachsmann planned the respective processes between the working groups with extreme precision: "Assuming that this team, divided into seven working groups, consists of 21 participants, and that seven individual problems of the study are chosen accordingly, a part of the available total working

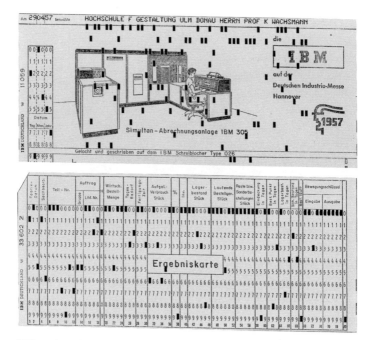

IBM punch cards by Konrad Wachsmann, Hanover Industrial Fair, 1957.
© Judith Wachsmann / Konrad-Wachsmann-Archiv, Akademie der Künste Berlin

time must be divided into seven equal working periods. These seven working periods will be separated from each other by seven discussion periods. Each of these discussion periods will be divided into seven equal time intervals, so that equal time is available to discuss each problem."[33] For Wachsmann, the design process was not like a schematic—it was a schematic. His goal was nothing less than the development and implementation of a comprehensive electrical database for industrial construction. All knowledge was to be stored on punch cards and made available to universities.[34]

To ensure the completeness of the stored knowledge, Wachsmann resorted to special measures: "The groups work best at four drawing boards pushed together, with a large folder on every fourth drawing board, in which all the sketches and other data produced during the work are collected. The folders must be accessible to all team members at all times and also be present during the discussions, so that earlier stages of development can always be reviewed. Therefore there should be no trash bins, because every sketch, drawing, or calculation and every written-down thought must be preserved, as one of the essential principles of this working technique lies in the later reconstruction of the entire development process of the seminar work."[35]

With descriptions such as these, Wachsmann illustrated what may very well be the most radical impact of automation on the practice of architecture: the rationalization, modularization, and ultimately the machine reproduction of architectural knowledge itself. Wachsmann had transferred the modulating logic of the machine to the human process of group work. The project of demythologizing architecture had reached another level. It was the step from industrial building to the industrialization of knowledge.

Aesthetics, Revolts, Calculations

In the final volume of the ten-volume *Enzyklopädie des technischen Jahrhunderts* [Encyclopedia of the modern sciences], Abraham Moles and Herman Grégoire sketched a "picture of the modern man."[1] In their volume on the "Era of the atom and automation" published in 1959—the question of the human being was a central topic. The mission of the Ulm School of Design was to educate the people of tomorrow. However, after the Nazi regime in Germany, the idea of enlightenment and fostering a new political awareness were clearly in the foreground. Moles and Grégoire thought on a much larger scale. For them, the increasing global networking enabled by communication technologies had long made the man of today a "citizen of the world," which was "something entirely new."[2] Furthermore, underpinning the concept of "humanity" was the "discovery of technology."[3] And yet, as Moles and Grégoire explained, mankind was leading a life "that was not adapted to or appropriate for the present."[4] Their criticism was not of individual lifestyles, but of the low mechanization in the built environment. How could modern man survive and profit from the fast pace of progress—as Moles and Grégoire would have asked—if architecture produced living spaces and urban spaces that did not reflect the latest technical and scientific developments? While a vision of the future was being drawn before mankind's very eyes in the form of cars and factories, the architecture of homes and cities was nothing more than a "defensive position of the past."[5]

The pattern of argumentation used by Moles and Grégoire was similar to those applied to industrial construction—recalling Konrad Wachsmann's hymns of praise for automation. It involved juxtaposing the construction of single-family homes with standardized automobile production, an emphasis on objectivity in science and technology, and the idea that the image of man could be measured by the speed of technical developments in architecture; history only stood in the way of an unflinching look to the future. Likewise, Moles and Grégoire were not only concerned with the development of a new architecture, but also asserted that tradition had to give way: "The major cities have to be rebuilt on a functional basis. We have the means to do so in our hands."[6] But instead of examples from the field of industrial construction, such as Wachsmann's space frames or Buckminster Fuller's Dymaxion House, which could be dismantled and rebuilt, Moles and Grégoire presented an illustration of Le Corbusier's Modulor. For them, the Modulor's abstract aesthetics and standardization symbolized the image of modern man better than the automation factories and modular systems of industrial construction. The search for the image of modern man was therefore not only a technical but also an aesthetic question.

A comparable dual orientation in architecture, combining aesthetics and technology, can be found in Max Bense's travelogues from Brazil. Bense recorded his impressions and observations in his diary, mostly in aphoristic form, from the four trips he made to Rio de Janeiro, São Paulo, and Brasilia with Elisabeth Walther between 1961 and 1964. His insightful observations were published in 1965 as a small book under the title *Brasilianische Intelligenz* [*Brazilian Mind*]. Bense was particularly taken with Brasilia, the country's new geometrically organized capital designed by the architects Lúcio Costa and Oscar Niemeyer. In his diary Bense noted: "Unexpectedly Brasilia takes on the character of an enormous room: everything in its place, intended, well ordered, spacious, immovable. A piece of savannah constructed and fully fitted out. The buildings are arrayed like furniture and their relationships to one another are almost

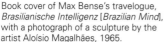

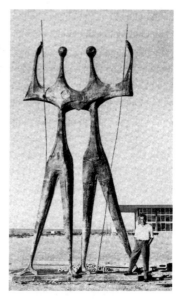

Book cover of Max Bense's travelogue, *Brasilianische Intelligenz* [*Brazilian Mind*], with a photograph of a sculpture by the artist Aloísio Magalhães, 1965.

Max Bense, *Brasilianische Intelligenz* (Wiesbaden: Limes, 1965) © Limes Verlag/Aloisio Manglhães

Os Candangos, a sculpture with two oversized human figures, by the Brazilian sculptor Bruno Giorgi. The courthouse designed by Oscar Niemeyer is visible in the background.

Max Bense, *Brasilianische Intelligenz* (Wiesbaden: Limes, 1965), 49 © Elisabeth Walther-Bense/Bruno Giorgi

more important than their individual selves. Less an architecture of facades than of arrangements. […] Modulated habitability. Cybernetic design."[7] The Brasilia project was planned as an aesthetic representation of a forward-looking Brazil and a symbol of modern man, which made Bense's concept of "modulated habitability" sound unintentionally dry.

Designed in the shape of two symmetrical wings along a gigantic axis, Brasilia was intended from the outset to represent a controlled aesthetic system, a model city of the future. Although there was an undeniable intellectual affinity between Bense and the automation dreams of industrial construction, he, like Moles, felt more obliged to the Cartesian aesthetics of classical modernism than to those of prefabrication, space frames, and construction nodes. The idea of a future machine culture, as Wachsmann constantly spoke of, for example, corresponded in principle to the ideas of Bense and Moles. But while Wachsmann was primarily concerned with fabrication and production processes, Bense and Moles initially adhered to a purely aesthetic and artistic approach to the world. In his philosophical treatise *Ungehorsam der Ideen: Abschluss der Traktat über Intelligenz und technische Welt* [Disobedience of ideas: concluding treatise on intelligence and the technical world], Bense made a distinction: "Technology is to be considered differently from art, in each case to a lesser degree. The degree of spirit that technology presupposes is principally less than the degree of spirit that art reflects upon. The opposite would indicate a degradation of art."[8] Although this statement might make the dialectical relationship between art and technology seem rather one-sided, for Bense, art and technology embodied two sides of the same production process.[9] In the search for the image of modern man, aesthetics (art included), was, in a sense, superordinate to technology, although the two were closely intertwined.

In his essay "Thesen über die Notwendigkeit der Ästhetik in der Architektur" [Theses on the necessity of aesthetics in architecture], published in 1977 in *Deutsche Architekten- und Ingenieur-Zeitschrift* [Journal of German architects and engineers], Bense explained what was important in his idea of cybernetic aesthetics for architecture: "In fact, we not only have modern art, but also modern technology, and not only modern architecture, but also modern aesthetics. Their propositions are not rooted in a hermeneutic metaphysics and are not formulated in beliefs but are based on certain well-fortified numerical mathematic procedures and the formally unambiguous and comprehensible representation and communication schemes of relational theory semiotics. And it is a very general principle of application practice that the degree of precision in application depends on the degree of precision in the presupposed theory."[10]

Going hand in hand with the so-called modern man was also a modern aesthetics; that was the real message behind Mole's and Grégoire's critique of the built environment. But what initially sounded like a creative challenge for architecture was actually a demonstration of their devout faith in science. Aesthetics had become a servant of methodical thinking. "Only the methods, the algorithms, which are conceived in science, span an arc from the realm of the mind to the realm of reality."[11] The question of aesthetics was declared to be a question of methodology, and this reasoning possibly explains both the originality and the limitations of this project in information aesthetics.

Computer Fodder

At the Ulm School of Design, efforts were made to integrate the computer into architecture. Together with Max Bense, Abraham Moles was responsible for the subjects of cybernetics, information theory, semiotics, and philosophy of science. In 1965, a few years after the publication of Moles and Grégoire's encyclopedia on the atom and automation era, Moles became head of the Ulm School's

Arbeitsgruppe 4 (2. und 3. Studienjahr Bauen)

Gliederung der Aufgabenbereiche
von Wohnung und Stadt

Gesichtspunkte	ERSCHLIESSUNG			GLIEDERUNG			BEREICHE					"Computer-futter"
	VERKEHR	VEE-u. ENTWÄSSERUNG	ENERGIE	VERSORGUNG	RÄUMLICHE	SOZIALE	WOHNEN	ARBEITEN	ERHOLEN	DIENSTE		
Wirtschaft‑lichkeit	x o	x o	x o	x o	x o	x o	x o	x o	x o	x o		Vergleiche
Bequemlichkeit	x o			x o	x o		x o	x o	x o	x o	GESETZE + NORMEN	Energie/Zeit
Soziologische					o	x o	x o	x	x o	x		Erhebung
Physiologische					x o		x o	x o	x o	x		Medizinisch Tests
Psychologische					x o	x o	x o	x o	x o	x		Befragung, Tests
Ästhetik	x				x o							

x = für Stadt

o = für Wohnung

Abraham Moles, "Table of functions for the dwelling and the city," Working Group 4, second and third-year architecture students, Ulm School of Design.

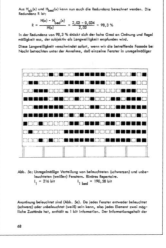

Book cover, Manfred Kiemle, *Ästhetische Probleme der Architektur unter dem Aspekt der Informationsästhetik* [Aesthetic problems in architecture under the aspect of information aesthetics] (Quickborn: Schnelle, 1967).

© Manfred Kiemle

Studies on Kenzo Tange's facade for Kurashiki City Hall (1960).

Manfred Kiemle, *Ästhetische Probleme der Architektur unter dem Aspekt der Informationsästhetik* (Quickborn: Schnelle, 1967), 68 © Manfred Kiemle

Working Group 4, which dealt with issues related to "housing and the city."[12] His countless seminar notes reveal that the question of where the computer could be used in architecture and urban planning was discussed particularly intensively. A table Moles prepared provides some interesting insight: different areas of human activity, such as "working" and "living," but also infrastructural aspects, such as "energy" and "transport," are classified according to their respective economic, sociological, psychological, and aesthetic aspects. The

Manfred Kiemle, analysis drawing of Ralph Rapson's Tyrone Guthrie Theater in Minneapolis (1963).

Manfred Kiemle, *Ästhetische Probleme der Architektur unter dem Aspekt der Informationsästhetik* (Quickborn: Schnelle, 1967), 119 © Manfred Kiemle

Manfred Kiemle, analysis drawing of the Bank of London and South America in Buenos Aires (1960) by SEPRA (Santiago Sánchez Elía, Federico Peralta Ramos, Alfredo Agostini) and Clorindo Testa.

Manfred Kiemle, *Ästhetische Probleme der Architektur unter dem Aspekt der Informationsästhetik* (Quickborn: Schnelle, 1967), 120 © Manfred Kiemle

rightmost column refers to the application of the computer. Under the heading "computer fodder" [*Computerfutter*], Moles listed aspects that the computer could presumably process in the future. In psychological examinations, for example, it could be used for "interviews and tests," in sociological analyses for "surveys," and in business audits for "comparisons." While a possible computer application was found for all the above areas, the field of "aesthetics" remained empty. This is surprising, since aesthetics was a regular focal point of Mole's research. Apparently, finding aesthetic applications for the computer in architecture and urban development was more difficult than assumed. Moles and the seminar participants in Ulm lacked ideas about where, and especially how, to collect data in architecture for computer use in the field of aesthetics. To put it bluntly: architecture could not be fed to the computer as easily as Mole's sweeping category initially implied.

Aesthetic Calculations

In 1967, two years after Mole's seminar, a book was published that seemed to provide an answer to the seminar table's apparent inconclusiveness. The book, *Ästhetische Probleme der Architektur unter dem Aspekt der Informationsästhetik* [Aesthetic problems in architecture under the aspect of information aesthetics], was based on a doctoral thesis by the architect Manfred Kiemle at the Technical University of Berlin.[13] An abstract black-and-white drawing adorns the dust jacket. Its myriad unevenly scattered hexagons form a multilayered, branching matrix, whose honeycomb structure is reminiscent of the additive ground plan forms of structuralist buildings. With the title of his work, Kiemle signaled that the two dry terms, "aesthetic problems" and "information aesthetics," did not conceal a historical or philosophical treatise—at least not one that was expected to follow familiar discourses in the history of architecture or art.

Information aesthetics—a term that can be traced back to a lecture by Bense on modern aesthetics at the University of Stuttgart in 1957[14]—was not to spring from the subjective fabric of "metaphysical reflections"[15] but from the objectivity of quantifiable data.

Any aesthetic judgements, for example, whether a work of art was "beautiful" or "ugly," were viewed from an allegedly mathematical perspective.[16] A picture, poem, or piece of music was no longer to be grasped and analyzed by the "technique of interpretation," but by the "technique of observation."[17]

Information aesthetics thus differed from aesthetics as a philosophical discipline, which was concerned with interpreting aesthetic experiences, sensations, and perceptual impressions. In contrast, information aesthetics was conceived as a kind of empirical aesthetics, the theorization of which was to be "exposed to the corrective of experimentation" and the conceptualization of which was to be adopted from mathematical definitions of "physics, information theory, communication theory, signal theory, and systems research."[18] It may be an irony of history that Kiemle's dissertation topic, which was so submissive to science, was supervised by O.M. Ungers, of all people, who was increasingly critical of the use of the computer in architecture (see the chapter of this book on "Drawing Machines, Machine Drawings") .

"Our bible," as architecture students at the Technical University of Berlin referred to Kiemle's book in the late 1960s,[19] is an inconspicuous work that has nothing in common with the voluminous habitus of the Bible, judging by its outward appearance and its small size. However—and in this function it may have fulfilled the grand gesture of its moniker—it offered intellectual support to the students at a time coinciding with one of the most fraught chapters in the university's history. Kiemle's book came out in 1967, the year that student riots shook the city. That June, the murder of Benno Ohnesorg during a protest against the Shah of Iran's visit to Berlin drove the students out of their drawing rooms.[20] The Technical University became an organizational hub of the Berlin protest movement, where cybernetic conceptual models converged with students' organizations and political goals to create a unique blend.[21] Their slogan was: "Critical reflection and scientific analysis for a democratic political practice."[22] The signs of a crisis in higher education policy could no longer be ignored.[23] Classes at the architecture department were de facto suspended, the usual academic routines of lectures and seminars interrupted, and the atmosphere politically charged.[24] The result was an explosive mixture of architecture, politics, and science, which was characteristic of the situation in its enthusiastic heterogeneity. The architecture critic Wolfgang Pehnt recalled that time as "the age of leaflets and functional diagrams, of occupied institutes and canceled lectures, of group exams and self-grading."[25] Pehnt may also have had Bense's poetic provocation in mind when he added, "Aestheticism was considered a mortal sin."

Kiemle divided his book into two main topics. In the first, the basics of "General information aesthetics" are described in detail.[26] This includes a chapter on "Aesthetics as cybernetic theory"[27] as well as a comprehensive overview of familiar concepts from the fields of semiotics, information theory, information psychology, and sociocybernetics, shedding light on the research fields from which Kiemle's work was derived. The substantive pillars of his investigation were based on the ideas of Bense, Moles, and one of their closest students, the mathematician Helmar Frank. With the exception of Elisabeth Walther, who only represented the field of philosophical semiotics,[28] the others relied in different ways on Claude Shannon's mathematical theory of communication.[29] Bense applied it to the field of semiotics.[30] Frank used it as the basis for his theory of perception in information psychology.[31] And Moles, whose was always active in multiple fields at the same time, made it the starting point for his ideas in both information psychology and sociocybernetics.[32] Together, they provided the theoretical foundation for Kiemle's attempt to transfer the principles of information aesthetics

to architecture. This meant that Kiemle already had a differentiated body of knowledge at his disposal. Information aesthetics was
almost ten years old. Bense, Moles, and later Frank, with his book on
"Cybernetic Analyses of Subjective Matters"[33] had already written
a series of weighty foundational works that Kiemle could fall back
on in his project.

Kiemle opened the second focus of his investigation, which
he gave the programmatic title "Application of Information Aesthetics to Architecture,"[34] with a discussion of semiotic aspects
in architecture. He attempted to show how certain architectural
elements, such as a column or window, could each be assigned
a syntactic, semantic, and pragmatic sign function.[35] With his
chapter on "Aesthetic information in architecture,"[36] the actual
project began from an architectural perspective, namely the question of how the theoretically and terminologically seemingly
impenetrable fabric of information aesthetics could be projected
onto perceptual processes in architecture. Kiemle's basic thesis was
that "large areas of modern architecture are or have become too
poor in information to enable an aesthetic process of perception,"
from which he deduced "at least one cause for the latest trends in
contemporary architecture."[37] Kiemle began by citing an axiom
of Frank's information psychology, which assumed that "the in-
formation-psychological parameters of human consciousness will
become aesthetically relevant criteria."[38] The underlying definition
of perception and consciousness was simple. The brain was thought
of as an information-processing machine that could absorb and
process a limited amount of information from the environment
in a given amount of time. Human consciousness was, similarly, a
"storage device that stores the incoming perceptual contents while
retaining the temporal order for a short time (T)."[39] The technical
tone and the reductionism conveyed in those sentences, which can

hardly be ignored, were the basic conditions and also the result of the information aesthetics project. The self-proclaimed authority of psycho-cybernetic models allowed the complexity of perception, consciousness—in short, human existence—to become a technically reproducible clone of a cybernetic system.

But Kiemle was not interested in further developing Frank's information psychology. Rather, he was concerned with identifying the role of information aesthetics in the current architectural discourse. This included developing an information aesthetics model to explain certain architectural styles. The term "information poverty," for example, took on a twofold meaning in his work: as a component of a cybernetic theory of perception, and as a presumably empirically founded vehicle for the formulation of further architectural theoretical considerations. To this end, Kiemle cited several case studies with which he attempted to show the relevance of information aesthetics for architecture—such as the facade of Kenzo Tange's city hall in Kurashiki (1960), Ralph Rapson's theater in Minneapolis (1963), and the bank by the architects Santiago Sánchez Elía, Federico Peralta Ramos, Alfredo Agostini (SERPA), and Clorindo Testa in Buenos Aires (1960). Kiemle pointedly looked to examples of Brutalism, an architectural movement of the postwar period. Among its icons is the Smithdon High School in Hunstanton designed by Alison and Peter Smithson (1949–1954).[40] There may have been two reasons why Kiemle chose Brutalism, of all things. On the one hand, it enabled him to prove that information aesthetics could be applied to a current architectural trend that was "typical of the new tendencies."[41] He was thus concerned with the significance of information aesthetics for contemporary architecture. On the other hand—and this aspect is revealing from an architectural perspective—Kiemle saw the architectural expression of Brutalism as being in line with the foundations of information aesthetics. "The Brutalists strive—in accordance with the demands of information aesthetics—to make it difficult to grasp the building quickly, thereby increasing the subjective information."[42] What Kiemle was referring to with this assessment is a building's ability to express visual complexity. In other words, Brutalism embodied an architectural movement that, through the design of multilayered spatial configurations and "labyrinthine vistas,"[43] counteracted the so-called lack of information. Kiemle argued his support of Brutalism through information aesthetics on various levels, for example in his descriptions of the "rough, coarse-grained, and contrast-rich surface texture," the "sculptural shapes of the individual forms," and the "readability and recognizability of the structural and, above all, of the functional connections."[44] From an architectural point of view, Kiemle's assessments of Brutalism initially provided little that was new. From the point of view of information aesthetics, however, the plasticity of Brutalist building forms and the materiality of raw concrete signified a "gain in semantic information and therefore an increase in the overall information offered."[45]

It is not surprising that, in the course of his work, Kiemle used examples from the International Style to explain so-called information-poor architecture, such as Ludwig Mies van der Rohe's Seagram Building in New York (1956–1958), and the One Shell Plaza skyscraper in Houston built by Skidmore, Owings and Merrill (1969–1971).[46] Although these buildings embodied the industrialization of the construction process particularly well, the smoothness of the mirrored high-rise facades and curtain walls stood in direct contrast to the differentiated structural play of Brutalist buildings, and therefore stood in opposition to the demand by information aesthetics to increase the semantic information a building should provide. Also, due to the widespread popularity of these high-rises, the "existing subjective information has been greatly diminished."[47]

As if aesthetics were a commodity that could be consumed and worn out, Kiemle wrote disparagingly of the International Style as an "aesthetically spent" architecture.[48]

Kiemle's criticism was not only directed at the architecture of the International Style, but also at the "decorative embellishments of many buildings from recent times."[49] Using Rapson's theater as an example, he tried to illustrate that a simple box was hidden behind the visually complex facade structure; that it was, to put it bluntly, a kind of architectural deception. "Since increasing the information content of the outer surfaces is only possible to a small extent, e.g., through certain irregularities within the grid, some architects look to the device of surrounding the actual building with an autonomous, perforated structure, which has no other function than to offer the possibility—completely independent of the actual building and as a purely ornamental ingredient—to create a sufficient offer of information through sculptural designs, which are freed from any connection to the building. The low-information building is wrapped in a shell of 'free art.'"[50] That Kiemle criticized the ornamental character of prefabricated facade structures is one thing, but that he spoke of "free art" in this context illustrates only too well that the alleged objectivity of information aesthetics concealed an undifferentiated use of terms and subjective conclusions. Why the theater's facade structure is relegated to the realm of "free art" is not explained, nor is the question of what this so-called free art actually encompasses. The boundaries between what is considered architecture and what is considered art could not be plausibly answered, even by the aesthetic calculations of information aesthetics.

Discourse Production

Kiemle's doctoral thesis was picked up for publication by the brothers Eberhard and Wolfgang Schnelle in the same year of its defense. Thematically, the book was in good company. The publishing house Schnelle was considered a vital source of cybernetic literature. Bense, Frank, and Moles were a driving force behind the editorial program, which was filled with cybernetic themes. Besides cybernetics encyclopedias and the two quarterly periodicals—*Grundlagenstudien aus Kybernetik und Geisteswissenschaft* [Basic studies in cybernetics and the humanities] and *Kommunikation: Zeitschrift für Planung und Organisation* [Communication: journal for planning and organization]—there were books and essays on architecture and urban planning, such as *Architekt und Organisator* [Architect and organizer] by Eberhard Schnelle and Alfons Wankum,[51] *Flexible Verwaltungsbauten* [Flexible administrative buildings] by Ottomar Gottschalk,[52] and Johannes Holschneider's *Schlüsselbegriffe der Architektur und Stadtbaukunst* [Key terms in architecture and urban planning].[53] Among the featured authors was Curt Siegel, who was already internationally known from his foundational work, *Strukturformen der modernen Architektur* [Structural forms of modern architecture], published in 1960.[54]

Although Kiemle was hardly the only architect in the editorial program, his book on architecture and information aesthetics still appeared in a special light on the cybernetic stage that the publishing house provided for many intellectuals at the time. There were at least three decisive reasons for this. First, by attempting to map the quantification mentality of information aesthetics onto the blur of aesthetic questions, Kiemle subjected architecture to an apparently rigorous self-diagnosis. Such an approach, it was assumed, would enable an assessment of the discipline's own scientification. At the same time, one could claim to look at architecture with scrutinizing eyes of enlightenment, which, in the context of cybernetics and information aesthetics, meant nothing other than mathematically illuminating both the architectural planning process and the perception of architecture. In the politically charged atmosphere of the late 1960s, this supposedly enlightened view was decisive for reformulating the question of what architecture's social function could be, and subsequently, what the social function of architectural theory and architectural criticism could be. Second, Kiemle's work drew attention to the still young research field of information aesthetics, and in this way contributed to its popularization in architecture. And third, with the help of Kiemle, the proponents of information aesthetics hoped to "open up" architecture as an "art form"[55]—something that had barely been considered until then—to meet the scientific demands of their information aesthetics.

The latter was favored by the emergence of yet another intellectual stage. In addition to Schnelle publishers, a second platform emerged that was much more influential for architecture. In 1967, the same year that Kiemle's doctoral thesis was published, a group of students and teaching assistants at the University of Stuttgart founded the architectural journal *Arch+*.[56] The aim of the journal—which initially circulated under the programmatic title, *Studienhefte für architekturbezogene Umweltforschung und -planung* [Studies on architectural research and design of the environment] and was strongly inspired by Bense—was to develop a scholarly basis for architecture. In the first four years after its foundation, cybernetics, semiotics, scientific theory, and systems theory were important thematic focal points for the magazine. Essays, reports, and opinion pieces in those fields were published regularly, such as Bense's essays on "Urbanism and Semiotics" (no. 3, 1968) and "The Semiotics of Color and Form"

Journal cover, *Grundlagenstudien aus Kybernetik und Geisteswissenschaft* [Basic studies on cybernetics and the humanities] 8, no. 4 (1967), ed. Max Bense, Helmar Frank, Gotthard Günther, Rul Gunzenhäuser, Abraham Moles, Elisabeth Walther, et al.

© Verlag Schnelle, Quickborn

Book cover, Eberhard Schnelle and Alfons Wankum, *Architekt und Organisator. Methoden und Probleme der Bürohausplanung* [Architect and organizer: methods and problems in office building design], (Quickborn: Schnelle, 1964).

© Verlag Schnelle, Quickborn

(no. 9, 1970), Walther's "A Brief Overview of Semiotics" (no. 8, 1969), an essay on information aesthetics by Georg Nees (no. 7, 1969), and a report on the founding of the Institute for Local, Regional, and National Planning (ORL) at ETH Zurich (no. 3, 1968). The minimalist typographic layout of the magazine and the absence of any illustrations signaled to readers that this was a magazine with an almost technical claim to enlightenment. The journal was full of

The journal *Arch+*, issues no. 1 (March 1968) and no. 6 (April 1969), including a feature on the Institute for Cybernetics in Berlin and a visual project by Max Bense and Reiner Kallhardt.

diagrams, statistics, and mathematical formulas and expressed the attempt to base architecture on scientific criteria—a direction that *Arch+* turned away from in 1972 when the content and editing underwent restructuring.

Automation of Criticism

Architecture was considered the last artistic field whose inner function was demystified by information aesthetics. While music, literature, visual communication, the fine arts, and even art education were already eager to illuminate their own disciplines from the standpoint of information aesthetics,[57] architecture stood on the sidelines like a problem child.[58] Some of Kiemle's statements in his dissertation make it clear how painstakingly serious, and even sometimes absurd, the attempt was to bring together architecture and information aesthetics. In his chapter on "Aesthetic information and architecture," for example, Kiemle described his vision of a liaison between architectural criticism and information aesthetics: "Information aesthetics attempts to work out the necessary criteria of beauty that an object must satisfy, in order to function as a work of art in a certain society during a certain period. Fulfilling these criteria is objectively ascertainable, so that the aesthetic critique is freed from subjectivity and the aesthetic judgement can be made unambiguously. Aesthetic criticism is objectifiable; it can therefore be performed just as well by an appropriate programmed automaton as by a human critic." As if that were not enough, Kiemle added a quote from Frank: "If information aesthetics wants to strive for objectivity, it must formulate its theses so that they lay the groundwork for the automation of art criticism."[59]

With that, it was official: criticism was to enter into the service of science and technology and become a rallying cry that was ideologically charged by early information technology. In architecture and art, information aesthetics seemed to become a philosophical campaign against everything that could not be specified, objectified, and formalized. As if with a precision instrument, the so-called field of technical aesthetics, with its abstract language, dissected the "comforting gestures" of the established cultural establishment of art, architecture, music, literature, and painting. The independence of each building, its cultural autonomy, and the historical context of its origin fell victim to an all-encompassing model-based science, whose aim was nothing less than to reduce architecture as a creative discipline to the controllable size of a scientifically analyzable fact.

A vivid impression of Bense's unflinching aggressiveness and pleasure in imparting criticism can be seen in footage of the legendary exchange of blows between him and Joseph Beuys in 1970 during a heated panel discussion at Werner-von-Siemens School in Dusseldorf.[60] As a committed intellectual, Bense was the embodiment of technical reason—the philosophical and political opposite of the rhetoric of mysticism that had been associated with the Nazi regime in Germany. As such, he brought a new and refreshing "theoretical sound" to art criticism.[61] Alongside Bense and Beuys, Max Bill and the sociologist Arnold Gehlen also sat on the podium. This truly historic discussion exemplified the intensity and rigor with which the notion of scientific criticism was to be spelled out in every detail. The inability to state exactly how and by what means an artwork qualified as being aesthetically effective was considered a conceptual weakness by artists and critics alike. Furthermore—and this weighed much more heavily—it left room for various forms of emotional manipulation. The fear of falling once again under the spell of mystical demagogies was still present among many intellectuals since the Nazi instrumentalization of art and architecture. In response to Beuys's repeatedly emphasized aim of aspiring to an indescribable "expansion of consciousness" in the viewers of his works of art, Bense replied—to the audience's applause—that he must at least know "in which direction" this expansion should develop: "Otherwise this is all pure nonsense!"[62]

Max Bense and Joseph Beuys during the panel discussion "Ende offen: Kunst und Antikunst" [Open end: art and anti-art], with Max Bense, Max Bill, Arnold Gehlen, and Joseph Beuys, held at Werner-von-Siemens School in Dusseldorf, February 6, 1970. Video still from the live broadcast for the television show Wochenendforum [Weekend forum] by German public broadcaster Westdeutscher Rundfunk Köln.

With this statement, Bense underscored the theoretical determination and conceptual rigor with which the creative process of an intuitively thinking artist could and, in his opinion, should be, addressed. Bense may have won over the audience with his inimitable linguistic acrobatics and the physicality of his delivery. But in the end, it was Beuys who won the duel, with his passionate and no less brilliant rhetoric, and who continued the discussion with the audience late into the night. The operationalized approach to art and architecture by information aesthetics, and its rhetoric of algorithms and calculations, were countered by Beuys with the methodical openness of his productive thinking that was no less provocative in its totality. In the legacy of the colorful happening culture of the Fluxus movement, Beuys—by interweaving art, society, and

Packed auditorium watching the panel discussion. Video still from the live broadcast for the television show Wochenendforum [Weekend forum] by German public broadcaster Westdeutscher Rundfunk Köln.

Max Bill during the panel discussion. Video still from the live broadcast for the television show Wochenendforum [Weekend forum] by German public broadcaster Westdeutscher Rundfunk Köln.

politics—exploded the traditional aesthetic debates with a radical-ism that was comparable to Bense's own philosophy, albeit in the opposite direction. Objectivity and scientification were replaced by an "expanded concept of art"[63] that was detached from technology and science and instead based on imagination and creativity, with which Beuys wanted to appeal to people's artistic, and ultimately also political, potential in shaping society.

Bense's constant insistence on criteria of measurability, his railing against any inkling of subjectivity in judging art and architecture, even his otherwise enjoyable radicalism in philosophizing—sud-denly seemed strangely antiquated, narrow, and ideological, not least in view of the approaching postmodern era. In Frieder Na-kes's words: "Information aesthetics, as a grandiose reproach by an aesthetics that was oriented entirely to the object, which sought to end the turgid gobbledygook of established art criticism, had to end [...] because it cut through the dialectic of the artwork; because its approach offered no space for development, only for constriction."[64]

Kiemle's plan to describe the impact of architecture with the aid of aesthetic calculations, and to use this means to develop an au-tomated approach to architectural criticism, was also bound to fail. Although his investigations were able to fill a remarkable gap in the discourse of information aesthetics, there was no significant response in architectural practice itself. At the time of the student protests and university reforms in Berlin, Kiemle was able to provide guid-ance to the agitated architectural discourse. However, no intensive debates or forms of critical discussion followed, such as those that repeatedly erupted in fear of the cybernetization of architectural design and planning. Not even a review published in 1970 in the *Journal of Aesthetics and Art Criticism* by the art psychologist Rudolf Arnheim, who was already internationally influential, could help Kiemle's book, which just a few years earlier had been considered the "bible," to gain wider acceptance. Kiemle's work was both the first and last systematic attempt to apply any kind of basic principles of cybernetic aesthetics to architecture.

Swinging Cybernetics

In September 1969, the influential British journal *Architectural Design* published an essay that offered fundamental clarification about the relationship between architecture and cybernetics. With its programmatic title, "The Architectural Relevance of Cybernetics," the article was not written by an architect, but by Gordon Pask, a prominent British cyberneticist of the postwar period.[1] Alongside Stafford Beer, who was the first to apply cybernetic models to management issues,[2] and W. Ross Ashby, who became known to a wider public in the mid-1950s with his books, *Design for a Brain* and *Introduction to Cybernetics*, Pask is regarded as the third important protagonist of the British cybernetics movement.[3]

He was arguably the most flamboyant figure in this trio. Pale, gaunt, and frail in appearance, he gave cybernetics a face that contrasted with Norbert Wiener's stocky stature and energetic aura. Pask was a bricoleur, a tinkerer who played with the circuits of homemade art machines in his laboratory. He also developed a series of sophisticated cybernetic spatial programs for the Fun Palace, an architectural project that emerged in 1961 from a collaboration between the theater director Joan Littlewood and the architect Cedric Price. Pask gave the impression of the daydreaming, yet ingenious scientist. Unlike Wiener, who thought little of cybernetic art,[4] he did not shy away from contact with the arts, on the contrary, he felt at home in the experimental worlds of the London art scene and sympathized with the pluralism of methods and media and technocentric forms of architecture and art—as expressed, for example, in the colorful and comic-like architectural collages by the Archigram group. Pask's essay "The Architectural Relevance of Cybernetics" must therefore be read against a triple backdrop: the development of cybernetic art machines, the beginnings of Pop Art, and the planning of the Fun Palace. This triple exposure reveals the extent to which Pask operated with a concept of communication in architecture that oscillated between psychological, sociological, and computer science-oriented interpretations. While the focus at the Ulm School of Design was mainly the serious search for scientificity and objectivity, for Pask, cybernetics functioned as an explanatory model of communication processes, which, because of his close relationship to theater, had more performative features.[5] But that did not mean that cybernetics was any more modest in its claims. Despite, or perhaps even because of, his close ties to the arts and entertainment, Pask saw in cybernetics the potential for becoming an all-encompassing social theory. Similar to Max Bense, Pask began his project of designing the world through aesthetics. But unlike Bense, who was more interested in formulating an object-oriented aesthetics that was independent of the subject, Pask's concept of aesthetics was directly linked to people's subjective experience and physicality. He thus represented a facet of cybernetics that operated with the conceptual instruments of communication and control coined by Wiener while remaining conceptually bound to a performative worldview. At the heart of his approach was the conviction that space could reflect and shape reality, could only be accessed through action, and could constantly open up new realms of interpretation.

Pask attributed a decisive role to architecture. Architectural spaces, because of their ability to create social spaces again and again, was an ideal field for liberating cybernetics from its purely analytical role and endowing it with a synthesizing and creative role. Viewed from a systems theory perspective, it did not matter whether it was about the cybernetic design of architectural spaces themselves or the digital tools that were used to design and organize architectural spaces:

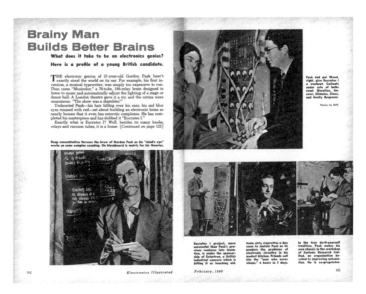

"Brainy Man Builds Better Brains," feature on Gordon Pask and his Musicolour machine, 1960.

Electronics Illustrated (February 1960): 102–103 © Electronics Illustrated

this was the subtle rigor of the approach. In the abstract world of cybernetic models, it seemed easy to operationalize and technically manage man, machine, and environment as homogeneous parameters of a single, all-encompassing system. This frightening formalism in Pask's thinking cannot be canceled out by the fact that his works were created against the backdrop of an urban and fun-loving zeitgeist, for which *Time* magazine coined the now long-popular term, "Swinging London" in its April 1966 issue.[6]

Systems Thinking

"The point I wish to establish is that nowadays there is a demand for system oriented thinking, whereas, in the past, there was only a more or less esoteric desire for it," Pask stated in his seminal essay, "The Architectural Relevance of Cybernetics."[7] In the late 1960s, the call for system-oriented architecture was not uncommon. Thinking in terms of prefabricated construction elements and flexible modular systems had gained in popularity, especially in industrial construction, which was driven by technical developments. The explosiveness of Pask's statement, however, lay in the idea that theory could be generalized: "Because of this demand, it is worthwhile collecting the isolated sub-theories together by forming a generalisation from their common constituents. [...] The common constituents are the notions of control, communication and system. Hence the generalization is no more nor less than abstract cybernetics interpreted as an overall architectural theory."[8]

The attempts to elevate cybernetics to an all-in-one unifying theory was a provocation to the methodological heterogeneity and cultural autonomy of architectural design concepts. Pask conceded a certain functionality to architectural theory, for example, in the critical discussion of historical representations. However, he was convinced that cybernetic concepts implied a much greater epistemological potential and a completely new methodological quality: "In contrast, the cybernetic theory has an appreciable predictive power."[9] With this, Pask expressed what many cybernetics enthusiasts thought: with the help of communication and control, not only could the behavior of technical and physiological systems be explained—as Wiener had popularized it before—but also that of cultural and social systems. "Human interaction is a major source of difficulties which can only be overcome by cybernetic thinking."[10] Pask thus started from the premise that the complexity of social actions could only be understood through the tools of cybernetics. At this point, it becomes drastically clear how far-reaching his trust in the cybernetic model world was.

In "The Architectural Relevance of Cybernetics," Pask remarkably illustrated his vision of a sociocybernetic approach to architecture. The underlying assumption was that cybernetic communication models could be applied to cognitive processes of perception, evaluation, and learning, such as those that occur when walking through and exploring a building. Pask took Parc Güell by Antoni Gaudí as an example; in doing so, he chose a historical example dating back to a pre-cybernetic time. Parc Güell was a project by Gaudí built from 1900 to 1914, but which was only partially completed. Situated on a hill above Barcelona, the park includes gardens and various freestanding buildings, and resembles a glittering fairytale forest populated by ornate objects covered in colorful mosaics. Visitors were meant to explore its many winding paths and surprising landscape like an unknown world. "Gaudi (intentionally or not) achieved a dialogue between his environment and its inhabitants. He did so using physically static structures. […] The dialogue can be redefined and extended with the aid of modern techniques which allow us to weave the same pattern in terms of a reactive environment."[11]

Pask, for whom Gaudí's complex embodied "one of the most cybernetic structures in existence,"[12] sought to illustrate that the relationship between architecture and cybernetics was not foremost a question of technology or tied to the use of the computer, nor was it only a question of history. Rather—and here the universal idea of cybernetics is particularly evident—cybernetics was presented as a systematic conceptual model focusing on the basic modeling of cognitive properties, such as perception or curiosity. The interactions between building and viewer, object and subject, could be understood—whether for the present or for history—as performative communication systems that could be interpreted cybernetically and described technically. For Pask, architecture's actual function consisted in the potential to enter into a physical interaction with people through the arrangement and design of spaces, and to engage with society as an environment: "[T]he concept of functionalism can be usefully refined in a humanistic direction. The functions, after all, are performed *for* human beings or human societies. It follows that a building cannot be viewed simply in isolation. It is only meaningful as a human environment. It perpetually interacts with its inhabitants, on the one hand serving them and on the other hand controlling their behaviour. In other words structures make sense as parts of larger systems that include human components and the architect is primarily concerned with these larger systems; *they* (not just the bricks and mortar parts) are what architects design."[13]

Pask used these considerations to emphasize that the consequence of a systems theory-based relationship between humans and architecture would require a correction, not only of the traditional notion of architecture but also of the architect's role in society. The architect would change from being a designer of concrete objects to a designer of abstract systems, or better: of communication systems. Material and form would no longer be in the foreground of the architectural design process, but rather the programming of an abstract system, based on the operability of its individual elements and their behavior. On the one hand, Pask interpreted Gaudí's aesthetic park from the standpoint of cybernetics. On the other hand, he transposed the idea of the reciprocal relationship between humans and structures onto the abstract world of cybernetics. Through his concept of mutualism, he provided this influence with a conceptual vessel and a performative role. With this form of double encoding,

Pask attempted to formalize a field of activity for which, strictly speaking, neither a generally valid definition nor an exact scientific definition existed, but which nonetheless played a central role in the history of architecture and cybernetics.

Colorful Light and Strange Sounds

In the early 1950s, Pask and a fellow student, the physicist Robin McKinnon-Wood, were already tinkering with several idiosyncratic devices in the computer laboratory at Cambridge University—such as a metronome that changed rhythm through a built-in feedback mechanism, and a typewriter that could produce sounds. They built them from whatever they could find; as McKinnon-Wood recalls, this included military technology machine parts that became available after the Second World War: "We usually had a cart-before-the-horse attitude to building things, partly because we had no money, and partly because we both liked junk. Gordon used to come back from Liverpool or the Isel of Man with bits of Calliope organ, I would come back from Lisle St., London with bits of bomb sight computer […]."[14] But the collage-like constructions were not considered the characteristic feature of these machines. Rather, it was the more or less understandable adaptive behavior they displayed towards their environment. It was not the physical materials, but the structure of the circuits for controlling behavior, that gave them their conceptual significance and effectiveness. One of these machines is considered particularly important in the history of British cybernetics,[15] and can also be seen as the conceptual starting point for the cybernetic program that Pask later developed for the Fun Palace.

View of the auditorium at Churchill's Club with projections by Gordon Pask's Musicolour machine.

The Musicolour, as Pask called his machine, was a soldered-together device which, apart from a jumble of cables, consisted mainly of two parts: a microphone, which was used to gather sounds as input, which were then converted into electrical signals; and a simple

Mechanism of the Musicolour machine.

lighting system, which was directly coupled to the microphone's circuits and projected colored light depending on the sounds. Pask linked both levels to a learning algorithm, which enabled the Musicolour to react to the viewer's behavior and adapt to the respective situation by changing the sound and light effects. In a way, the Musicolour can be seen as an early form of multimedia technology.

Between 1953 and 1957, Pask toured England's theaters with the Musicolour machine and its accompanying computer system. As spaces for experimentation and representation, theaters offered ideal conditions for generating new multimedia atmospheres through the interplay of music, dance, and drama. While Pask was initially inspired by theories on the physiological effects of synesthesia, which involves the brain's coupling of two or more physically separate areas of perception, the idea of a "learning machine" became increasingly more important to him. The latter had a much greater pull than the existing research on synesthesia, which dated back to the late-19th century. A machine that could learn was considered a greater challenge, and not only from a technical standpoint. Conceptually, the idea of a learning machine was also associated with a somewhat arrogant view of humans; this may have been a source of the fascination with this form of anthropotechnical transgression. "By that time it was clear that the interesting thing about Musicolour was not synaesthesia but the learning capability of the machine. Given a suitable design and a happy choice of visual vocabulary, the performer […] could become involved in a close participant interaction with the system. He trained the machine and it played a game with him. In this sense, the system acted as an extension of the performer with which he could co-operate to achieve effects that he could not achieve on his own. […] The 'learning' mechanism, in particular its strategy, was chosen as one of many alternatives which foster the transfer of information around the entire feedback loop […], i.e. the loop involving visual display, performer, musical instrument and 'learning' machine."[16] The *Musicolour* machine could thus serve as a mechanical model for a neurophysiological, behavioral pattern of adaptivity. Furthermore, the use of light and music created a spectrum of impactful multimedia atmospheres. Cybernetics functioned in this case as a kind of system integrating art, science, and entertainment. Through individual feedback steps, man and machine could be interpreted and regulated as seemingly equal influencing variables in a single feedback loop. Subject and object became parameters in a common abstract system.

In terms of media history, the Musicolour may initially be reminiscent of the art machine by László Moholy-Nagy, the Light–Space Modulator, a kinetic sculpture he developed around 1930.[17] Driven by small electric motors, the Light–Space Modulator was, in the words of Moholy-Nagy, an "apparatus for demonstrating light and motion phenomena,"[18] which he demonstrated in his short film *Lichtspiel—Schwarz-Weiss-Grau/ Light Play—Black-White-Gray*.[19] The fundamental difference between Moholy-Nagy's machine and Pask's was that the former produced a shadow pattern that moved uniformly, while the latter comprised a self-organizing mechanism whose behavior, from the viewer's perspective, did not follow a controlled pattern. The Musicolour was a black box whose input was known, but not its inside circuitry. The resulting output was therefore calculable, but not predictable. Pask had created a self-organizing art machine whose hidden cybernetic machinery became a new abstract model for a machine uniting science and art, while demonstrating a new manifestation of technical anonymity. It is the subtlety of these two aspects that explains—also with regard to Pask's early fusion of cybernetics, theater, and entertainment—the charm, but also the rigor of the later Fun Palace project.

In 1947, the writer Herbert Read, the art critic Roland Penrose, and the publisher Geoffrey Grigson, among others, found the Institute of Contemporary Arts (ICA) in London. In the same year, György Kepes—artist, theoretician, and student of the Bauhaus master Moholy-Nagy—established the first academic program on visual design at the Massachusetts Institute of Technology (MIT), which 20 years later would give rise to its Center for Advanced Visual Studies, which still exists today. Shortly after its founding, the ICA was already considered an intellectual hub of the British art scene. It hosted a multitude of exhibitions, happenings, and actions, making the institute an avant-garde oasis in conservative British society. Four years after its founding, the artist Richard Hamilton curated the groundbreaking ICA exhibition *Growth and Form* in 1951.[20] It was inspired by the study *On Growth and Form* from 1917 by the biologist D'Arcy Thompson.[21] Thompson's work addressed the geometric transformability of forms in nature— apparent, for example, in the structural similarities of bones and skeletons and the dynamic growth processes of cells. The question of visual form was therefore always also a question of the underlying morphological laws. Increasingly, Thompson's focus turned to the visualization and conceptual representation of force curves and other abstract organizational patterns. At the ICA, Hamilton took up Thompson's methodical reorganization of the concept of form from the standpoint of the arts. In the structural turn this involved, he saw a conceptual orientation that not only enabled different complex forms to be interpreted in terms of Gestalt psychology, but also shed new light on visual correlations between art, science, and technology.

Thompson's structural theory had a major influence on the field of science. The idea that there was a "unitary principle which correlates all observations and experiences within the range of human perception and understanding"[22] was attractive to many. For this reason, ICA produced an accompanying book called *Aspects of Form*, which advanced the ideas of the exhibition and Thompson's legacy in a theoretically sophisticated yet generally accessible manner. Edited by the science historian and theoretician Lancelot Whyte, the essay collection featured contributions by notable scientists, such as the crystallographer S.P.F. Humphreys-Owen, the geneticist Conrad Hal Waddington, the behavioral scientist Konrad Lorenz, and the art psychologist Rudolf Arnheim.[23] The cyberneticist William Grey Walter was also represented, with his essay "Activity Patterns in the Human Brain."[24] His involvement is a revealing detail for at least two reasons. Walter played an important role in the neurophysiological branch of British cybernetics discourse. Since the 1930s, he had been researching the development of neuronal patterns in the human brain and had developed an apparatus for the electroencephalographic measurement of brain activity, better known as the EEG machine. The second reason, which is of greater importance for the context discussed here: Walter was the father of the first cybernetically controlled, autonomous robots.

The two machines, which Walter affectionately called "Tortoises," were contained in two tin boxes, barely knee-high tall, which crept along the ground with the help of three small wheels. These simply wired machines mark the beginning of situated robotics, an engineering tradition that extends to the entertainment industry of the present day.[25] Simply put, situated robots are machines that determine their path through their respective environment by interacting with it. Equipped with simple sensors, such as photocells or contact switches, they explore the surrounding space using a simple trial-and-error

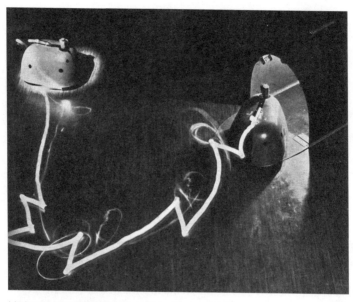

Motion tracking with William Grey Walter's cybernetic "Tortoise."

method. Situated robots are in this sense performative machines—machines that act recognizably in the world through their behavior. That Walter was featured in a book dealing with universal principles and a transdisciplinary notion of form and structure combining art and science testifies to the willingness to accept cybernetic models in art and architecture. Although the arts often approached cybernetics independently and detached from the attempts to appropriate it in architecture, the boundaries were fluid. This was related to a notion of space that was not understood as preexisting, for instance, as a neutral, geometrically defined container, but which is discovered and constructed interactively.[26] From a systems theory perspective, this applied to both humans and machines.

In 1968, the same year that the Ulm School of Design was closed, the ICA showed an exhibition focusing on cybernetics. The show *Cybernetic Serendipity*,[27] which was partly the result of an initiative by Max Bense and was curated by Jasia Reichardt,[28] provided the first large-scale survey of the still young field of cybernetic arts. It featured computer graphics by William Fetter, Georg Nees, Frieder Nake, and Michael Noll; compositions by John Cage, Karlheinz Stockhausen, and Herbert Brün; "electronic television" images by Nam June Paik, programmed choreographies, computer-generated poetry, and a cybernetic sculpture by Nicolas Schöffer.

The show also featured an architectural project, titled *Indeterminate Dimensions in Architecture*,[29] and included drawings of Northwick Park Hospital, a large hospital complex on the northern outskirts of London. The facade structure of the building, designed by John Weeks, had been generated with the aid of a computer program, resulting in an irregular random pattern that showed "the direct expression of an objective ordering process," according to the exhibition description.[30] Weeks used the computer as an automatic composition machine, which helped to operationalize indeterminacy and turn it into a design parameter—a method John Cage had already spoken of ten years earlier in his lecture on "indeterminacy."[31]

Although Weeks's project is considered the first "explicitly indeterminate building"—at least that is how Charles Jencks interpreted it shortly afterwards in his book *Architecture 2000*[32]—it played a rather subordinate role in the exhibition. This was not so much due to the architectural quality of the project. However, the use of the computer was limited to the automatic arrangement of flat facade

135

Cover of the exhibition catalogue for *Cybernetic Serendipity*, featuring a collage of programmed graphics by Donald K. Robbins (1968).

Jasia Reichardt, ed., *Cybernetic Serendipity: The Computer and the Arts* (London: Studio International, 1968) © Institute for Contemporary Art, London

elements of a building that had already been designed. The project thus had more the character of "art in construction." For visitors, it was not immediately obvious what role the computer played. The actual point of the project—"the appearance of the buildings was not determinable until the results of the calculations were seen"[33]— was not provocative and spectacular enough compared to the other artworks in the exhibition. One could also venture to say that the project lacked the performative playfulness that distinguished the works by Nam Jun Paik, for example. Weeks's experiment also reflected the general methodological difficulty of architecture to convincingly integrate the facets of indeterminacy and chance into the design process. While earlier exhibitions at the ICA, such as *Man and Machine* from 1955, displayed industrial everyday objects from the increasingly pervasive world of media and consumption, *Cybernetic Serendipity* transformed the exhibition space into a crowded enclosure of self-made machines, abstract graphics, and cryptic circuits—almost as if it had penetrated the mathematical interior of the objects themselves.

The term "serendipity" used in the title and borrowed from literary history—which also means "happy coincidence" or "unexpected discovery"—lent the exhibition a positive and cheerful note.[34] Cybernetics and computers were to be freed from the dubious reputation as the technical core of an authoritarian culture of thinking machines. The aim was to bring out technology's experimental and artistic sides. Yet even the charming metaphor of "cybernetic serendipity" could not distract from one technical aspect in particular, which was undeniably clear when cybernetic systems thinking was applied to social processes: that of social control. Visitors could experience this aspect, albeit on a small scale, at the exhibition's entrance: "Visitors are caught up in a carnivalesque March of Progress from the moment they enter. At the door, they find that their bodies have been sighted by an electric eye, which in turn triggers the computer-generated voice that welcomes them in a deep monotone."[35] Visitors therefore functioned as both a catalyst and a component of a technical feedback cycle, which they set in motion but could not control.

Pask also participated in the exhibition with a contribution. More than a decade after the *Musicolour*, he introduced a second cybernetic machine, the *Colloquy of Mobiles*, which was considerably more complex in its structure.[36] This time it was not a single object, but an entire ensemble of objects. Pask's work, along with Schöffer's cybernetic sculpture, *CYSP 1*, occupied a prominent place in the ICA's cramped quarters.

Cybernetic light tower

A project by Nicolas Schöffer, intended for the Rond-Point de la Defense in Paris
An open structure 307 metres tall, having an average span of 59 metres, is built of square steel tubes filled with reinforced concrete, based on the same techniques as a skyscraper frame. The structural elements of this skeleton will be covered either with polished stainless steel sheets, or with polished aluminium. Within this structure, 15 curved mirrors are placed at different heights between the 180 parallel arms protruding in four directions. 100 revolving axes are installed, on which 330 mirrors are fixed. The relationship between the curved mirrors and the revolving plane mirrors produce a great number of reflected and diffused rays around the sculpture.

Each of the 100 axes will be driven by electric motors at variable speeds. The combined controls for these motors are connected to a central computer.

The sound, temperature, traffic flow, and humidity will affect the movement and luminosity of the tower.

But on certain days and at certain hours, the tower can serve as a barometer, announcing bad weather, for example, through emission of red beams, and fine weather by the slowing up of its movements and the predominance of blue.

It will also be able, say at 1 p.m., to give the stockmarket trends: increasing brightness for a rising market, a more or less accentuated slowing-up for a falling market.

For road traffic, every evening from 5 to 8 p.m., it can be made to serve as the co-ordinator and broadcaster of information for car-drivers, communicating data by radio, and also by conventional visual signals, indicating the directions to take or to avoid.

In certain urgent cases, it will be able to broadcast warning sounds or orders.

CYSP 1

CYSP 1 (a name composed of the first letters of cybernetics and spatiodynamics) is the first 'spatiodynamic sculpture' having total autonomy of movement (travel in all directions at two speeds) as well as axial and eccentric rotation (setting in motion of its 16 pivoting polychromed plates).

Nicolas Schöffer has executed this spatial composition in steel and duraluminium, into which an electronic brain, developed by the

44

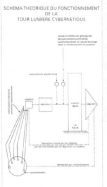

SCHEMA THEORIQUE DU FONCTIONNEMENT DE LA
TOUR LUMIERE CYBERNETIQUE

SCHÖFFER

Nicolas Schöffer's "Cybernetic Light Tower" sculpture.

Jasia Reichardt, ed., *Cybernetic Serendipity: The Computer and the Arts* (London: Studio International, 1968), 44

An architectural project

Indeterminate dimensions in architecture

John Weeks

Works of architecture, recognized as such, normally have their dimensions determined by their designers. However, in a hospital building under construction at Northwick Park, North London, by Spring, 1968,* the visible structure has its appearance determined wholly as a result of a computer-orientated programme.

The rational basis for the decision to abandon an architect-designed dimensional system stems from the need to produce a structure made up of as large a number of identical units as possible, to enable economies to be obtained out of standardization.

The building complex comprises a cluster of buildings of different heights and shapes, but the same structural elements, a mullion and a beam, are used throughout. Design parameters such as height and loading characteristics were fed into the stress computations. This was the only design process which controlled the external appear-

ance. The impact of the standard analysis on the varying conditions has resulted in buildings which are everywhere different, since the design parameters differ, even though they are made of identical structural elements. The standard structural mullions are grouped at intervals which enable them to be equally stressed whether they are at the bottom of multi-storey buildings or on the upper level of a two-storey building. The apparently random intervals between the mullions are the direct expression of an objective ordering process. The appearance of the buildings was not determinable until the results of the calculations were seen; the designers of the building did not intervene.

*Architect: John Weeks of Llewelyn-Davies Weeks Forestier-Walker & Bor; Engineers: Peter Dunican; Nigel Thompson of Arup & Partners.

Below, two buildings from a hospital complex under construction—a research building and an ambulant patient department. Identical structural elements are used throughout and the intervals between structural elements follow a stress computation without architectural modification.

69

Architectural project by John Weeks with a computer-generated facade structure.

Jasia Reichardt, ed., *Cybernetic Serendipity: The Computer and the Arts* (London: Studio International, 1968), 69

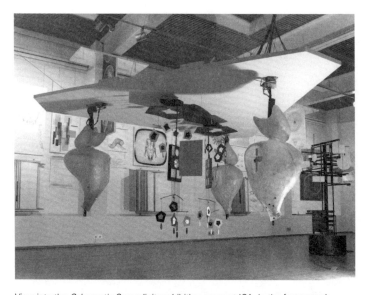

View into the *Cybernetic Serendipity* exhibition space at ICA. In the foreground: Gordon Pask's installation *Colloquy of Mobiles;* in the background (right) Nicolas Schöffer's *CYSP 1* sculpture. Computer graphics by Frieder Nake can be seen on the walls.

http://www.medienkunstnetz.de/works/colloquy-of-mobiles/images/8/ © Amanda Pask Heitler/Gordon Pask/ Gordon-Pask-Archiv, Institut für Zeitgeschichte, University of Vienna

Pask's installation was an interactive structure whose behavior users could directly influence via a series of mirrors. The individual objects of this ensemble, the so-called mobiles, hung from the ceiling like oversized mosaic stones and giant plastic drops. Pask had metaphorically divided his ensemble of machines into "male" and "female." Corresponding "female" and "male" circuit diagrams showed only too well the universal claim of cybernetics in aiming to answer anthropological questions through purely technical models.

Document by the Fun Palace Cybernetics Committee, March 17, 1965.

FUN PALACE CYBERNETICS COMMITTEE

MINUTES OF THE MEETING
HELD AT THE ARCHITECTURAL ASSOCIATION,
34 BEDFORD SQUARE, W.C.1. 17/3/65.

The intricately interconnected machines of the *Colloquy of Mobiles* interacted with each other through light and sound: "It is a group of objects, the individual mobiles, that engage in discourse, that compete, cooperate and learn about another. [...] Each individual has a set of programs that determine its motions and its visible state. Each individual learns how to deploy its programs in order to achieve a goal [...]. Its level of 'satisfaction' is reflected partly in its behaviour and partly in a visual display."[37] What was interesting about the installation was not only the behavior of the individual elements, but the performance of the entire ensemble, which Pask described in the exhibition catalogue as an "aesthetically potent environment."[38]

Cedric Price at the drawing table.

Viewers of the installation could intervene in the play of light that the machines produced. With the help of small mirrors, they could reflect and redirect the rays of light that the objects produced, thus intervening in the machines' "communication process" and entering into a dialogue with them. "An aesthetically potent environment is an environment of any sort [...] that people are liable to enjoy and which serves to shape their enjoyment. [...] The quality of 'aesthetic potency,' although it determines the framework of which artistic communication can take place, is primarily attached to a relation between the environment and the hearer or viewer. An aesthetically potential environment encourages the hearer or viewer to explore it, to learn about it, to form an hierarchy of concepts that refer to it; further it guides his exploration; in a sense, it makes him participate in, or at any rate see himself reflected in, the environment."[39] From Pask's brief description, it is hardly clear that his installation involved programmed objects comprising circuit diagrams, codes, and an all-managing database operating in the background, which could form their own "computational environment" seemingly detached from humans. With his work, Pask sketched the symbolic contours of a multimedia world of technically produced and reproducible didactic entertainment, in which the technical was no longer called by its name, but which was thoroughly technical in its essence.

Triumph of the Theater

"It is probably fair to describe Miss Littlewood's Fun Palace project as an attempt to provide a form of environment that is capable of adapting to meet the possibly changeful needs of a human population and capable, also, of encouraging human participation in various activities."[40] With this sentence begins the minutes of a meeting of cyberneticists called the Cybernetics Committee, chaired by Pask. The committee played a central role in the development of the Fun Palace, an ambitious building project, which—despite remaining unbuilt after a seven-year planning phase—became an influential architectural project of the postwar period. The project was launched in 1961 by the theater director Joan Littlewood, together with Cedric Price. Price, who was busy with the construction of a geometrically complex bird aviary for the London Zoo, was one of the most original minds on the British architectural scene, and therefore an ideal partner for the Fun Palace project. Pask joined them a short time later, his role becoming something like the cybernetic control center of the entire planning process. Other protagonists from the British cybernetics scene were also involved in the project, such as Stafford Beer, the neuropsychologist Richard Gregory, the economist Richard Goodman, the artist Roy Ascott, the sociologist Leslie Wilkins, and the cognitive scientist Frank George.

In the countless drawings, collages, and sketches that Price continuously produced throughout the planning process, the Fun Palace usually appears as a stage-like structure made of oversized trusses. Price often used a central perspective for the drawings, allowing viewers to look straight into the construction interior, which seemed to be the real highlight of the project. The Fun Palace interior was essentially a vast, nearly empty space, which, together with a series of variable and flexible ramps, stairs, platforms, and arenas, was to guarantee a wealth of possibilities for perception and movement. The Fun Palace was conceived as a structure that would allow for the constant redefinition of these possibilities. Accordingly, it represented a notion of architecture that was composed of experimental spaces of activity. In short, the Fun Palace was a multifunctional spatial structure of gigantic dimensions, designed with flexible dividing walls.

The spatial program of the Fun Palace comprised six zones. The first zone clearly bears Pask's signature, meant as a place where visitors could experiment with cybernetic "teaching machines."[41] The second zone was devoted to participatory concepts and "new forms of expression."[42] The third zone was for film screenings and public lectures. The fourth zone accommodated a laboratory for scientific experiments. The fifth zone was an art studio for painting and sculpture; and the last zone was devoted entirely to music. Visitors to the Fun Palace could not only experience every imaginable form of entertainment but also produce it themselves. "In London we

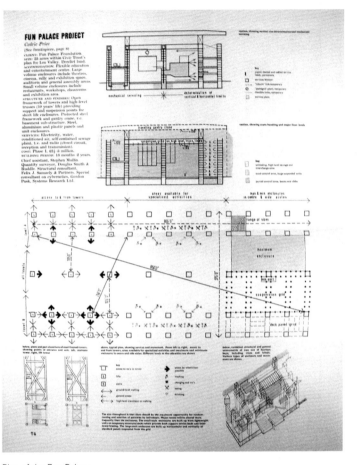

Plan of the Fun Palace.

Perspective of the interior of the Fun Palace.

are going to create a university of the streets [...]. It will be a laboratory of pleasure, providing room for many kinds of action. [...] For example the 'fun arcade' will be full of the games and tests that psychologists and electronics engineers now devise for the service of industry or war—knowledge will be piped through juke-boxes."[43] War technologies were to be placed in a positive light and transformed into playful instruments of entertainment. Cybernetics itself was the best example of this.

The origins of the Fun Palace project can be found in the experimental theater of the 1960s, whose well proclaimed aim during this time was to blur the boundaries of the arts, such as literature, music, or theater itself. This so-called performative turn[44] is generally characterized by an increasing focus on the production of events rather than the creation of works. One aim of the Fun Palace project was to spatially remove the dichotomy between subject and object that was characteristic of traditional theatrical concepts. Theater should no longer legitimize itself through the representation and performance of a fictitious other world, which the audience had to interpret and understand. Instead, the theatricality of the Fun Palace was that it fostered unexpected and surprising encounters and connections between the visitors and the building, and between the visitors themselves, leading to ever new processes of action.

Performance as a principle creates a situation that redefines two relationships that are fundamental to semiotic aesthetics: first, the relationship between object and subject, viewer and viewed, spectator and performer; and second, the relationship between corporeality or materiality and the symbolic quality of the elements, i.e., between signifier and signified.[45] In the logic of semiotic aesthetics, as in that of Bense's information aesthetics, the separation of subject and object is essential. The artist creates a work of art as a detached and detachable artifact, thus granting it its own existence, independent of the artist. This was also the issue at stake in the 1970 debate between Max Bense and Joseph Beuys described earlier (see chapter on "Aesthetics, Revolts, Calculations"). While Bense insisted on a sharp separation of subject and object in the sense of semiotic aesthetics, Beuys challenged this view by repeatedly pointing to the individual interpretive ability of human beings—using the somewhat grandiose expression of "expansion of consciousness." Just like Beuys, Littlewood, Price, and Pask were not concerned with a semiotic foundation for aesthetics or any other forms of its systematization. Their aesthetic concept was closely tied to the performative nature of consciously staged action.[46] At its heart was a performative aesthetics concerned not with the analysis of architecture, but its physical experience.

But visitors were not supposed to perceive and interpret the Fun Palace as a building only. That would require the architectural space to exist independently of its observers and users, with an a priori meaning and function. Instead, the Fun Palace was to evoke wonder, fascination, and curiosity in its visitors and appeal to them aesthetically: "The organization of space and the object occupying it should, on the one hand, challenge the participant's mental and physical dexterity and, on the other, allow for a flow of space and time, in which passive and active pleasure is provoked."[47] Whether on the level of simple affects or cognitive functions, the architectural space of the Fun Palace was conceived as an action that could shape reality, but which first had to be activated by the visitor as a protagonist. The materiality of architecture was not to be translated into semiotic spheres but enabled each visitor to have his or her own individual, unsymbolic experience.

If the impact of an architectural space is no longer dependent on the architect's intended meaning but on the meaning that users evoke through their behavior, this also results in a different image of the architect. According to Pask, "[…] The architect will no more know the purpose of the system than he really knows the purpose of a conventional house. His aim is to provide a set of constraints that allow for certain, presumably desirable, modes of evolution."[48] The focus was no longer on the design of forms, but on sets of rules for the generation of forms. Pask explicitly wrote of a "set of constraints" and of "evolution."[49] Analogous to the indeterminacy of the machine behavior of Pask's *Musicolour* or Walter's *Tortoises*, Pask's aim was to establish a new paradigm in the sense of an architectural design strategy.

1965 marked a turning point in the Fun Palace project. That year, Pask made a proposal to the planning team that raised doubts about cybernetics, especially in Littlewood's mind. Littlewood feared cybernetics would become too dominant in the project; Pask had developed an engineering schematic to regulate and control behavior within the building. The reductionist approach of cybernetic thinking was particularly prominent here. Pask had made a complex organizational diagram of feedback loops, which he called the "organisational plan as programme."[50] It was like a huge circuit diagram, which would record all the behavioral processes and movement profiles of the Fun Palace visitors. There were three parts to the process. In the first step, the individual preferences, interests, and wishes of the arriving visitors would be fed into a computer system, referred to simply as "individual preference valuations"[51]—it was a matter of accumulating raw data. In the second step, the data would be sorted and evaluated; the results would be used to generate user profiles. In the third step, these user profiles would be used to vary and adapt the spaces within the Fun Palace accordingly. A computer would continuously monitor this process in the background, and, through a feedback loop, reconcile it with the number of visitors arriving and leaving the Fun Palace. Pask referred to the former as "unmodified people" and the latter as "modified people."[52] In this conceptual confrontation, the cybernetic logic of control is clearly visible. Taken as a whole, Pask's project resembles a sophisticated personalization program, which would record, index and then transform human behavior into a modifiable parameter for designing a personalized technical environment.

"It will be necessary to consider the Fun Palace as a vehicle for social and psychological experiments. It will be also necessary to regard

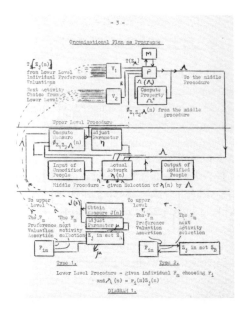

Gordon Pask's cybernetic schematic for the Fun Palace.

Stanley Matthews, *From Agit-Prop to Free Space: The Architecture of Cedric Price* (London: Black Dog Publishing, 2007), 120 © Cedric Price Fonds/Canadian Center for Architecture, Montréal

the Fun Palace as a test bed for novel art forms and novel media," wrote Pask in a report by the Fun Palace Cybernetics Committee.[53] Rigid spatial concepts would be replaced by free experimentation with new forms of entertainment and communication. With a view to the history of theater, one could also speak here of a "performative turn" for architecture. If no architectural space exists independently of its design by the architect, but architecture is instead an event, i.e., an action that shapes reality—so that the production and reception of space occur simultaneously—then operating with categories of spatial separation, such as functional separation, or a rigid spatial program, becomes questionable.

At the same time—and this is where the utopian potential of the Fun Palace becomes apparent—the concept of performance, originally borrowed from theater, was to be technically regulated by cybernetics and reproduced and acted out on a larger scale. While the Fun Palace project falsely assumed that performance could be guaranteed through feedback loops, it was precisely this expanded notion of space that bore much of the project's groundbreaking significance for architecture. The originality of Littlewood, Price, and Pask was that they opened up a new performative reception aesthetics for architecture based on early information technology, whose conceptual origins lay in theater and the development of cybernetic art machines.

Drawing Machines, Machine Drawings

"This cannot be left to a device that can make if/then or yes/no decisions and nothing else!"[1] This sentence, uttered unequivocally in an interview in 1986, was by Oswald Mathias Ungers, one of the most internationally successful German architects of the postwar period. The human activity at stake, and one that should by no means be left to a computer, he asserted, was the act of drawing. Ungers based his critique on the assumption that the digitalization of drawing would not only have direct effects on the practice of design but also on the concept of architecture under these new technical conditions: "Architecture becomes graphic through the means it uses. CAD is, after all, a graphical tool, two-dimensional. It would therefore come as no surprise if architecture, which already appears flat at present, were to become even flatter with the spread of CAD: a mere facade, two-dimensional like the drawing. [...] Today we think and design in miniatures. What we build, we first scale down. But this reduction in size also alters the concept we have in our mind. Space and material only occur in the imagination, in simulation [...]."[2]

While Ungers tried to appeal to architecture's collective conscience with his above assessment of architectural drawing, the first gray calculating machines were already standing on the drawing boards of architecture departments and planning offices. Thin computer graphic lines flickered on small screens that were originally created for the military industry. Traditional notions about the coupling of drawing with seeing, but also drawing as seeing, were subjected to scrutiny by a new kind of technical knowledge and its accompanying criteria of operationality with the invasion of the computer. The intuitive dialogue between the executing hand and the creative eye was dramatically disrupted. But there was more at stake than uncertainty in the face of this new technical dimension. Unger's vehement statement can be understood as a late attempt to rescue architecture from abandoning the productive contradictions of the human spirit in favor of the computer's promises of efficiency. At the core was the uncertainty about what instruments would be available for the theory and practice of architecture to critically confront the ephemeral worlds of software programs and databases, computer codes and simulation models.

Despite his critical stance towards the computer, Ungers had already been occupied with its possible applications in architecture at an early stage. He began experimenting with planning software in the late 1960s, around the same time that he withdrew from the politically charged protest atmosphere in Berlin's university landscape and accepted an appointment at Cornell University.[3] One of the earliest examples is a study he conducted on mass housing. In the interdisciplinary project on "Optimal Residential Area Planning,"[4] Ungers and the economist Horst Albach examined the density of the Märkisches Viertel housing development on the outskirts of Berlin (built from 1963 to 1974), which was still under construction. Following a detailed analysis of statistics provided by the state housing finance institution, Ungers concluded that high-density housing developments tended to be less effective than those with low density. This was a revealing and somewhat uncomfortable assessment for the state housing association—not least because Ungers was himself involved in the gigantic housing project with the design of a high-rise apartment building.

Another example is his "Series of Interactive Planning Programs" (SIPP).[5] The program, developed in 1972 with Tilman Heyde and Tom Dimock, resulted from a joint research project and was based on the premise that in the future, the growing complexity of planning

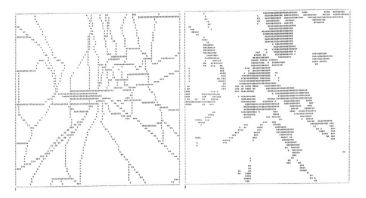

Computer-generated schematic maps by Oswald Mathias Ungers.

Oswald Mathias Ungers, Tilman Heyde, and Tom Dimock, "Eine Serie von interaktiven Planungsprogrammen—SIPP," in *Werk*, no. 6 (1972): 348 © UAA Ungers Archiv für Architekturwissenschaft

tasks would become essentially unmanageable for architects, both mathematically and graphically. Ungers and his team of developers were confident that they had found an appropriate means of dealing with this new situation in the computer with its ever-increasing computing abilities.

With SIPP it was possible to calculate large amounts of data and present the results as schematic maps. The computer functioned as a visualization machine for statistics, showing, for example, the relationship between a certain quotient for the geographical distribution of schools and the resulting travel network for students. Each of these maps was based on a true-to-scale grid, which could be filled with various index numbers depending on the statistics. This made it possible to generate many specific maps in a relatively short time.

For Ungers, the computer was a powerful machine that could optimize calculation processes. However, he was critical of any idea that went beyond this. Ungers rigorously rejected the provocative thesis that a kind of design expertise or intelligence could be attributed to the computer. He therefore opposed the view that the computer represented a new creative medium and not merely an automatic calculating machine. During the design process, the role of the computer should be to solve purely computational tasks, while the level of designing and drawing should be reserved for the architect.

It can be assumed that Ungers was familiar with the work of the computer specialist Donald Greenberg, who was also conducting research at Cornell—for example, with the 3D model of the Johnson Art Museum by I.M. Pei, printed on the May 1974 cover of *Scientific American*. It was Ungers's concern, however, precisely because drawing was so closely connected to the design process and architectural thinking, that the mechanization of the one would also mean the mechanization of the other. The drawing is considered the architect's central medium. Through "geometry and line"[6] implicit knowledge is articulated, communicated, and honed. In terms of the instrument, the process of drawing has much to do with the gesture of writing[7]—through the free movement of the hand, in the crystallization of one's own thoughts, or in the individual character of the handwriting.[8] Writing and drawing are therefore related. Architectural design was considered synonymous with creative thinking, and in this function was intrinsically tied to the gesture of drawing. For Ungers, every step toward the mechanization of drawing, however described, was seen as a deliberate attempt to invalidate creative thinking through technology: "The beauty of designing is that you think, see, and design something that has never existed before. That is what makes it so exciting. To take over what has already been developed, what already exists—that is not designing, that is mere production. An essential characteristic of design is the attempt to achieve perfection. To leave this to the machine means only relying on what already exists, never daring to embark on the adventure of the birth of something new. [...] Imagine, for a moment, what it means if I use programs to develop a design, with the 'retrieval' of certain data instead of the concrete material. It follows that I could be replaced by anyone who can do it better. You know that there have been attempts to have computers produce poetry. Can you imagine poetry without the experience of the writer?"[9] Ungers offered a host of criticisms to caution against the threatening supremacy of the digital. From the very beginning, the idea of digitizing drawing was seen as a twofold instance of cultural devaluation—weakening both the role of the architect as the sole decision-maker and that of the design process as a cultural technique. Unger's reference to poetry was not least a targeted critique of an artistic genre that had emerged in the early 1960s through the likes of Theo Lutz and became known as "concrete poetry."[10] At the core of this art movement were so-called stochastic texts, i.e., swathes of words created by playing with random generators and probability calculations. The idea of being able to produce poems by programming simple sets of rules could also be applied to the production of architecture.

The ambivalence with which Ungers confronted the potential of the technical is palpable in his work. On the one hand, his experimentation with software opened up a spectrum of genuinely new and promising branches of research. Terms such as "planning tool" and "drawing tool" suddenly took on a procedural timbre in the context of programming, databases, and feedback concepts. The question of how the man–machine interface must be designed so that the architect could operate the computer and "communicate" with it as easily as possible became one of the greatest challenges. On the other hand—and Unger's defensive attitude can also be interpreted as such—all the talk about providing the designing architect with an intelligent partner in the form of the computer seemed like a dark premonition that architectural production would become entirely automated and anonymized. A rhetoric of the feasible loomed overhead, in which scenarios of humans liberated by technology were constantly being generated. Many of the discussions that took place during this time were on a purely hypothetical basis. It was not uncommon to hear arguments based on utopian promises and the power of technology to transform the entire architectural profession. At the same time, voices remained modest, acknowledging that they were only at the beginning of the technological revolution. In this respect, the computer enjoyed the status of both a wishing well and a technical nightmare. To put it pointedly, the processes of rapprochement between architecture and the computer can be told as a course of countermovements: every moralizing concern about the effects of computer-aided design immediately produced a new ideal of faith in progress. Likewise, every techno-optimistic reverie about the efficiency of intelligent design machines was followed by an emphasis on the intuitive qualities of the architect as an artist and creator of the world.

Architectural Assistants

At the beginning of the 1960s, the computer was still uncharted technological territory for architects. Most architects could not yet imagine exactly how and especially where the computer should be integrated into the complexity of the creative design and planning processes of architectural practice. They saw it primarily as an artifact of technicians for technicians. The idea of what a computer was, or what it looked like, was predominantly shaped by photographs depicting massive computers bathed in bright light, stylized as representatives of a sober, rational world of applied mathematics. It was an alien world of codes and programs, and yet, because of its mysterious and seductive technological glamor, it was also fascinating. Nevertheless, the idea of being able to draw with a computer and even conduct a dialogue with it must have sounded to many like a strange harbinger of an architectural practice still in the distant future. "If the use of computers by architects is inevitable, then, clearly the problem must be faced of how architects are to 'talk' to the computers,"[11] was therefore one of the central challenges in the history of computer-aided design. How architects could use the computer at all, what knowledge they needed, whether they had to gain this knowledge on their own, or whether they needed the help of specialists for this—in a way, this spectrum of questions marked the birth of the history of architecture and the computer.

"Will it [...] be necessary to educate a new profession of architectural assistants for the purpose of articulating the problems to be solved into the proper language of the computer?"[12] asked Walter Gropius of the audience at "Architecture and the Computer," the Boston Architectural Center's first conference in 1964. The visitors were curious, and not only because the Bauhaus founder, one of the most famous architects of the 20th century, was on the list of participants at the first architecture conference focusing on computers. In fact, Gropius—who at the time was planning a new residential district in Berlin, Germany that was named after him[13]—was, at 81, also the oldest guest speaker at this historic colloquium, which was the first of its kind dedicated to discussing both the potentials and the limits of the use of the computer in architecture. "Our topic, the computer, seems the most timely, the most urgent, the most

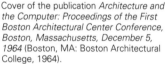

Cover of the publication *Architecture and the Computer: Proceedings of the First Boston Architectural Center Conference, Boston, Massachusetts, December 5, 1964* (Boston, MA: Boston Architectural College, 1964).

© Boston Architectural Center

View of the conference room at Sheraton Plaza Hotel, Boston.

Architecture and the Computer: Proceedings of the First Boston Architectural Center Conference, Boston, Massachusetts, December 5, 1964 (Boston, MA: Boston Architectural College, 1964).

serious subject that we could bring to the profession," said H. Morse Payne, president of the Boston Architectural Center and Gropius's collaborator, in his welcome speech.[14] His diagnosis followed: "Our profession is steeped in time-honored traditional methods of approaching architectural assignments, but this machine, a product of our day and our time, might require us to change and approach our task in some new manner. So, we must begin to explore the subject immediately."[15] Payne's brief speech was more than just an invitation to the architects gathered in the room. It had the character of a public appeal, addressed to architecture as a discipline. The message: architects should finally embrace technological progress and explore the computer and its possibilities for architecture.[16] So what did exploring the computer, which Payne called for, entail? Gropius embodied the voice of an architect who was both technically and aesthetically minded, which had certainly been a strategic reason for his invitation to the conference. His purpose was to mediate between artistic expression and machine-generated form. That the organizers—supported by the Graham Foundation and IBM—could win over one, if not *the* symbolic figure of the Bauhaus era, must have been seen as a special stroke of luck. Gropius's opinion weighed heavily, considering that the subject he would address—architecture and the computer—was a young and in no way coherent or developed branch of architecture. Until then, there had been little public discussion about the relationship between architecture and computers, although some people were already thinking about it. It was in Boston that these loose threads of discourse first came together. The atmosphere was one of innovative exchange, with encounters between academia and industry, technology companies exhibiting their latest computer models, and Bell Laboratories presenting the first digitally produced animated films. A small exhibition of printed computer graphics was also part of the conference.

The public interest was accordingly great. According to *the New York Times*, twice as many visitors came to the conference as expected, which was immediately interpreted by the organizers as a sign of how urgent this conference was for architecture—and this was one of its greatest promises—to finally be part of the discussion on par with science and technology.[17] In fact, however, the number of those in the know was small and belonged to the inner circle of the American scientific elite. Most of them were mathematicians and electrical engineers, such as Steven A. Coons and Marvin Minsky, who, during the Cold War era, often combined their research careers with a science policy or military-related appointments. Computer research was the exclusive domain of research departments at a few aircraft and automobile companies and of select universities supported by the military. Although, or precisely because, the conference was an event where previously hidden technical knowledge was made accessible to the public, it provides a good impression of what ideas there were at the time for a realistic, practical division of tasks between the architect and the computer.

For Gropius, the question of the balance of power between architect and machine had already been decided: "Still I believe, if we look at those machines as potential tools to shorten our working processes, they might help us to free our creative power."[18] Gropius's view of the computer was that of a practicing architect. His question at the conference of whether a new profession of architectural assistants would first have to be created in order to use the technology underscores two fundamental aspects. First, Gropius saw the computer as a new kind of tool that could be used to solve architectural problems, but which required special knowledge that not everyone possessed. Second, in order to use this tool adequately for architecture, a translator was necessary. This person would have to speak the language of both the architect and the machine.

Gropius's view was that the computer was primarily an automated drawing machine, and that the creative moment should remain with the architect. There was a clear hierarchy between the thinking head and the executing hand: first the architect would develop a design, which would then be fed into the computer by an assistant and optimized, modified, and visualized. If the architects, as Payne demanded in his welcoming speech, did not want to close their minds to the computer any longer, the so-called architectural assistant had to be given a decisive role. Without this, an essential link would be missing in the "architect–assistant–machine" working scheme that Gropius outlined. Accordingly, the discourses on architecture and the computer dealt with two aspects: the question of how the computer could be used as a design and planning tool, and how the division of labor between architect, assistant, and computer could be articulated. The intrusion of this new type of machine thus implied not only a question of application but also a question of knowledge; this is where the true significance of Gropius's question for architecture lay.

A young Christopher Alexander also spoke at the conference in Boston, challenging the audience with a way of thinking that was, to an extent, contrary to that of Gropius. Despite the widespread focus on the new drawing tools being developed for computer graphics, Alexander emerged early on as a vehement critic of this trend. At the conference in Boston, which took place in the same year that his book, *Notes on the Synthesis of Form*, was published,[19] Alexander presented his ideas to a broad public for the first time: "In my opinion the question [...] 'How can the computer be applied to architectural design?' is misguided, dangerous, and foolish. We do not spend time writing letters to one another and talking about the question, 'How can the slide rule be applied to architectural design?' We do not wander about houses, hammer and saw in hand, wondering where we can apply them. In short, adults use tools to solve problems that they cannot solve without help. Only a child, to whom the world of tools is more exciting than the world in which those tools can be applied, wanders about wondering how to make use of his tools."[20] For Alexander, the strength of the computer lay primarily in its extraordinary computational capacities. He strongly opposed the otherwise popular idea of attributing to computers any kind of machine intelligence. In response to the popular argument among architects that digital drawing programs could generate a wide variety of floor plans or facades for the architect in a very short time, he dryly explained: "A digital computer is, essentially, the same as a huge army of clerks, equipped with rule books, pencil and paper, all stupid and entirely without initiative, but able to follow exactly millions of precisely defined operations. There is nothing a computer can do which such an army of clerks could not do, if given time."[21] According to Alexander, "At the moment, the computer can, in effect, show us only alternatives which we have already thought of. This is not a limitation in the computer. It is a limitation in our own ability to conceive, abstractly, large domains of significant alternatives."[22] The expert understanding and theoretical acumen that Alexander already possessed in the nascent research field of digital architecture were remarkable. Whatever one may think of Alexander's later views on the role of the computer as an architectural design instrument, his ideas were groundbreaking.

In the closing words of his lecture, Alexander made a statement that proved why he was also regarded as a serious participant in debates on architectural theory: "There is really very little that a computer can do, if we do not first enlarge our conceptual understanding of form and function."[23] In his view, the machine should play a secondary role, after the architect had thought about the conditions for the development of form and function, and after the complexity of the design task had been broken down into individual, solvable subsets. Alexander thus saw the benefit of the computer for architecture as being mainly on a structural level.

Behind this was an attempt to reverse the directional vector between architecture and technology: the social logic of an architectural design and the associated idea of diversity should not be adapted to the logic of the computer and its possibility of producing countless variants, but the other way around. For Alexander, the computer was a powerful calculating machine that could technically simplify research into basic human needs, but which should in no way relieve architects of their social responsibility.

Drawing

Steven A. Coons, who was also a participant at the conference in Boston, was considered one of the driving forces in the still young research field of computer-aided design. The electrical engineer and pioneer in the field of interactive computer graphics was aware of the fears many architects had regarding the computer and the new working methods it represented. His motto was simple, yet effective: "No architect wants to become or should want to become an expert computer programmer. Architects want to do architecture. City planners want to do city planning. They don't want to have to invent and manufacture the pencils they use. They want to have them at hand. The computer is a tool. We want to arrange matters so that the computer can be used as naturally and easily as a pencil [...]. The computer can act as a super-tool."[24] Architects would therefore not need to know about the inner workings of the computer or how a program's code was structured. An understanding of the new tools should only be needed at the level of their use, not on the level of their programming. In architecture, such a statement was very well received since architects were traditionally regarded as designers who communicated by drawing. In his plea, Coons looked to a very specific technical development.

Ivan Sutherland, one of Coons's former students and at the time a doctoral student under Claude Shannon, had developed a computer graphics program a few years earlier that was to make its mark under the name Sketchpad.[25] In Sutherland's view, users should be able to operate the computer on a visual and descriptive level and not, as was usually the case, on a mathematical and symbolic one. The instructions, which until then could only be written in the form of computer codes, could now be represented and supplemented by

Ivan Sutherland drawing with the light pen on the screen of the TX-2 computer, 1962.

Ivan E. Sutherland, "Sketchpad: A Man–Machine Graphical Communications System," (1963), *Technical Report* No. 574, University of Cambridge Department of Computer Science and Technology, 2003, 20 © Ivan Sutherland

drawn instructions. "The Sketchpad system uses drawing as a novel communication medium for a computer. The system contains input, output, and computation programs which enable it to interpret information drawn directly on a computer display. It has been used to draw electrical, mechanical, scientific, mathematical, and animated drawings; it is a general purpose system."[26]

Sutherland, who developed his system from 1961 to 1963, made use of a device from military radar research called the "light pen." Com-

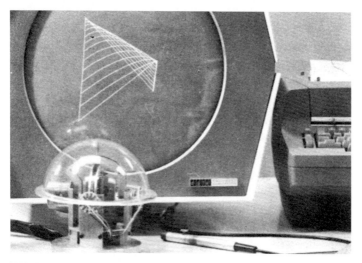

With the *MIT 3D Ball*, architects could rotate a three-dimensional model on the screen using intuitive gestures.

Murray Milne, ed., *Computer Graphics in Architecture and Design: Proceedings of the Yale Conference on Graphics in Architecture held in New Haven, Connecticut, April 1968* (New Haven, CT: Yale School of Art and Architecture, 1969), 4
© Yale School of Architecture

parable to an ordinary pen on paper, this enabled users to "draw" directly on the screen. Once a drawing had been produced in this way, it could be modified by a repertoire of transformation rules and the corresponding operation of the necessary equipment: "If we point the light pen at the display system and press a button called 'draw,' the computer will construct a straight line segment which stretches like a rubber band from the initial to the present location of the pen [...]. Additional presses of the button will produce additional lines until we have made six, enough for a single hexagon. To close the figure we return the light pen to near the end of the first line drawn where it will 'lock on' to the end exactly."[27] The materiality of the drawing paper and the physical sensation of the pen were replaced by an interactive surface that could be manipulated by a few controlled gestures of clicking, pushing, pulling, or pressing. With this new tool, architects could continue to move in the familiar, visual world of drawing while simultaneously operating from the new, foreign realm of codes and programs. Sutherland laid the groundwork for a field of research that would be defined by the development of the widest possible range of application scenarios for increasingly powerful tools for the architect of the future.

Efficiency Rhetoric

Douglas Engelbart, an electrical engineer, experimented with systems very similar to Sutherland's in the laboratories at Stanford University. Engelbart worked on the H-LAM/T system, an acronym for "Human using Language, Artifacts and Methodology in which he is Trained." Behind this was a hybrid man–machine concept, which Engelbart called "Augmenting Human Intellect."[28] Its special feature was the machine's alleged ability to both expand and reinforce the cognitive abilities of the human being. "Man's population and gross product are increasing at a considerable rate, but the *complexity* of his problems grows still faster, and the *urgency* with which solutions must be found becomes steadily greater in response to the increased rate of activity and the increasingly global nature of that activity."[29] Engelbart's statement reveals a pattern of argumentation that can be seen throughout the history of digital tool research: the belief that an apparently growing lack of clarity about increasingly complex global interrelationships in people's lives could be managed through increasingly innovative technological concepts. "By 'augmenting human intellect' we mean increasing the capability of a man to approach a complex problem situation, to gain comprehension to suit his particular needs, and to derive solutions to problems. Increased capability in this respect is taken to mean a mixture of the following: more-rapid comprehension, better comprehension, the possibility of gaining a useful degree of comprehension in a situation that previously was too complex, speedier solutions, better solutions, and the possibility of finding solutions to problems that before seemed insoluble. And by 'complex situations' we include the professional problems of diplomats, executives, social scientists, life scientists, physical scientists, attorneys, designers—whether the problem situation exists for twenty minutes or twenty years. We do not speak of isolated clever tricks that help in particular situations. We refer to a way of life in an integrated domain where hunches, cut-and-try, intangibles, and the human 'feel for a situation' usefully co-exist with powerful concepts, streamlined terminology and notation, sophisticated methods, and high-powered electronic aids."[30] The machine functioned not only as an augmenting means but also as a therapeutic means of reorganizing cultural, social, and political structures—in this twofold benefit of the computer lay the appeal of Engelbart's concept of "Augmenting Human Intellect."

To illustrate the practicality of his system, Engelbart envisioned the architect of the future. "Let us consider an augmented architect at work," he wrote, introducing the workflow of an architect assisted by the machine.[31] This "augmented architect" had a screen and a small keyboard at his workstation, with which he could communicate with the machine: "With a 'pointer,' he indicates two points of interest, moves his left hand rapidly over the keyboard, and the distance and elevation between the points indicated appear on the right-hand third of the screen."[32] It was also possible to spatially rotate a drawing constructed in this way. The architect could also enter metric data on the keyboard. After several steps, the first outlines of the building would appear. At the same time, the computerized architecture assistant would calculate the possible impacts of the designed building and test them under different parameters. All the data produced during such a workflow—under which Engelbart interestingly understood not only "the building design and its associated 'thought structure'"[33]—could finally be stored on a "tape" and retrieved at any time. Like Marshall McLuhan, Engelbart understood computers as a mechanized prosthesis, an extension with which the cognitive and physical abilities of the architect could be expanded and technically reinforced.[34] Engelbart's concept of the computer as a tool was, therefore, compensatory in nature. The term "augmented architect" makes it clear that the architect should be integrated into an information technology milieu and that the technical should wrap itself around the architect like a second skin. The architect's drawing table was transformed into an apparatus-based world of devices, surfaces, and databases.

Programming

While work at high-tech laboratories in the United States focused on the user-friendliness of ever more useful tool systems for the architect of the future, in postwar Europe an artistic and philosophical branch of computer graphics was flourishing. This contrasted in many ways with a pronounced pragmatic approach to the computer taken by the likes of Coons and Sutherland. In the productive twilight of cybernetics, art, and philosophy, an experimental and inventive culture of programming emerged, which initially had little influence on architecture, but which played a decisive role as a theoretical framework.[35] Computer graphics were not "drawn" in this discourse, but "programmed." Central figures of this so-called code culture were the young mathematicians Frieder Nake and Georg Nees and—as their philosophical godfather, so to speak—Max Bense. Nees and Nake began experimenting with Konrad Zuse's Graphomat in the early 1960s.[36] Playing with the machine led to the creation of small line drawings featuring irregular patterns. With the help of programmed random generators, they could generate clusters and overlays of points, lines, and circles. Often, these were interference patterns caused by faulty programming. But the visual results amazed Nees and Nake. It quickly became clear to the two young mathematicians what explosive power their small black-and-white drawings could have for art theory.[37] With Nake and Nees, programming was declared a modern form of aesthetic craft,[38] and Bense elevated this craft to a philosophical level. The idea of the artist as a "technician of theory" was not only a provocative but also innovative image of the artist, which took on concrete form with the emergence of the first programmed computer graphics.

In a letter to Bense, Nees described the ambivalence and simultaneous fascination he felt when looking at the machine drawings he produced: "At first, I had great difficulty in grasping the full impact of what I had the machine produce. Then I came to realize that they were actually models of the process of artistic production."[39] For Nees, it was neither about the development of new drawing tools nor the optimization of the drawing itself, such as the possibility of creating three-dimensional models. At the core of the matter was nothing less than the surreal notion of being able to generate models of the creative design process itself through programming. That this concept could be illustrated through the traditional medium of drawing—thus immediately raising questions about aesthetics—was initially considered a productive side effect. Nevertheless, the graphic element played a decisive role. The possibility to visualize programs and give an aesthetic face to their obscurity showed that the use of electronic computing machines was not only "bound to the use of numbers"[40] but also implied an aesthetic facet. This went so far that Nake and Nees exhibited their small black-and-white drawings in galleries, a decision that provoked a wave of outrage and enthusiasm in equal measure. The programmed graphics hung on the wall like works of art. That they also signed their works—with name, date, title, version number, and machine type—and had some of them screen printed, must have intensified the already provocative gesture of their works. At the same time, Nake's drawings seemed to bear a resemblance to "modern architectural drawings."[41] This observation had not even escaped the attention of Konrad Wachsmann. During a lecture he gave in the spring of 1965 at the philosophy department of the University of Southern California, Wachsmann referred specifically to Bense's philosophy and Nake's computer graphics: "A German philosopher, Max Bense, who is probably not too well known in the United States, has written quite a number of modern books about […] the language of form, the language of structure. I wish I could read many passages of his work, even though, in many instances I feel, myself, in complete opposition to his basis of approach, but Max Bense has created certain images of formulation which are based on some kind of […] equations in which he tries to calculate form, not on the emotional and not on the reaction basis, but on the segments of consequential deductions, which are derived from certain observations, resulting in his stating that he believes he is capable of producing a machine which would be capable of producing Clay paintings [note: "Clay" was crossed out and corrected as "Klee"] for instance, exactly as original Clay paintings [see previous comment] in consideration of all those factors which are recognizable, which made Clay act and he goes on to say that even if this machine were to exist, this would not be enough that such a machine would be capable in time, after our Clay no longer exists, it would continue to produce the paintings in regard to the continuation of accumulation and experience […] whatever it may be so that in 100 years after his death he would still be able to produce such work under the assumption that the energy which creates this work, once known, can never die."[42]

The computer graphic Wachsmann was referring to is *Hommage à Klee* (1965), for which Nake analyzed the structural features of Paul Klee's 1929 painting, *Haupt- und Nebenwege* [Highways and Byways] and then reproduced them with the help of an algorithm.[43] Wachsmann seems to have been less taken with the production process behind the image. In his lecture, he barely touched on the actual core of Bense's information theory considerations, except for the mention of "consequential deductions, derived from certain observations." Wachsmann was much more taken with the idea of being able to program information about a human being—in this case Paul Klee—into the artificial memory of a machine and retrieve it as often as desired. It was therefore a question of the computer's capacity as a database—an idea that was hardly new to Wachsmann either. In Ulm, he himself had attempted to store all the information for a design process in a database for industrial construction. For Wachsmann, the computer embodied foremost a machine for the production of industrially producible architecture, and not an avant-garde theory of art. Nevertheless, he saw generative computer graphics as a categorical change for the technical self-understanding

Frieder Nake shows his computer graphics at an auction organized by Stuttgart-based artists to support the Viet Cong (National Liberation Front of South Vietnam) in Vietnam, Stuttgart, 1966.

http://dada.compart-bremen.de/node/68#/ © Frieder Nake

of architecture and art. Unable to conceal his quibble with the Bauhaus's idea of unity, which he criticized for its romanticism, he explained that it should no longer be called (as it had been at the Bauhaus) "art and technology—a new unity, but rather: science and technology—a new art."[44]

Indeed, "artificial art,"[45] as the computer graphics were initially called, caused a great stir among conservative artists, art scholars, and especially the media. That art could be programmed was a provocative idea. The programmed works removed the conservative sound of the question on the relationship between art, authorship, and technology, and seemed to pursue it ad absurdum with unprecedented intellectual rigor. A considerable part of the public criticism

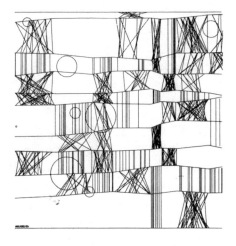

Frieder Nake's computer graphic, *Hommage à Paul Klee, 13/9/65 No. 2.*

Jasia Reichardt, ed., *Cybernetic Serendipity: The Computer and the Arts* (London: Studio International, 1968), 155 © Frieder Nake

was naturally aimed at the "design process" behind the graphics, i.e., the fact that they were programmed. In the eyes of many critics, that a simple computer program was behind the small, aesthetically pleasing line drawings turned them into something alien, something that sprang from the rational logic of the machine and not from the creative spirit of human beings. The works therefore represented a double demystification: that of the creative process of the artist and that of the logic of the machine. That the disclosure of the machine's functional logic was, paradoxically, also part of the provocation that emanated from computer graphics, becomes understandable, considering that the demystification of the machine was linked to the demystification of the author. The question of creativity and intuition in an artwork was deprived of its conceptual basis when it became clear that the author was not only a machine but also a simple set of rules made of signs.[46]

To program a drawing meant to think in terms of the computer, i.e., in terms of the logic of a "semiotic machine."[47] As Georg Trogemann, explains, "In the narrower, mathematical sense, a code is a rule for the unambiguous assignment of the characters of one set of characters to those of another set of characters. […] The term 'code' is used in a twofold way: first for the mathematical mapping rule, and second for the strings of characters produced by the encoding."[48] A code therefore consisted of symbolic signs and yet, as Nake himself pointed out, was in this respect nothing more than "text, essentially text."[49] In short, drawing with code meant operating with text. A computer graphic could be seen as the aesthetic trace of a text, distinguished by the fact that it consists of signs that can be read from two directions: on the one hand by humans, although not without certain difficulties, and on the other hand by machines, as an operational code. At the same time, code was no longer seen merely as a means to an end, in order to calculate a large amount of data in as short a time as possible, but now also formed the conceptual foundation for an aesthetic avant-garde.[50]

Max Bense, for whom an epistemological approach to the world lay in the emblematic nature of drawings, elevated the programmed graphics of Nake and Nees to the first proof of the future technological world he championed. In his essay "Projects of Generative Aesthetics," included in his groundbreaking book from 1965, *Aesthetica*, Bense wrote: "On the whole […] the 'artificial' category of production differs from the 'natural' category of production by inserting a mediating system between creator and work, consisting of the program and the programming language, which leads to an unusual division of labor in the aesthetic process."[51] In the aesthetic impact of this intermediate level of the computer code—which Bense here referred to matter-of-factly as a "mediating system," and which Nees and Nake used as the starting point of their considerations—lay the provocation, but also the expansion and originality, of the German postwar art scene that Bense had emboldened.

At first, programming had limited influence on the practice of architecture. Wachsmann's database project is an example of how broad the spectrum of ideas and applications was in this context. Admittedly, there had already been isolated architectural projects where specific parts of the planning or design were programmed, such as the facade of Northwick Park Hospital in London (see Chapter on "Swinging Cybernetics"), which John Weeks had generated with the help of a random algorithm.[52] But often, the concept of programmability in architecture functioned more as a general theoretical framework, whose productivity could frequently be found in the accompanying conceptual ambiguity and an often questionable desire for rationalization—one example was Wolfgang Döring's nebulously formulated goal of declaring communication as an "organizational tool" for programming architecture.[53]

Besides this more metaphorical level, there were attempts to establish programming as a transdisciplinary design method. However, the impetus for this did not come from architecture, but again from the field of graphics. Karl Gerstner, an influential representative of Swiss graphic art in the 1950s and a protagonist of Concrete Art, worked in the immediate environment of Max Bill and Richard Paul Lohse.[54] Gerstner differed from artists working in a similar way at the time, in that he not only spoke of and worked with computer programs but also attempted to elevate the process of "programming" itself to an independent and generally applicable design methodology. Gerstner's book *Programme entwerfen* [Developing programs], published in 1964, became an influential work shortly

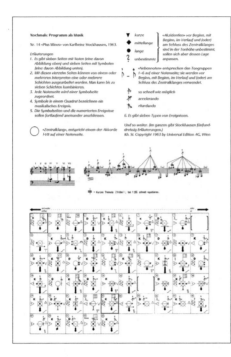

The "program as music," score of Karlheinz Stockhausen's composition *No. 14. Plus Minus* from 1963.

Karl Gerstner, *Programme entwerfen: Statt Lösungen für Aufgaben Programme für Lösungen* (1964) [Developing programs: not solutions to tasks but programs for solutions] (Baden: Lars Müller, 2007), 31 © Karl Gerstner/Karlheinz-Stockhausen-Stiftung

after its publication.[55] He regarded the idea of not only being able to apply programs, but even to design them himself, as a "specific method of engaging with creative design,"[56] which, he claimed, implied a "systematic approach to a task instead of hoping for inspiration from higher realms."[57] In this sense, the subtitle of his book, *Statt Lösungen für Aufgaben Programme für Lösungen* [Programs for solutions instead of solutions for tasks] became a transdisciplinary design axiom bridging art and architecture.

"Programm als Entwurf für die Zukunft" [The program as a design for the future], Kapitel aus *Programme entwerfen* [Designing programs]. Building system by Rudolf Doernach, Hans-Joachim Lenz, and Eckhard-Schulze-Fielitz, Ideas Competition, University of Bochum, 1963.

Karl Gerstner, *Programme entwerfen: Statt Lösungen für Aufgaben Programme für Lösungen* (1964) [Developing programs: not solutions to tasks but programs for solutions] (Baden: Lars Müller, 2007), 31
© Karl Gerstner / Karlheinz-Stockhausen-Stiftung

Programm als Entwurf für die Zukunft

Mit den «Stadtbausystemen» sind nicht nur Wohnhäuser zu erstellen. In die Tragsysteme sollen je nach Verkehrsbedarf auch Wege und Strassen eingehängt werden. Alle erforderlichen Installationsleitungen für Warm- und Kaltwasser, Heizung, Strom, Telefon, Antenne und Abwasser sind in den Stützen und Trägern eingezogen.

Die untenstehenden Abbildungen zeigen das System als Projekt für die Universität Bochum. Auf dem oberen Bild ist dies deutlich zu sehen: auch das Nichtvorhandensein ist programmiert: Dank der vollständigen Flexibilität der Struktur kann sich die Universität sowohl nach innen als auch nach aussen in alle Richtungen verändern – je nach der Entwicklung der Bedürfnisse. An diesem Beispiel wird das Prinzip deutlich: ein diesem neuen Städtebaukonzeption passt sich nicht mehr der Mensch dem Gebäude- und Stadtanlagen an, sondern diese passen sich dem Menschen an.»

Doernach, Lenz und Schulze-Fielitz sehen ihr Programm in der Perspektive der totalen Urbanisation der Erde. Heute leben 50% der Menschheit in Städten; gegen Ende des Jahrhunderts wird sie (dann nahezu verdoppelt) zu 90% in Städten leben. Die Bevölkerungsprogression konzentriert sich ausserdem auf die vorhandenen Grosstädte und Ballungsräume.

Unter dem Druck dieser Entwicklung werden sich neue soziale Strukturen bilden – die Ausdruck in neuen Städtebau-Programmen finden müssen. Schulze-Fielitz: «Unsere Aufgabe ist die Entwicklung und Fertigung räumlicher Stadtbausysteme mit einer möglichst grossen Anpassungsfähigkeit.» Die Nutzungsdichte sieht er nicht nur aus ökonomischen, sondern auch aus psychologischen Gründen möglichst hoch: «Zur Erhöhung der Sozialintensität, als Mittel gegen die Entmischung.» Vor allem geht es auch um geistige Dichte: Die Stadt der Zukunft ist im wörtlichen Sinne ein Rahmen, objektiv und neutral, der mit Lebensraum von beliebiger Individualität gefüllt werden kann.

"Programming apartments is first and foremost an economic issue," was Gerstner's sober opening to his chapter "Program as Architecture."[58] He continued: "The smaller the number of elements, the more economical the system."[59] To explain this, Gerstner referred to the housing system by the Zurich-based architects Schwarz + Gutmann + Gloor. In the 1960s, they had developed a building system whose additive logic was inspired by the systems thinking of industrial building and the field of megastructures that evolved

179

Leonardo Mosso, Testimonianza, structural model, 1966/67.

from it. As a further example of architecture programmed in this sense, Gerstner cited the *Stadtbausysteme* [urban building systems] designed by Rudolf Doernach, Hans-Joachim Lenz, and Eckhard Schulze-Fielitz in 1964 for a competition held by the University of Bochum.[60] However, the concept of the program was not only to

Leonardo and Laura Mosso, Continuity, city model, 1968/69.

Leonardo Mosso, in *Programmierte Architektur* [Programmed architecture], ed. Umbro Apollonio and Carlo Belloni
(Milan: Studio die Informazione Estetica and Vanni Scheiwiller, 1969), 69 © Leonardo und Laura Mosso

refer to questions of architecture and urban planning, but also to
typography, graphics, literature, music, and photography. Gerstner
wanted to show that not only the aesthetic dimension of abstract
graphics[61] and music but also the functional and therefore social dimension of architectural spaces could be programmed. He illustrated

the chapter "Program as Music" with abstract slides and circuit diagrams as accompaniment to John Cage's *Variations I* from 1958 and Karl Stockhausen's *No. 14 Plus Minus* from 1963.[62] Under the universal notion of the program, it seemed as if every disciplinary difference and creative peculiarity could be minimized and homogenized. In such a programmed world, the designer—whether architect, artist, or musician—was left only with the role of "algorithm creator."

In 1969, only a few years after Nake and Nees caused a sensation with their computer graphics and Gerstner's *Programme entwerfen* [Developing programs] was embraced as a groundbreaking book, the idea of "programmed architecture" actually seemed to come true. An exhibition in Zagreb claimed to show computer-generated architecture for the first time. *Computer and Visual Research*,[63] the title of the exhibition curated by Abraham Moles, was the fourth of six exhibitions held in Zagreb between 1961 and 1978, each in conjunction with a symposium.[64] Although the hospital project programmed by John Weeks and exhibited in London a year earlier at the ICA[65] was also seen as computer-generated architecture, it was a facade structure (albeit one that was actually built), not an entire building.

In Zagreb, the Italian architect Leonardo Mosso, who had previously worked for Alvar Aalto, presented two projects under the overarching title, "Computers and Human Research: Programming and Self-Management of Form."[66] *Testimonianza*, the title of the first project, was a competition entry designed in 1966–1967 for the Chamber of Deputies, Italy's lower parliament, in Rome. The second project, *Continuity*, was a study he developed in 1968 on an urban scale. Both projects were based on a three-dimensional spatial structure. The former operated with an oversized grid structure. The latter had a modular structure and formed an urban topography out of myriad cubes. For his *Continuity* project, Mosso presented a drawing that depicted different modular variations next to each

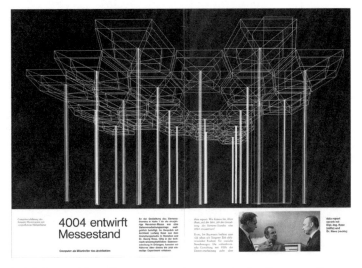

Ludwig Rase and Georg Nees, programmed computer drawing, Siemens pavilion, Hanover Trade Fair, 1970.

"4004 entwirft Messestand: Computer als Mitarbeiter des Architekten" [4004 Designs Exhibition Stand: Computer as Architect's Assistant], *Siemens Data Report* 4/70, July 1970: 2–7

other in a grid. "This study deals with the problem of programmed architecture aided by computer technology as an integrated system of relations between linguistic structures as they occur in the complex ecological and eco-social system:—life/architecture and man/environment—namely, as hypothesis of a general programming for the auto-programming of the human being."[67] In essence, Mosso was interested in a relational system for programming self-organizing structures.

Only one year after the exhibition in Zagreb, another computer-generated architecture project was produced—this time much more

```
'BEGIN'
'COMMENT' AORD ENTHAELT DATEN FUER EINE ANZAHL VON GERADEN UND IHRE
VERMESSUNG IM SINN VON EINGER, ENGZEICHEN IST GROESSER 1'6, INBORD
WIRD WAHR WENN RINGER FUER ALLE GERADEN IN AORD ZUTRIFFT,,
'INTEGER' I,, 'BOOLEAN' V,, V,=TRJE!,,
'BEGIN'
'FOR' I,=I+5 'WHILE' ABS(BORD(I/I)) 'LESS' I'6 'DO'
'BEGIN'
V,=V 'AND' RINGER(X,Y,A,B,C,BORD(/I/),BORD(/I+1/),AORD(/I+2/),
BORD(/I+3/),BORD(/I+4/)),,
'END',,
INBORD,=V,,
'END' INBORD,,
'BOOLEAN' 'PROCEDURE' EXOBSTI(X,Y,A,B,C,OBSTAC),,
'VALUE' X,Y,A,B,C,, 'REAL' X,Y,A,B,C,, 'ARRAY' OBSTAC,,
'BEGIN'
'COMMENT' OBSTAC ENTHAELT DATEN FUER EINE ANZAHL VON KREISFOERMIGEN
HINDERNISSEN XM,YM,R, ENGZEICHEN IST GROESSER 1'6, EXOBST WIRD WAHR
WENN OBSTACK X,Y,A,B,C AUSSERHALB ALLER HINDERNISSE IN OBSTAC,,
'INTEGER' I,, 'BOOLEAN' V,,
'BOOLEAN' 'PROCEDURE' KEXTRA(XM,YM,R,X1,Y1,X2,Y2),,
'VALUE' XM,YM,R,X1,Y1,X2,Y2,, 'REAL' XM,YM,R,X1,Y1,X2,Y2,,
'BEGIN'
'COMMENT' KREIS XM,YM,R, KEXTRA WIRD WAHR, WENN KREIS DIE
STRECKE X1,Y1,X2,Y2 NICHT SCHNEIDET,,
'REAL' DIS,S,ALF,BET,A,B,C,BEM,MIR,DI2,D1K1,D1K2,D2K1,D2K2
,,XK1,YK1,XK2,YK2
,,
'BOOLEAN' B0,B1,B2
,,
R,=ABS(R),,
'IF' ABS(X2-X1) 'GREATER' ,01 'THEN' 'GOTO' HY,,
DIS,=R*R-(X1-XM)*(X1-XM),,
'IF' DIS 'LESS' 0 'THEN' 'BEGIN' B0,='TRUE',, 'GOTO' FIN 'END',,
S,=SQRT(DIS),,
XK1,=XK2,=X1,, YK1,=YM-S,, YK2,=YM-S,, 'GOTO' CUT,,
HY,, 'IF' ABS(Y2-Y1) 'GREATER' ,01 'THEN' 'GOTO' AG,,
DIS,=R*R-(Y1-YM)*(Y1-YM),,
'IF' DIS 'LESS' 0 'THEN' 'BEGIN' B0,='TRUE',, 'GOTO' FIN 'END',,
S,=SQRT(DIS),,
XK1,=XM-S,, XK2,=XM-S,, YK1,=YK2,=Y1,, 'GOTO' CUT,,
AG,, A,=Y1-Y2,, B,=X2-X1,, C,=-(X1*A+Y1*B),,
ALF,=-B/A,, BET,=-C/A,, BEM,=BET+XM,,
DIS,=(ALF*ALF+1)*R*R-(ALF*YM+BEM)*(ALF*YM+BEM),,
'IF' DIS 'LESS' 0 'THEN' 'BEGIN' B0,='TRUE',, 'GOTO' FIN 'END',,
S,=SQRT(DIS),, MIR,=YM-ALF*BEM,,
YK1,=(MIR+S)/(ALF*ALF+1),, YK2,=(MIR-S)/(ALF*ALF+1),,
XK1,=ALF*YK1+BET,, XK2,=ALF*YK2+BET,,
```

Georg Nees, Algol program code for generating roof modules, Siemens trade fair pavilion, Hanover Trade Fair, 1970.

"4004 entwirft Messestand: Computer als Mitarbeiter des Architekten" [4004 designs exhibition stand: computer as architect's assistant], *Siemens Data Report* 4/70, July 1970: 2–7 © Georg Nees

concrete, but also more small-scale. In conjunction with the Hanover Trade Fair, the architect Ludwig Rase developed the first computer-programmed architecture in the German-speaking world. Rase had designed the official trade fair pavilion for the company Siemens.[68] The pavilion had a simple structure, consisting only of a modular roof surface and the necessary supports. The roof's basic structure had honeycomb-like pattern made of a series of six-sided modules.

Nees, who was not acting as an artist in this case, but as a technical specialist and architectural assistant in Gropius's sense, had written a computer program for Rase, which calculated the optimum size of the basic roof module. The highlight of the program was that Nees could generate different variations of the basic module and, depend-

Ludwig Rase with Georg Nees, Siemens trade fair pavilion (built structure), Hanover Trade Fair, 1970.

"4004 entwirft Messestand: Computer als Mitarbeiter des Architekten" [4004 designs exhibition stand: computer as architect's assistant], *Siemens Data Report* 4/70, July 1970: 2–7 © Ludwig Rase, Georg Nees

ing on the module size, calculate a corresponding three-dimensional model of the pavilion's construction. Although Rase had developed the pavilion's overall concept, the design of the individual variations was no longer in his hands. In the project by Nees and Rase, two different aspects of the architectural history of the computer coincided. On the one hand, Nees, in his function as a computer specialist, embodied the "architectural assistant" that Gropius had previously called for at the conference in Boston in 1964.[69] On the other hand, the project provided evidence for Bense's assumption that the so-called "artificial" category of production would be distinguished from the "natural" category of production by inserting a mediating system between creator and work, i.e., a computer code.[70]

Looking back, Nake recalls: "In the discussions about the field, which combined art, computer graphics, programs, computers, computer art, and creativity, it was always important to show not only how simple, formal and exacting but also how powerful the program and programming were, through clear, straightfowrad examples."[71] Here, Nake was again referring to the aspect that distinguished Coons's and Sutherland's drawing machines from his own programmed art worlds. The work of Coons and Sutherland treated the computer as a technical artifact, focusing on the creation of ever more powerful machines and clear user interfaces. Meanwhile, Nake focused on programming as a purely mathematical and intellectual method of formalization, detached from the technical performance of the computer as a tool and object.

Individualization Systems

"What man makes, nature cannot make. What nature makes, man cannot make. How far can we entrust the machine to design?"[1] This was the question architect Louis Kahn skeptically asked his audience in the large lecture hall of the architecture department at Yale University in April 1968. The occasion was a panel discussion at the Yale Conference on Graphics in Architecture, which promised to be a special event, both because of its well-known participants and the choice of its topic. Kahn, certainly the most prominent participant on the podium, was nevertheless in stellar company. The three other participants in the discussion were Charles Moore, then Dean of the department of architecture there; Steven A. Coons, the electrical engineer and pioneer of computer-aided design; and the cyberneticist Warren McCulloch, who, as a founding father of neuroinformatics and chairman of the legendary Macy Conferences, was one of the most important intellectual minds in the American postwar scientific landscape. The discussion on "The Past and Future of Design by Computers," as the title aptly described, focused on the question of whether and, if so, how the computer could be integrated into the architectural design process. The explosive nature of this question was enough to rattle not only the self-image of the architect in his role as creative demiurge, but also the time-honored foundations of the discipline. Kahn therefore made it clear, right at the beginning of the discussion, how little he thought of the optimization rhetoric that accompanied the development of digital technologies:

"The machine can communicate measure, but the machine cannot create, cannot judge, cannot design. This belongs to the mind. [...]

If measure is accepted only when absolute, how could one measure realization, concept, truth, desire, silence?"[2] Kahn was extremely critical of the idea that the individual handwriting of the architectural design process could be fundamentally influenced by the anonymous perfection of computers. He was by no means alone in this. In his seminal two-volume work *The Myth of the Machine*[3]—the first part of which was published just a few months before the conference— the influential architectural historian Lewis Mumford also made it clear that he thought little of the futuristic visions being conjured up in the computer laboratories and at the architects' drafting tables. In his view, "Obviously, computers cannot invent new symbols or conceive new ideas not already outlined in the very setting up of their programs. Within its strict limits, a computer can perform logical operations intelligently, [...] but under no circumstances can it dream of a different mode of organization than its own."[4]

Coons's glorifications of the power of machine intelligence and computer graphics in particular must have seemed like a provocation to Kahn. At the podium, Coons nevertheless addressed his plea directly to Kahn: "I suppose that I am far away from all of you in spirit, and very close to the machine. But you bring to this task the viewpoint that I cannot furnish. You bring the viewpoint that no scientist, no engineer can fully fulfill. [...] You think of a machine, and computers are machines as rather rigid mechanisms like automobile. [...] Computers are indeed, machines, but they are not like automobiles, they are not like electric stoves, they are not like telephones that have specific functions. They are far more magic and general than that. [...] They are, perhaps, the most congenial mechanical device ever envisioned by human beings."[5] And as if he had to account to Kahn, Coons concluded by stressing that it was only the beginning of a transformational computer culture that was yet to come: "We are only at the beginning [...] Computers will be different tomorrow.

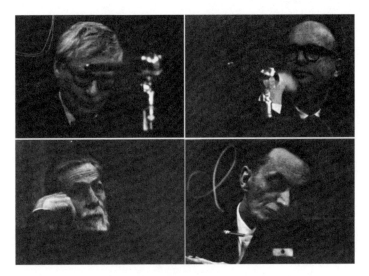

Louis Kahn (top left) arguing with Charles Moore (top right), Steven A. Coons (bottom right), and Warren McCulloch (bottom left).

"Panel Discussion: The Past and Future of Design by Computer," in *Computer Graphics in Architecture and Design: Proceedings of the Yale Conference on Graphics in Architecture held in New Haven, Connecticut, April 1968*, ed. Murray Milne (New Haven, CT: Yale School of Art and Architecture, 1969), 98–103 © Yale School of Art and Architecture

They will be more capable, they will be cheaper, and they will be far more congenial to human beings than they are today."[6]

Kahn's harsh criticism was a direct reaction to the rapid progress being made in the field of digital architectural production. His expression, "this belongs to the mind,"[7] made it obvious where the sore spot was for him. Given the increasing encroachment of the digital into ever more areas of the architect's work, Kahn saw nothing less than the importance of thinking itself as being in danger. Without speaking directly of a crisis of thought, it was no longer just a question of the pros and cons of some calculating machine. Rather, the

189

entire creative foundation of architecture as a discipline suddenly seemed at stake. Designing was considered synonymous with individual thinking. Every step in the direction of the digitalization of design, however described, was seen as a deliberate attempt to invalidate creative thinking through technology. It was not uncommon to hear talk of a "symbiosis" between man and machine, and of the computer as an "intelligent partner"—technoid metaphors that were characteristic of the mythologizing mentality in research in artificial intelligence; this also led Kahn to ask critically at Yale about the trustworthiness of the computer for the design process.

The Machine as a Protagonist

Kahn's fears of the institutional weakening of the architect by the computer may seem exaggerated today. However, they were by no means unfounded. One of Coons's most distinguished students, the architect Nicholas Negroponte, played an instrumental role in mythologizing the machine. In 1967, one year before the Yale conference on Graphics in Architecture, Negroponte launched the Architecture Machine Group at the Massachusetts Institute of Technology (MIT). It would become one of the most influential think tanks for architecture and urban design in research at the intersection of humans and machines. In short succession, Negroponte then published two books—*The Architecture Machine* in 1970 and *Soft Architecture Machines* in 1975—which were considered manifestos for computer research in the field of architecture.[8]

Establishing a research institute of that kind was not a matter of course. Computers cost a fortune and often filled entire rooms

View into the rooms of the Architecture Machine Group, founded by Nicholas Negroponte at MIT.

Nicholas Negroponte, *Soft Architecture Machines* (Cambridge, MA: The MIT Press, 1975), 160 © Nicholas Negroponte/ Architecture Machine Group

because of their size. During the Cold War, the US government's science funding increasingly focused on the development of mainframe computers. The field of applied mathematics became a powerful research complex, whose closest advisory circles often included exceptional mathematicians, such as Norbert Wiener, Claude Shannon, Warren McCulloch, and John von Neumann, a pioneer of the discrete modeling of dynamic systems, the so-called cellular automata.[9] While the computer was already familiar as an administrative calculating machine, scientific research on the computer was almost exclusively reserved for the research departments of a few aircraft

The name "Architecture Machine" adorned the outside of the computer like a trademark.

Nicholas Negroponte, *Soft Architecture Machines* (Cambridge, MA: The MIT Press, 1975), 160 © Nicholas Negroponte/ Architecture Machine Group

and automobile companies and select universities that received military funding, such as the Moore School of Electrical Engineering at the University of Pennsylvania. The latter's research lab was home to the first electronic universal machine, a computing colossus built in 1942 for solving complex ballistic computing tasks known as ENIAC—the Electronic Numerical Integrator and Computer.[10] As an intellectual center for math-based military science, MIT in particular was home to a large number of research institutes which, despite belonging to different disciplines, all had the common goal of further developing the computer. This included the Mechanical Engineering Department, where Coons was involved in the development of computer-aided design; the Lincoln Laboratory, where Ivan Sutherland earned his doctorate in mid-1963 with Shannon's

Sketchpad program; and the Research Laboratory of Electronics,[11] where McCulloch had been tinkering with the development of artificial neural networks since the early 1950s.[12]

As a key Cold War technology, the computer was one of the central scientific research subjects. Wiener's (famously fruitless) efforts to develop a cybernetic control system for air defense are a vivid example of how closely science and war were intertwined.[13] Negroponte and the Architecture Machine Group were, in a sense, at the "hub of power that linked military control systems to cold-war strategies."[14] In the words of Friedrich Kittler, one could even say that, with the Architecture Machine Group, Negroponte was the first to institutionalize an architectural form of the "misuse of army equipment."[15] One of the things that made the work of the Architecture Machine Group so special was its playful attitude toward the computer. The group's focus was on the development of projects in which the computer would be integrated into the particular habits and needs of designing architects. Negroponte knew that it was better to get architects excited about new technologies through practice than theory. The computer's scope of possibilities was to be explored as experimentally as possible, through a reciprocal game of developing and testing. The art installation *SEEK*, produced by Negroponte in 1970 for the exhibition *Software*, impressively demonstrated how such a game was to be understood conceptually. In a large glass vitrine, a computer-controlled robot arm monitored the spatial order of over 100 stacked cubes. Mice ran around between the cubes, sometimes knocking them over with their movements, and in this way continually upset the order of the cubes. The computer's task was to restore the original order. At the same time, it was to calculate a behavioral model based on the chaotic movement pattern of the mice—something Negroponte metaphorically called a "cybernetic world model."

Nicholas Negroponte, *SEEK*, installation at the exhibition *Software*, held at the Jewish Museum, New York, September 16 to November 8, 1970.

Although there was always talk of machine intelligence, for Negroponte the key to the digitization of architecture lay elsewhere. In the foreground was not the idea of artificial intelligence—a chapter in modern computer history outlined by Alan Turing in his essay

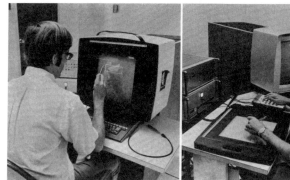

Computer-aided design, around 1969: architects could draw directly on the screen (left) or on an interactive surface (right) using a "light pen."

Nicholas Negroponte, *Soft Architecture Machines* (Cambridge, MA: The MIT Press, 1975), 160 © Nicholas Negroponte/ Architecture Machine Group

"Computing Machinery and Intelligence," first published in 1950,[16] and expanded upon shortly thereafter by the mathematicians John McCarthy and Marvin Minsky together with Shannon.[17] Nor was Negroponte concerned with an aesthetic approach to code as a new artistic craft, for instance, in the sense of Frieder Nake's and Georg Nees's computer graphics created with the aid of random generators. Instead, Negroponte's ambitious goal was to develop machines that would not only make architects' work easier, but even do it for them completely. While the focus until then had been more on graphic concepts at the intersection of humans and machines, now, for the first time, the question was up for debate as to what extent the architect's planning and design activities could be transferred to a computer. The basic idea behind Negroponte's architectural concept was the procedural individualization of man–machine interaction.

"Imagine a machine that can follow your design methodology and at the same time discern and assimilate your conversational idiosyncrasies. The same machine, after observing your behavior, could build a predictive model of your conversational performance. Such a machine could then reinforce the dialogue by using the predictive model to respond to you in a manner that is in rhythm with your personal behavior and conversational idiosyncrasies. What this means is that the dialogue we are proposing would be so personal that you would not be able to use someone else's machine, and he would not understand yours. [...] The dialogue would be so intimate—even exclusive—that only mutual persuasion and compromise would bring about ideas, ideas unrealizable by either conversant alone."[18]

With Negroponte's concept of the computer as a learning machine, i.e., a machine that can independently adapt to its environment and vary its own behavior through feedback, the focus was no longer on visual user interfaces and descriptive computer graphics. Instead, it was on the individual cooperation between man and machine. One of the first computer experiments designed according to these criteria was URBAN5, a planning program developed in 1967, whose aim was to enable a dialogue between man and machine that was as simple as possible in terms of language, thanks to the help of learning algorithms.[19] Without specialist expertise or previous knowledge, users of URBAN5 could interact with the computer through a graphic interface. This technical approach to the architectural medium was considered a popular field of research, at the latest since Ivan Sutherland's Sketchpad. While computer graphics was still a mystery to most architects, it was assumed they would not be intimidated by the rhetoric of optimization, thanks to the appealing simplification of work it promised. The real highlight of Negroponte's computer experiment, however, lay elsewhere. URBAN5 users would not only be able to communicate visually with the machine, but also linguistically. It would be possible to enter specific questions, considerations, and instructions about a planning project, such as the optimal position of the house entrance or windows, in the form of complete sentences. The computer would understand the meaning of these sentences and calculate corresponding solutions, formulate counter-questions, and even make recommendations about what should be done next in the planning process or what should not be forgotten. Negroponte had long since left behind the doubts voiced by Kahn as to whether the computer could be trusted in the design process. The machine had been elevated to the status of a techno-scientific oracle, and the fantasy and intimacy of the interpersonal exchange of ideas replaced by the myth of mechanical perfection. Technical omniscience took the place of wisdom and experience. Negroponte's computer experiments were radical and innovative, and perhaps for this very reason, they represent one of the most vivid chapters of fascination and longing in the architectural history of the computer.

"[W]e, the Architecture Machine Group at MIT, are embarking on the construction of a machine that can work with missing information. To do this, an architecture machine must understand our metaphors, must solicit information on its own, must acquire experiences, must talk to a wide variety of people, must improve over time, and must be intelligent. It must recognize context, particularly changes in goals and changes in meanings brought about by changes in context."[20] At the core was the search for the meaning of communication and the semantic determination of the complex relationship between available and missing information within an architectural planning process. Based on this, a simulation model of individual communication could be generated: "a predictive model of your conversational performance."[21] Such a model not only provided clues about what information played what role at what point in the planning process. Rather—and this was the actual aim of the Architecture Machine Group—this model would form the technical foundation on which the machine could stand alongside the architect as a social actor and equal partner. Not only was it about the architect's knowledge of the computer, but also the computer's knowledge of the architect. In this anthropotechnical mirroring of man and machine, which resembled a cybernetic fusion of nature and culture, lay the originality, but also the frightening potential of Negroponte's ambitious project. As an independently acting machine, the computer would become a reality-constituting actor in the interpersonal sphere. The idea that computers would not only be able to observe and analyze individual human behavior but also to model it technically, makes it clear how thin the borderline of innovation was between technical service and social control.

Negroponte sketched the contours of a machine world that liberated the computer from its passive status as a purely administrative machine. It is therefore no surprise that the theoretical foundation of the Architecture Machine Group was not based on architectural theory but on sociocybernetic machine theory. Negroponte referred to none other than Warren McCulloch and his thoughts on the social behavior of "ethical robots," a term McCulloch had already coined in the mid-1950s in an article of the same name.[22] "Given that the physical environment is not in perfect harmony with every man's life style, given that architecture is not the faultless response to human needs, given that the architect is not the consummate manager of physical environments, I shall consider the physical environment as an evolving organism as opposed to a designed artifact. In particular, I shall consider an evolution aided by a specific class of machines. Warren McCulloch calls them ethical robots; in the context of architecture I shall call them architecture machines."[23] As a cyberneticist, McCulloch was initially interested in the "behavior of artifacts" rather than their materiality or substance. In contrast to Wiener, for example, for whom the focus was primarily on the technical interpretation of man and machine, McCulloch also explicitly asked about behavior within machine groups, i.e., intermachine behavior patterns. The hypothetical question was about "what machines, by cooperation and competition, can constitute a society…"[24] To put it pointedly, at the heart of the matter was the social behavior of cybernetic machines.

McCulloch was no stranger to architecture. As an expert in sensory physiology and spatial perception, he had been a frequent guest at various architecture departments since the 1950s, for example in 1954, as part of the Laboratory of Lighting Design at the Massachusetts Institute of Technology.[25] McCulloch's actual professional expertise, however, did not seem to matter to Negroponte. His idea of a world opened up by learning machines fitted better into Negroponte's technoscientific image of the future. McCulloch's thoughts on the construction of a future machine world were more concrete than they may initially seem, even if his projects were in many respects less concerned with the systematic development of market-ready applications than with the experimental exploration of the potentials information technology could offer architecture.

Negroponte's interest was primarily in the development of digital design and planning tools. This was not about the perception of architectural space or its material composition, but the design of technical operation chains at the juncture of physical and virtual space. That Negroponte cited McCulloch's idiosyncratic concept as one foundation of the Architecture Machine Group also says something about how its projects were to differ from traditional architecture and the architectural image that was to be associated with it. On the one hand, Negroponte gave the debate on computer graphics and machine intelligence in architecture a sociological bent, and thus a new radicality. On the other hand, the question of the architect's role, in a world in which the computer was declared an equal player in the design and planning process, became all the more insistent.

Negroponte identified three basic ways to integrate the computer into the architectural design process. The first was by automating the design process itself. In this regard, the focus was mainly on quantitative questions, such as the increase in machine computing power and the resulting reduction of labor costs. Second, by aligning creative thinking with the mathematical logic of the computer. In this case, architects would have to become familiar with the intangibility of computer codes and learn to program accordingly. They would thus give up their role as generalists to become algorithm creators and programming specialists. As a result, the only architectural concepts that would be considered significant would be those compatible with the symbolic world of the computer, which could be described through algorithms. Third, by accepting the idea that man and machine were two different, yet equal, actors in a communication system—a radical idea in which Negroponte was particularly inspired by Gordon Pask's cybernetic theory of learning machines.[26] While this would not remove the dualism of human intuition and mechanical calculation, it could be overcome by the allegedly playful technical dimension they both shared.

Although various aspects of these three possibilities overlapped with the work of the Architecture Machine Group, Negroponte conceded the greatest potential to the last point: "I shall consider only the third alternative and shall treat the problem as the intimate association of two dissimilar species (man and machine), two dissimilar processes (design and computation), and two intelligent systems (the architect and the architecture machine). By virtue of ascribing intelligence to an artifact or the artificial, the partnership is not one of master and slave but rather of two associates that have a potential and a desire for self-improvement."[27] Attention was therefore drawn to the specific behavior of the computer user, who, until then, had been a relatively neglected parameter in computer research. This aspect was the only human constant in Negroponte's world of individualized computing machines. There were similar projects involving the personalization of machines, such as that of Douglas Engelbart and his concept of the "augmented architect." Joseph C.R. Licklider's concept of a "Man-Computer Symbiosis"[28] can also be seen as one of the building blocks for Negroponte's work. The computer user—and in this respect Negroponte's approach differed from other research in the field of computer graphics—did not have to be a trained architect. On the contrary, it was by championing the power of the individual that Negroponte believed he could break up entrenched power structures in the planning process and change them in favor of the user.

Power of the Individual

Both facets—that of individuality and that of playfulness—may also have been the reason the Architecture Machine Group's book was featured in the influential *Whole Earth Catalog*.[29] The writer and entrepreneur Stewart Brand launched the large-format magazine in 1967, as the hippie movement swept across California. Because of its enormous influence, the magazine constantly grew in size until its last issue in 1974.[30] The *Whole Earth Catalog* stood for a programmatic combination of theories on tools and individualization, grounded in faith in progress and optimism about technology. The subtitle of the catalogue is simply: *Access to Tools*. It became a counterculture gospel for an entire generation and the ultimate guide to an alternative lifestyle.

This probably also led Reyner Banham at the Design Participation Conference, organized by the Design Research Society in Manchester, UK in 1971—which included Negroponte and Yona Friedman among the speakers—to describe the *Whole Earth Catalog* as an "alternative network for the alternative culture."[31] The *Whole Earth Catalog* did not list the world as it was. Rather, the things it collected and catalogued—such as everyday tools, books, and manuals of all kinds—were what seemed necessary to create a new, better world. Its underlying premise was the preservation of intellectual autonomy for individual self-interpretation, a concept that ties in with the 19th-century tradition of American transcendentalism, for example, the philosophical reflections of Ralph Waldo Emerson and Henry David Thoreau.[32] In Banham's words, "It is what the *Whole Earth Catalog* is all about—where to find the resources to do what you want to do, with your own set of rules. The indication which I deduce from this, is that do-it-yourself, is the only real design participation. When the resources are in the hands of the 'the people' and 'the people' invent their own rules for the game, then I think design participation is getting somewhere."[33] The notion of freedom expressed by the catalogue was inextricably linked to individual action. Given the right tools, individuals could make the world a better place for themselves and others. "Most of our generation scorned computers as the embodiment of centralized control," Brand recalled in a 1995 *Time* magazine article. "But a tiny contingent—later called 'hackers'—embraced computers and set about transforming them into tools of liberation. That turned out to be the true royal road to the future. 'Ask not what your country can do for you. Do it yourself,' we said."[34] Brand thus named the two transformation processes that would give the computer a new cultural meaning, and which were also decisive for the Architecture Machine Group: the shift from being a computing machine to a tool, and from representing control to representing liberation. In this way, the computer as an artifact, while by no means de-ideologized, was culturally transcoded. It became something playful, with which everyone could design their own world, and also change it again. It may therefore come as no surprise that Yona Friedman's participatory planning models exerted a major influence on the Architecture Machine Group.

Circuit Diagrams of Participation

"Modern man wants and needs to make use of technology in order to become independent and highly mobile within the loose framework of a social order. The offer of prefabricated goods as well as periodically changing habits and tools make it easier for him," wrote Yona Friedman early on, in his 1957 essay "Ein Architektur-Versuch" [An architectural attempt].[35] With this statement, Friedman touched on a core idea of his understanding of architecture. With systems of stackable furniture made of inexpensive materials, Friedman believed he had found an appropriate architectural concept for a society characterized by industrialization and mobility. Using a few prefabricated building elements, he proposed to generate new variations of multifunctional structures.

Ville du Bois de Boulogne in Paris (1957), La Ville Spatiale (1958/1962), and the Seven Bridge Towns to Link Four Continents (1963) are projects worth mentioning in this context.[36] However, this was not the reason Friedman aroused Negroponte's interest; the latter had no intention of designing oversized spatial structures

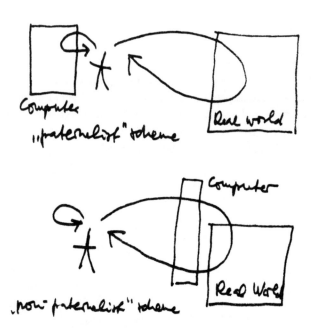

Yona Friedman, relationship diagram, "Paternalist Scheme" (top) and "Non-Paternalist Scheme" (bottom).

with suspended living capsules. Friedman, however, differed from the other protagonists of participatory construction—such as N. John Habraken and Ottokar Uhl[37]—in that he used a whole series of mathematical concepts to link the level of information and communication with that of spatial mobility, such as theories of probability theory, topology, and graphs. His goal was to find a language that

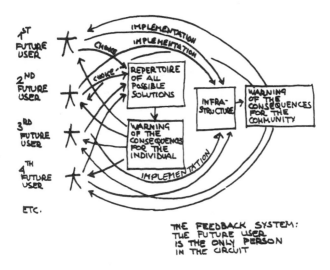

Yona Friedman, "The Feedback System: The Future User is the Only Person in the Circuit."

Yona Friedman, *Toward a Scientific Architecture* (Cambridge, MA: The MIT Press, 1975), 8 © Yona Friedman

was as objective as possible for the planning process, and to present it with the help of easy-to-understand diagrams.

Friedman's starting point was a participatory concept that could be described as a form of group decision-making in third-party planning processes.[38] Three aspects were fundamental: interaction, influence, and information exchange. The first aspect established the principle of involving the user in important planning decisions from the very beginning of the process. The second was the resulting possibility of influencing the outcome of decisions made in this way, and thus of always being able to change and correct them. The third aspect—the exchange of information—went beyond being the basis for the first two aspects. It was also that aspect of the participatory planning process which Friedman attempted to describe using cybernetics. "Human behavior and action, progress and the changeability of any civilization, […] are always based on the transformability of information and communication and thus on the mobility of semiotic systems, and it is undoubtedly true when Yona Friedman points out in his manifesto on *L'architecture mobile* that 'any completely immutable object is non-existent to our senses'," Max Bense explained in his essay "Urbanism and Semiotics," published in *Arch+* in 1968.[39] At first glance, this might seem to be an abstract formulation, but it reveals how much Bense tried to connect the concepts of information and mobility. Although Friedman was not concerned with the development of semiotic models or the scientification of aesthetics, Bense's idea about the transformability of information and communication was of central importance to him. The idea of changing these independently with the help of suitable tools (among which Friedman counted mathematical theories) harbored the conditions of participatory construction that Friedman advocated: the technically guaranteed independence of individual existence through the regulation of information and communication—and that meant with the help of cybernetics, information theory, and computers.

Architecture from the Machine

It is no coincidence that, in his second book, *Soft Architecture Machines*, Negroponte had Friedman write the introduction to the chapter "Computer-Aided Participatory Design," one of the emerging areas of research in the field of architecture and computers: "It is evident that the term machine has a general meaning and that it can stand for practically anything related to some temporal process [...] What I consider more important is to introduce this part of the book I like and to stay consistent in this introduction with my personal views and my own research; and for this purpose I had to underline the fact that no 'machine' could be imagined that did not 'contain' an intelligent observer. Thus I don't consider the 'hardware' machine as the machine. I consider as 'machine' only and exclusively a system containing 'the machine and me.' The theme 'computer-aided participatory design' is clearly contained his definition [...]."[40] On the one hand, Friedman made clear how relative the concept of machine can be considered in this context. On the other hand—and this was also how it connected to Negroponte's research on the man–machine interface—he emphasized that the computer as a tool should not be considered without the user. Friedman also regarded the relationship between humans and computers as a partnership—although for him, the focus was less on the technology of the machine and more on people's needs.

In 1970, Friedman developed the design concept "Flatwriter: Choice by Computer," which he originally conceived for an IBM pavilion at the Osaka World Expo. The Flatwriter was a machine designed to help users automatically generate an apartment (i.e., a "flat," as its name implies) in just a few steps. Friedman based the Flatwriter on a drawn diagram comprising a complex network of feedback loops, representing its processes as a kind of cybernetic circuit diagram. "This process […] made up of a transmitting station (the future user), a channel (the architect and the builder together), a receiving station (the hardware, or finished building), and information return or feedback (the usefulness of the product made available to the client). This system allowed for no corrections, no adjustments in case the feedback was unsatisfactory. Therefore, if the receiving station (the finished building) had not received the message (the specific needs of the client) from the transmitting station (the client), the responsibility lay with the channel (the architect and the builder)."[41] The highlight of this diagram, however, was hidden in the individual connections. Not only would the Flatwriter create a spatial program, it would also enable its modifications and calculate the resulting spatial and social effects on the immediate environment, showing this to the user—what Friedman called "direct feedback from the user."[42]

"Thanks to a machine which I call the Flatwriter, each future inhabitant of a city can imprint his personal preferences with respect to his apartment (flat) to be, using symbols which put in visual form the different elements of his decision so that the builder as well as his neighbours can understand what his choice is. In other words, this machine contains a repertoire of several million possible plans for apartments, knows how to work out instructions about the characteristic consequences of the way each future inhabitant would use an apartment, and finally, can determine whether or not the site chosen by a future inhabitant will risk upsetting the other inhabitants."[43] While the initial task was simply to arrange and connect rooms, and determine basic shapes and the basic furnishings required for an apartment, the system provided a brief feedback as the planning progressed, i.e., an initial calculated evaluation of the previous decisions. If, after this evaluation, the future user was satisfied with his or her choice, an empty chessboard-like grid would be displayed on the screen, which represented the infrastructure. Friedman spoke in this context of a "picture of the plan of an infrastructure, an empty framework."[44] Within this grid, the user could define the exact location of the apartment by entering numerically defined parameters. The system then independently checked whether the planned building project could lead to restrictions for the neighbors and the environment—for example, in terms of natural light, views, access, and noise. A feedback mechanism then informed the user a second time whether the choice was spatially and socially feasible. If this was the case, it meant that nothing stood in the way of building the apartment. Finally, the Flatwriter calculated a performance diagram (called "effort-chart") for the entire infrastructure that the flat was connected to. If the computer system did not signal a problem in the planning at this point either, all other occupants would be informed about the planned building project.

Although the Flatwriter was never produced for the Expo `70 world's fair, Friedmann now had a formalized, well thought-out concept with illustrative diagrams. Only a few years later, Friedman embarked on a second project, this time much more technological and complex in its scope. "I was turned on by a soft-spoken but persuasive argument, for removing the architect as middleman between a user's needs and their resolution in the built environment,"[45] Negroponte later recalled about his first meeting with Friedman. Together with Guy Weinzapfel, another member of the Architecture Machine Group, Negroponte and Friedman developed a computer experiment, called "Architecture-by-Yourself: An Experiment with Computer Graphics for House Design."[46] The basis of this experiment was the YONA software that Negroponte had developed, which could generate a variety of floor plans. Similar to the Flatwriter, the user's technological freedom was in the project's foreground. "As its title suggests, 'Architecture-by-Yourself' is concerned with the development of sign aids for 'do-it-yourself' designers—people designing their own homes or apartments. We see these users as designers, but designers who, unlike architects, are not trained or practiced in the skill. For this reason, their requirements for design aids differ significantly from those of aids created for architects. [...] The goal of Architecture-by-Yourself is to allow people to design their own homes without either a middleman or a middle machine creating whole solutions for them."[47]

Negroponte and Friedman reduced the complexity of the architectural design and planning process to a linear sequence of only five steps. Simple instructions on the screen guided users step by step through the program. They could define basic criteria, such as room size, room height, and the desired light or shade conditions using a series of controls. The program then generated a network of spaces in the form of a topological vector diagram, whose node connections could be individually changed and rearranged like rubber bands. In the last step, and after an automatic check for spatial overlaps or other planning errors, YONA calculated a final corresponding layout.

What the Flatwriter and Architecture-by-Yourself had in common was their technical implementation of the same underlying concept: the idea of architecture without architects. With a view to cybernetics and information theory, Friedman spoke unmistakably of the "elimination of the designer."[48] This also put the traditional self-image of the architect back in the crosshairs. Negroponte also made the issue abundantly clear: to "remove[ ] the architect and his design function more and more from the design process; the limit of this progression is giving the physical environment the ability to design itself, to be knowledgeable, and to have an autogenic existence. The general assumption is that in most cases the architect is an unnecessary and cumbersome (and even detrimental) middleman

YONA software: Working
with topological diagrams
to generate apartments.

Nicholas Negroponte and Guy
Weinzapfel, "Architecture-by-Yourself:
An Experiment with Computer Graph-
ics for House Design," *SIGGRAPH
'76, Proceedings of the 3rd Annual
Conference on Computer Graphics
and Interactive Techniques* (New York,
NY: ACM Press, 1976), 76, 77
© Nicholas Negroponte, Guy
Weinzapfel

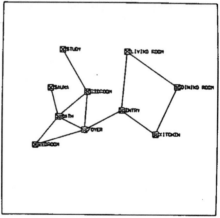

between individual, constantly changing needs and the continuous incorporation of these needs into the built environment. The architect's primary function, I propose, will be served well and served best by computers."[49] Both Friedman and Negroponte were concerned with exposing the mythologized mechanisms of the architectural creation process. However, the planned disempowerment of the architect took place under two different auspices: Negroponte approached the project from a purely technological standpoint, while Friedman approached it from a more sociological perspective. For Negroponte, the architect was to be replaced by the universality of a learning machine, for Friedman by the participation of the occupants. Friedman's idea of "direct feedback from the user" was covered by Negroponte's concept of the "individual designer."[50]

However, what may initially read like a seamless success story of computer-aided participatory design was considered by both sides to be a failed project. Negroponte and Weinzapfel already indicated in the conclusion of their article from 1976 that they were quite critical of the project: "In summary, we see Architecture-by-Yourself as a worst-case exercise in man–machine interaction."[51] And Friedman also later recalled: "My experience with MIT made me understand a fundamental disadvantage of using computers for design: they are too fast. People have their own thinking speed and computer-thinking is too fast, too intransparent for them."[52] What Negroponte saw as an advantage of technological progress, Friedman saw as a disadvantage. And so, it is perhaps the later computer works by the architect Lucien Kroll that actually carried on the legacy of participatory building, which emerged in the 1960s and 1970s between the desire for democratization and the fever of mechanization. This includes his planning software Paysage, which he developed between 1981 and 1987, and his book, *CAD-Architektur: Vielfalt durch Partizipation* [CAD architecture: diversity through participation], published in 1985.[53]

Lucien Kroll, computer simulation for residents as part of the renovation of a residential block in Étouvie-Amiens.

Lucien Kroll, "Paysage," in *Lucien Kroll: Bauten und Projekte* (Stuttgart: Hatje, 1987), 138–141.

In a way, Kroll resumed the project that Negroponte and Friedman had begun with great hope, but soon abandoned, of linking concepts on participatory construction with the tool-based worlds of computer-aided design. With the help of increasingly powerful simulation models, more and more parameters could not only be visualized but also varied and then discussed by the future occupants of a building project.

In 1959, Abraham Moles spoke of the arrival of a new world—the "world of machines"[54]—and in the same breath proclaimed that 20th-century science would be "above all the science of models."[55] The projects by Negroponte and Friedman can be understood as an architectural interpretation of this thesis. While Negroponte was interested in the technical modeling of communication at the intersection of man and the machine, Friedman created a diagrammatic world of "operative imagery" under the claim of participatory construction.[56] Not only do their different approaches clearly demonstrate how broad the spectrum of cybernetic thinking in architecture was, but also the originality and radicalism with which certain projects were launched in the name of individualization.

Epilogue: Return of the Material

Cybernetics was euphorically received in architecture, where it was transformed in a productive way, until a short time later, it almost completely disappeared from view. The idea that cybernetics would enable us to penetrate any kind of deep structure of the world merged with the hope of being able to speak objectively about the comprehensive nature of architecture and urban planning. Given the increasingly digitalized production of architecture over the years, it is impossible to deny that the considerations of that time—regarding information, structure, and complexity—are highly relevant today. They are omnipresent as fundamental concepts. The media scientist Manfred Fassler went one step further to write of a so-called cybermodernism.[1] Cybernetics seduced architecture not only through its allegedly universal scientific terminology; it also promised to elegantly overcome another, much more fundamental problem: the question of whether architecture was closer to the arts or sciences. The strategic highlight of cybernetics was to provide architects with a set of interdisciplinary theoretical models that promised to single-handedly solve the conflict between a purely technical, scientific notion of architecture and a purely artistic one. This was not done by combining, merging, or otherwise linking parts of both approaches. As is well known, cybernetic model-based thinking operated on an entirely new level of abstraction. Norbert Wiener's influential maxim of examining the world from the perspective of communication was transformed into a universalist conceptual model in architecture. Cybernetics was regarded as a new cognitive instrument, a mixture between a magnifying glass and an X-ray machine. It was hoped that this would make hidden structures and invisible processes not only visible but also objectifiable and formalizable. It is not by chance that Abraham Moles wrote of cybernetics as a "microscope of complexity."[2]

Ultimately, cybernetics failed in architecture with its universal scientific claim and a much too narrow corset of methods.[3] By the late 1970s, the theoretical concepts on automation and communication technology no longer suited the practice-oriented approaches required by universities and industry. Instead of an analytical machine theory, the idea of the computer as a tool gained the upper hand. "Instead of teaching a general theory of modeling and control, an academic field was established to master the key instrument of the 'technoscientific revolution': the computer."[4] Not only did this open up new realms of possibility in terms of technology for architecture, but also new areas of research. It is no coincidence that today's fields of media studies and cultural technology research are demanding a revision of the concept of tools and discussing the many definitions of "designing" in the age of computer simulation.[5]

The era of cybernetics is once again very much in vogue in other respects, too. A few years ago, two remarkable art installations attracted the public's attention. The first was a work by the artist and filmmaker Lutz Dammbeck. In 2007, he reconstructed Nicholas Negroponte's cybernetic robot experiment *SEEK*, true to the original, at a gallery in Berlin[6]—almost four decades after Negroponte caused a sensation with it in the groundbreaking exhibition *Software*, at the Jewish Museum in New York.[7] The second art installation was a project by the architects Fabio Gramazio and Matthias Kohler. As a contribution to the Swiss Pavilion at the 2008 Architecture Biennale in Venice, they exhibited a fabrication robot.[8] This robot autonomously produced a brick wall measuring nearly three meters high and one hundred meters long, with multiple curves, before the public, and after its completion meandered through the entire pavilion as a walk-in sculpture. While Dammbeck's homage to Negroponte fascinated visitors with the cybernetic competition between human and machine, Gramazio and Kohler's robot installation was impressive in the precision with which its machine arm could layer individual bricks into a complex spatial structure. The charm of the utopian potential and the oversized metaphorical gesture of Negroponte's "cybernetic world model" shrank in Gramazio and Kohler to the size of a constructive detail. Yet, although the interplay of architecture and technology in both art installations—regardless of their respective historical backgrounds—was conceived on different scales, a common thread can be found. It was not by chance that Dammbeck chose to revive this installation rather than one of Nicolas Schöffer's kinetic sculptures. *SEEK* was originally developed as an art installation addressing the systemic behavior of living beings and machines, but besides aspects of communication and control, it also questioned the meaning of materiality. As a metaphor, the installation implied a physical model highlighting both the interaction of computer and material and the behavior of a cybernetic machine in a representational environment. That Dammbeck took up Negroponte's metaphor can therefore be understood as a critical reference to architecture's ongoing quest, for nearly half a century now, to find a corresponding "cultural form" for the "structural form" of the computer.[9]

On this point, the conceptual rigor of Negroponte's project overlaps with that of Gramazio and Kohler. It is not difficult to see in their construction robot a reformulation of the efforts by Konrad Wachsmann and Walter Gropius to transform the field of architecture into a fully automated and thoroughly rationalized construction industry. In this sense, Gramazio and Kohler's machine can be seen as a symbol of a continuation of the project of industrial construction by new means. At the same time, the installation embodies a fundamental attempt to reformulate the architecture of modernism. Whereas in industrial building the emphasis was on serial production, today the focus is increasingly on the digital fabrication of complex geometries and irregular structures. In contrast to the Cartesian simplicity of modernist architecture, in recent years there has been increasing talk of "nonstandard structures"[10] or, in reference to the book by Charles Jencks, of an "architecture of the jumping universe."[11] It is hardly surprising that, in a 2010 exhibition paying tribute to Wachsmann's legacy, called *Turning Point(s) of Building: From Serial to Digital Architecture*, Gramazio and Kohler's robot was seen as a promising example of processes of transformation in building technology that are described in terms of "mass customization," "parametrization," and "digital fabrication."[12] One of the basic mechanisms in the organization of digital architecture is that the use of the computer for design increases the complexity of the built geometries so that the only way they can be economically produced is by digital means. Gramazio and Kohler's contribution to the Venice Biennale, therefore, had a twofold message. On the one hand, it became unmistakably clear that even the oldest prefabricated building element—the clay brick—can no longer escape processing by information technologies. On the other hand, it showed that the exactingly calibrated production process for a complex twisted wall curve can only be realized thanks to the use of a high-tech machine. Construction process and art object, control and material, were given equal importance.

Contrary to many ideas about how dematerialization, however conceived, will lead to the dissolution of the architectural object, current form-finding processes are increasingly beginning, once again, with the study of specific materials. The fears that have been repeatedly expressed since the beginnings of computer-aided design, that increasingly intelligent design automata would remove humans from the decision-making processes of architectural production—one only has to recall the passionate debates with Louis Kahn or O.M. Ungers—are emerging again with the return of the material. Renewed attention to materials, however, is not understood as a targeted antidote to the alleged virtualization of the design process, but as an adequate supplement. Material properties, joining techniques, and manufacturing possibilities are being systematically explored and used as parameters at the starting point of geometric optimization processes. In this context, one should mention the work by the computer scientist Fabian Scheurer,[13] and the so-called material systems by architect Achim Menges and engineer Jan Knippers.[14] Not only do they use the computer for the visualization and calculation of complex surfaces, but also for the structural description of material behavior. It is certainly not too much to say that architecture today is confronting the advent of a new technical culture of description, at the intersection of human, machine, and material.

It remains to be seen what understanding of technology this will lead to when "digital craftsmanship"[15] and "digital materiality"[16] are discussed in the future. With the return to the physical behavior of individual building materials, the cultural history of construction is once again coming to the fore. A view of architecture from the perspective of technology history demands to be acknowledged, asking about the characteristics of a new material aesthetics and the revision of the traditional concept of "engineering art." After the abstract circuit diagrams of model cybernetic worlds, what is at stake today is a technical way of thinking concerned with the knowledge of the material and the corresponding design tools, and with the cultural spectrum of their interaction.

Epilogue to the 2nd edition (2020)

After the large-scale cybernetics wave of the second half of the last century, the once heavy computing machines have lost weight but gained power. Social forms and ways of living are emerging that can no longer be expressed without the computer. Sensors are migrating, populating the environment, and creating their own algorithmic ecosystems. While smart dust blows like a warm technological wind through buildings, cities, and landscapes, human behavior, communication, experiences, and emotions are stored, analyzed, and evaluated as quantifiable patterns. It is the quiet murmur of data that is constantly audible yet, so far, can hardly be experienced or used.

In 2017, the United Nations therefore published a series of reports describing various applications of big data technologies for public-sector purposes and community projects. The publications are part of the Global Pulse initiative, founded by the United Nations Secretary-General, and are based on two noteworthy assumptions. First, that data will be "harnessed safely and responsibly as a public good" in the future, and second, "that digital data offers the opportunity to gain a better understanding of changes in human well-being."[17] Contrary to the still widespread idea that big data technologies[18] can only be used by individual companies, this highlights the enormous potential and benefits data holds as a community resource if it is freely available to the public. One of the UN's central questions is therefore: "How can citizens be involved in collecting community-level data and mapping their own living environments, and how can they then use this information in planning for the future?"[19] What new emancipatory possibilities would result from such an approach? What would a digital world look like, for example, in which big data technologies were actually freely available?

What would such a step mean for society—culturally, scientifically, socially, and politically? What new methods and perspectives would this open up for the design of the built and natural environment? What does "public" mean, for example, when there are digitally and globally networked, yet inherently fragmented, plural sub-publics? What "citizens" are we talking about here? And who designs the so-called living environment? One thing is certain: because of new possibilities in information technology for data storage, management, processing, and transmission, the concept of data apparently liberated itself from the traditional scientific notion of data as only a measurement value.[20] When data changes, suggesting certain trends, it can either warn of the future or promise better times.[21] In doing so, it has both prognostic and utopian potential and is characterized by an almost universal pluralism of origin and use. The term storage has become synonymous with the automated accumulation and analysis of enormous amounts of data. What will be remembered in the future, and in what form, therefore depends on who organizes and controls the storage media and in which medium the individual and collective experiences are transported and passed on. Information fragments are constantly generated, stored, retrieved, updated, and stored again—a seemingly endless cycle of coding and recoding history and the present.[22] What is transmitted on "thousands of computers, copied, and becomes part of our everyday world through constant repetition, stabilizes itself and eventually becomes a cultural sediment of the system."[23] Increasingly, social, political, and ethical issues of planetary proportions are dominating the debate, breaking down and recomposing established regulatory structures of modern Western societies. The accelerated datafication of society is shaking the foundations of the traditional privilege of interpretation and collective forms of cooperation. Not least, this calls into question historically entrenched cultural, political, and economic values and production systems. Forms of technological unrest are emerging, which require not only new hypothetical and critical thinking but also alternative approaches to shaping the future data society. How will spaces of production change, and with that the concept of work, if our physical and cognitive actions are increasingly replaced by automation and artificial intelligence? How will housing and everyday life in cities change, if the concept of urbanity is no longer a synonym for a certain segment of the urban community, but—in the sense of smart cities—for an efficiently regulated, permanently controlled matrix of life, synchronized with a multitude of other data? What spaces for education, teaching, and research must be created if creativity is no longer the focus of design and the sciences no longer concerned with forming hypotheses and theories, but with a new kind of digital data empiricism, in which traditional thinking in terms of causality is replaced by thinking in terms of correlation?

It is indisputable that the rapid development of datafication processes, especially in the last two decades, has resulted in transformation processes throughout society. The book *The Stack*, written by the sociologist and design theorist Benjamin Bratton and published in 2016,[24] presents one of the most theoretically differentiated models to date, interweaving many of the aspects outlined above. Going beyond traditional horizontal principles of social organization, such as those in Fritz Haller's study on the *totale stadt* [total city], Bratton designed a vertical counter-model organized along technical platforms. The image of the "stack" attempts to connect numerous phenomena from current data technologies to illustrate territorial power shifts. Referring to the "design of political geography" and "planetary-scale computation,"[25] Bratton developed a multilayer model consisting of six levels: Earth, Cloud, Address, City, Interface, and User. In short, Bratton's *The Stack* presents an elaborate theoretical structure for the world as a vertical database, an "accidental megastructure."[26] The question of which perspectives may emerge for the design of this data society, however, remains unanswered.

It seems necessary to deal more intensively with the emancipatory potential of design data technologies and artificial intelligence in architecture in the future, in order to once again, in a renewed recourse to the era of cybernetics, pursue the famous question of (cultural) technology, and with it, the significance of architecture in our increasingly automated data society.

The Re-Invention of (the) Building: Epilogue 2022

The datafication of today's world makes us realize what it means to be part of a globally operating industrial complex. This is especially true for architectural design and production. Materials, objects, and capital circulate in an infrastructural matrix whose scale and impact we are only gradually beginning to understand. Thanks to more precise simulation models of material and substance cycles, we are increasingly able to document and research the consequences of an environment that humans have fundamentally transformed. Digital mappings are now emerging that will lead us to new insights and simultaneously question traditional supply and production systems. We are only beginning to grasp, for example, that the way buildings are manufactured and constructed around the world is a process that no longer takes place only on the earth's surface but also leaves traces deep inside it. Sandstone, iron, copper, and lithium are mined using elaborate, destructive methods and then processed for the global construction industry. The oceans have changed from a once mythical realm into little more than a vast geopolitical infrastructure project whose story can no longer be told without oil platforms, undersea cables, floating server farms, and forensic oceanography.

How can construction, raw materials, and digitalization be brought together in a productive way? What will be the geological footprint of data-based design? These are tricky yet crucial questions that are not only about innovation but also collaboration and co-creation. In the coming decades, they will undoubtedly have a more profound impact on design than we can imagine. For the future, the significance of these questions lies in our collective responsibility to constantly and critically question and renegotiate the concept of "openness." An open society is one of the most significant civil society-oriented projects we have inherited from the last century. However, the definition of an open society changes depending on the context. It makes a difference, for example, whether the topic of discussion is the political basis of a democracy, the economic principle of a market economy, or the handling of personal data. This is also indicated by reports issued by the UN Global Pulse initiative (mentioned in the Epilogue to the 2020 edition of this book). The initiative advocates an "open data" society that harnesses big data for the benefit of the common good. In such a future, architects would have access to all current data concerning our built and natural environment—for example, about the global consumption of sand, the accumulation of microplastics in our oceans and groundwater, the toxic properties of building materials, or how people behave in cities. The cultural technology of designing would be based on a new technological, but also environmental, foundation of planetary proportions.

It is perhaps possible to mention the UN initiative in the same breath as Buckminster Fuller's World Game simulation of 1960, even if such juxtapositions seem somewhat awkward given the rapid technologization of the world. Both Fuller's World Game and the UN study are mental experiments that use an agenda of enlightenment, lending them a certain social relevance, and they indicate the direction architecture might take. Dreaming of an open data society as a project is one side of the coin. The question of what it means to design in such a data-driven society, or how we can produce meaning at all from the vast amounts of environmental data that will be collected, is the other side. At some point, we will not be able to avoid tools like machine learning or computer vision in architecture because human intuition will reach its natural limits when faced with so much data. The faster we collect ever-more data on materials, the environment, and the climate, the likelier we are to run up against the limitations of our ability to deal with it. We will have to admit that humans will neither be able to assess nor evaluate the complex structure of an open-data society without automated analytical capabilities.

Unlike early cyberneticist notions that envisioned buildings as bifurcated communication networks, in today's age of artificial intelligence, building design has become more a matter of data management: from building standards and participatory user behavior to integrating sensors and climate data. A smart building, for example, is not just a collection of disparate devices or computational protocols but of ones that function in concert as a remotely controllable infrastructure system. People and buildings, but also buildings and buildings, are interconnected, creating new types of architectural sensor networks. Buildings are no longer merely passive objects displaying signs or symbolic forms. They become active producers: building data generates more data, transforming buildings into urban databases.

This datafication of buildings offers us a thought-provoking opportunity to rethink and reposition fundamental architectural design concepts such as shelter, comfort, privacy and security, or even human behavior, climate control, and energy efficiency. How will we—and should we—reinvent the building of the future?

Notes

Introduction

1 Salomon Klaczko, "Einführende Bemerkungen zur Kybernetik für zukünftige Architekten und Urbanisten," lecture, in *Systemdenken: Dokumentation einer Vorlesungsreihe: Kurs OEL 1, 1972/1973*, ed. W. Custer und H. Imesch (Zurich: ETH Zurich Department of Architecture, 1972/1973, 3. Salomon Klaczko was a visiting professor for Cybernetics at the ETH from 1972 to 1975.

2 Jacques Herzog, Pierre de Meuron, Georg Giser, presentation on Helmar Frank's book, „Kybernetische Grundlagen der Pädagogik (1962)," in *Systemtechnik: Arbeits und Unterrichtshilfsmittel zur Übung "System"* (Zurich: ETH Zurich Department of Architecture, 1972), 71–73.

3 Antoine Picon, "Architecture and the Sciences: Scientific Accuracy or Productive Misunderstanding?," in *Precisions: Architektur zwischen Wissenschaft und Kunst/Architecture between Sciences and the Arts*, ed. Ákos Morávanszky and Ole W. Fischer (Berlin: Jovis, 2008), 79.

4 One exception is an insightful study into the history of American corporate culture that includes the role played by cybernetics: Reinhold Martin, *The Organizational Complex: Architecture, Media, and Corporate Space* (Cambridge, MA: The MIT Press, 2003).

5 Erich Hörl, *Sacred Channels: The Archaic Illusion of Communication*, trans. Nils F. Schott (Amsterdam: Amsterdam University Press, 2018), 38.

6 Claude Lévi-Strauss, *Structural Anthropology* (1958), trans. Claire Jacobson and Brooke Grundfest Schoepf (New York, NY: Basic Books, 1963), 283.

7 Niklas Luhmann, "Kybernetische Regelung," in *Zweckbegriff und Systemrationalität* (Frankfurt am Main: Suhrkamp, 1977), 157.

8 Claus Pias, "The Age of Cybernetics," in *Cybernetics: The Macy Conferences 1946–1953: The Complete Transactions*, ed. Claus Pias (Zurich: Diaphenes, 2003), 11.

9 Norbert Wiener, *Cybernetics: Or Control and Communication in the Animal and the Machine* (1948), 2nd edition (Cambridge, MA: The MIT Press, 1963), 1.

10 See Eberhard Lang, *Zur Geschichte des Wortes Kybernetik: Beiheft zu Band 9 der Reihe Grundlagenstudien aus Kybernetik und Geisteswissenschaften* (Quickborn: Schnelle, 1968).

11 Wiener, *Cybernetics*, 11.

12 Norbert Wiener, "Cybernetics," *Scientific American* 179, no. 5 (November 1948): 14–19.

13 Norbert Wiener, *A Life in Cybernetics: Ex-Prodigy: My Childhood and Youth and I Am a Mathematician: The Later Life of a Prodigy* (Cambridge, MA: The MIT Press, 2018), 465.

14 Norbert Wiener, *The Human Use of Human Beings: Cybernetics and Society* (1950) (London: Free Association Books, 1989).

15 Ibid., 16.

16 Claus Pias, "Jenseits des Werkzeugs: Kybernetische Option der Architektur zwischen Informationsästhetik und Design Amplifier," in *Kulturtechnik Entwerfen: Praktiken, Konzepte und Medien in Architektur und Design Science*, ed. Daniel Gethmann and Susanne Hauser (Bielefeld: transcript, 2009), 269.

17 Otto Walter Haseloff, *Kybernetik als soziale Tatsache: Anwendungsbereiche, Leistungsformen und Folgen für die industrielle Gesellschaft* (Hamburg: Decker, 1963), 9.

18 See Slava Gerovitch, *From Newspeak to Cyberspeak: A History of Soviet Cybernetics* (Cambridge, MA: The MIT Press, 2002); Jérome Segal, "Kybernetik in der DDR: Dialektische Beziehungen," in *Cybernetics/Kybernetik: The Macy-Conferences 1946–1953*, vol. 2: *Essays und Dokumente*, ed. Claus Pias (Zurich: Diaphanes, 2004), 227–253.

19 W. Ross Ashby, *Design for a Brain: The Origin of Adaptive Behavior* (New York, NY: Wiley, 1952).

20 W. Ross Ashby, *An Introduction to Cybernetics* (London: Chapman & Hall, 1956).

21 See Andrew Pickering, "Cybernetics and the Mangle: Ashby, Beer and Pask," *Social Studies of Science* 32 (2002): 413–437; see also Eden Medina, "Designing Freedom, Regulating a Nation: Socialist Cybernetics in Allende's Chile," *Journal of Latin American Studies* 38, no. 3 (2006): 571–606.

22 See Fred Turner, *From Counterculture to Cyberculture: Stewart Brand, the Whole Earth Network, and the Rise of Digital Utopianism* (Chicago, IL: University of Chicago Press, 2006); see also Georg Vrachliotis, "Whole Earth Catalog: Die Katalogisierung der Welt," in *Versuche das Glück im Garten zu finden*, ed. Franziska Bark-Hagen (Baden: Lars Mueller Publishers, 2011), 120–138.

23 See Philipp Aumann, *Mode und Methode: Die Kybernetik in der Bundesrepublik Deutschland* (Göttingen: Wallstein, 2009).

24 Klaus Brake, "Hochschuldidaktik und politische Realität in der Ausbildungsreform der Architekten und Planer," in *Hochschuldidaktik und politische Realität*, seminar at ETH Zurich, Department of Architecture, November 7 to 11, 1971 (Zurich: Architektura Publikationsladen, 1971), 162.

25 Ibid.

26 "Mit dem Latein am Ende: Spiegel-Serie über Krise und Zukunft der deutschen Hochschulen (Architekten)," *Der Spiegel* (September 8, 1969): 74–80.

27 See David Gugerli, "Kybernetisierung der Hochschule: Zur Genese des universitären Managements," in *Die Transformation des Humanen: Beiträge zur*

Kulturgeschichte der Kybernetik, ed. Michael Hagner and Erich Hörl (Frankfurt am Main: Suhrkamp, 2008), 414–439.

28 Klaczko, 1.

29 Ibid., 3.

30 Ibid.

31 Jay Wright Forrester, *Urban Dynamics* (Cambridge, MA: The MIT Press, 1969).

32 This book focuses mainly on how cybernetics was applied to the field of architecture in Europe. The complex architectural universe of Buckminster Fuller or individual protagonists in the field of computer-aided design, such as Michael Noll or Ron Resch, were intentionally not addressed.

33 The terms "man" and "mankind" to refer collectively to all people regardless of gender, and in the combinations "modern man" and "man and machine," were commonly used during the period in history this work focuses on and has therefore been used throughout this book.

Universalization of the Machine

1 Nicholas Negroponte, *The Architecture Machine: Toward a More Human Environment* (Cambridge, MA: The MIT Press, 1970).

2 Wiener, *Cybernetics,* 43.

3 See David Mindell, *Between Human and Machine: Feedback, Control, and Computing Before Cybernetics* (Baltimore, MD: Johns Hopkins University Press, 2002).

4 Wiener, *Cybernetics,* 38.

5 Ibid., 39.

6 Sigfried Giedion, *Mechanization Takes Command: A Contribution to Anonymous History* (New York, NY: Oxford University Press, 1948).

7 See Edward Shanken, "Cybernetics and Art: Convergence in the 1960s," in *From Energy to Information: Representation in Science and Technology, Art, and Literature*, ed. Bruce Clarce and Linda Dalrymple Henderson (Stanford, CA: Stanford University Press, 2002), 255–279.

8 See Michael Hagner, "Bilder der Kybernetik: Diagramm und Anthropologie, Schaltung und Nervensystem," in *Konstruierte Sichtbarkeiten: Wissenschafts und Technikbilder seit der frühen Neuzeit*, ed. Martina Hessler (Munich: Wilhelm Fink, 2006), 383–405.

9 Ibid., 386.

10 Lily E. Kay, "Diskursproduktion: Kybernetik, Information, Leben," in *Das Buch des Lebens: Wer schrieb den genetischen Code?* (Frankfurt am Main: Suhrkamp, 2005), 157.

11 Claus Pias, "Unruhe und Steuerung: Zum utopischen Potential der Kybernetik," in *Die Unruhe der Kultur: Potentiale des Utopischen*, ed. Jörn Rüsen and Michael Fehr (Weilerswist: Velbrück, 2004), 302.

12 Wiener, *Cybernetics*, 42.

13 See Kisho Kurokawa, "Helix Structure, 1961," in *Metabolism in Architecture* (London: Studio Vista, 1977), 56.

14 See Hans-Peter Schwarz, "Die Mythologie des Konstruktiven: Zerstreute Gedanken zur Naturgeschichte der Maschine," in *Vision der Moderne: Das Prinzip Konstruktion*, ed. Heinrich Klotz, exhib. cat., German Architecture Museum, Frankfurt am Main, June 6 to September 17, 1986 (Munich: Prestel, 1986), 46–56.

15 See Jakow Tschernichow, *Konstruktion der Architektur und Maschinenformen* (1931), trans. from Russian into German by N.A. Jepantschin (Basel: Birkhäuser, 1991).

16 Ibid., 54.

17 Ibid.

18 Ibid.

19 See Giedion, "Springs of Mechanization: Movement," in *Mechanization Takes Command*, 14–29.

20 W. Ross Ashby, *An Introduction to Cybernetics*, 1.

21 Ibid.

22 Dirk Baecker, "Kommunikation," in *Ästhetische Grundbegriffe: Historisches Wörter-buch*, vol. 3, ed. Karlheinz Barck, Martin Fontius, Dieter Schlenstedt, Burkhart Steinwachs, and Friedrich Wolfzettel (Stuttgart: J.B. Metzler, 2001), 384–423.

23 "Bürolandschaften," in *Lexikon der Planung und Organisation*, ed. Hans Niewerth and Jürgen Schöder (Quickborn: Schnelle, 1968), 26 ff.

24 Eberhard Schnelle, foreword to *Flexible Verwaltungsbauten* by Ottomar Gottschalk (Quickborn: Schnelle, 1963), 14.

25 Ibid.

26 Ibid.

27 Ibid.

28 Ibid.

29 Pierre Bertaux, *Mutation der Menschheit: Diagnosen und Prognosen* (Frankfurt am Main: Fischer, 1963).

City Plan, Escape Plan

1 See Carola Hein, "Trauma und Stadtplanung: Der Wiederaufbau von Tokio und Hiroshima nach dem Zweiten Weltkrieg," in *Stadt und Trauma: Annäherungen, Konzepte, Analysen*, ed. Bettina Fraisl and Monika Stromberger (Würzburg: Königshausen & Neumann, 2004), 112.

2 Günter Anders, *Die Antiquiertheit des Menschen*, vol. 1: *Über die Seele im Zeitalter der zweiten industriellen Revolution* (Munich: C.H. Beck, 1956); vol. 2: *Über die Zerstörung des Lebens im Zeitalter der dritten industriellen Revolution* (Munich: C.H. Beck, 1980), 19.

3   Norbert Wiener, "Moral Problems of a Scientist. The Atomic Bomb," in *I am a Mathematician: The Later Life of a Prodigy* (Garden City, NY: Doubleday, 1956), 293–313.

4   Ibid., 300.

5   "How U.S. Cities Can Prepare for Atomic War: MIT Professors Suggest a Bold Plan to Prevent Panic and Limit Destruction," *Life*, December 18, 1950, 77–86.

6   See Michael Hagner and Georg Vrachliotis, "Die Stadt als kybernetische Kommunikationsmaschine," in *Text & Stadt: Eine ideeengeschichtliche Analyse der Quellentexte zur Stadt und Städtebau des 18. bis frühen 20. Jahrhunderts*, ed. Vittorio Magnago Lampugnani, Katia Frey, and Eliana Perotti (Berlin: Gebr. Mann, 2011), 127–137.

7   "What the Scientists are saying," *Bulletin of the Atomic Scientists* 6 no. 3 (March 1950): 71–76. With statements by Albert Einstein, Edward Teller, and Robert Oppenheimer, among others.

8   Wiener, *The Human Use of Human Beings*, 128.

9   See Günter Anders, "Über die Bombe und die Wurzeln unserer Apokalypsen-Blindheit," in *Die Antiquiertheit des Menschen*, vol. 2, 233 ff.

10   Norbert Wiener, quoted in Robert Kargon and Arthur P. Molella, "The City as Communications Net: Norbert Wiener, the Atomic Bomb, and Urban Dispersal," *Technology and Culture* 45, no. 4 (October 2004): 770.

11   "The United States Strategic Bombing Survey: The Effects of the Bombing on Hiroshima and Nagaski" (1946), quoted in Kargon and Molella, 765.

12   Ludwig Hilberseimer, *The Nature of Cities: Origin, Growth, and Decline, Pattern and Form, Planning Problems* (Chicago, IL: Paul Theobold & Co., 1955), 257.

13   Ibid., 282.

14   Eugen Rabinowitch, "Civil Defense: The Long-Range View," in "Civil Defense Against Atomic Attack," special issue, *Bulletin of the Atomic Scientists* 6, no. 8–9 (August/September 1950): 226–230.

15   See Reinhold Martin, "The Organizational Complex: Cybernetics, Space, Discourse," *Assemblage* 37 (December 1998): 102–127.

16   Ibid., 121.

17   Ibid., 114.

18   See "Ideale Stadtkonzepte," in *Anthologie zum Städtebau*, vol. 1.1, ed. Vittorio Magnago Lampugnani, Katia Frey, and Eliana Perotti (Berlin: Gebr. Mann, 2008), 7–205.

19   Wiener, quoted in Kargon and Molella, 772.

20   Ashby, *An Introduction to Cybernetics*, 1.

21   Wiener, Karl W. Deutsch, Giorgio de Santillana, "Cities that Survive the Bomb," quoted in Kargon and Molella, 774.

22 Wiener, quoted in Kargon and Molella, 774.

23 Ibid., 769.

24 See Kisho Kurokawa, "The Origin and History of the Metabolist Movement," in *Metabolism in Architecture* (London: Studio Vista, 1977), 41–45.

25 Noboru Kawazoe, "Material and Man" (1960), in *Anthologie zum Städtebau*, vol. 3, ed. Vittorio Magnago Lampugnani, Katia Frey, and Eliana Perotti (Berlin: Gebr. Mann, 2005), 230–232.

26 Ibid., 230.

27 Max Bense, foreword to Louis Couffignal, *Denkmaschinen*, trans. Elisabeth Walther with Max Bense (Stuttgart: Klipper, 1955), 7. See also Mortimer Taube, *Der Mythos der Denkmaschine: Kritische Betrachtungen zur Kybernetik* (Reinbek: Rowohlt, 1966).

28 Ibid.

29 Kawazoe, "Material and Man," 231.

30 Kenzo Tange, "Function, Structure and Symbol," (1966) in *Kenzo Tange 1946–1969: Architecture and Urban Design*, ed. Udo Kultermann (Zurich: Artemis, 1970), 240.

31 Ibid.

32 Ibid., 241–242.

33 Ibid., 240.

34 See Arnulf Lüchinger, *Strukturalismus in Architektur und Städtebau* (Stuttgart: Krämer, 1981).

35 Tange, "Function, Structure and Symbol," in Kultermann, 243.

36 Ibid., 245.

37 See Thomas Gnädi, "Die Stadt als Verkehrs- und Kommunikationssystem," in *Anthologie zum Städtebau*, vol. 1.2, ed. Vittorio Magnago Lampugnani, Katia Frey, and Eliana Perotti (Berlin: Gebr. Mann, 2008), 1081–1161.

38 Kenzo Tange, "A Plan for Tokyo, 1960," in Kultermann, 117.

39 Ibid., 117–118.

40 Hans-Joachim Flechtner, *Grundbegriffe der Kybernetik: Eine Einführung*, 4th edition (Stuttgart: Wissenschaftliche Verlagsgesellschaft, 1969), 10.

41 Colin Cherry, *On Human Communication: A Review, a Survey, and a Criticism* (1957), 2nd edition (Cambridge, MA: The MIT Press, 1966), 21.

42 See Lauritz Lauritzen, ed., *Städtebau der Zukunft: Tendenzen, Prognosen, Utopien* (Dusseldorf: Econ, 1969); see also Reyner Banham, *Megastructure: Urban Futures of the Past* (London: Thames & Hudson, 1976).

43 Arata Isozaki, "Computer-Aided City," *Kenchiku Bunka* 310 (August 1972), 138–149.

44 Fritz Haller, *totale stadt: ein modell* (Olten: Walter Verlag, 1968); Fritz Haller, *totale stadt: ein globales modell / integral urban: a global model* (Olten: Walter Verlag, 1975).

45 Fritz Haller, *totale stadt: ein modell*, 8.

46 Gernot Feldhusen, *Soziologie für Architekten: Wissenschaft in der Planungspraxis* (Stuttgart: Deutsche Verlags-Anstalt, 1975), 11.

47 Wolfgang Döring, *Perspektiven einer Architektur* (Frankfurt am Main: Suhrkamp, 1970), 13.

48 Ibid., 108.

49 Ibid., 84–85.

50 Reyner Banham, "A Clip-on Architecture," *Design Quarterly* (1965): 9.

51 Sigfried Giedion, *Space, Time and Architecture: The Growth of a New Tradition* (1967), 5th revised and enlarged edition (Cambridge, MA: Harvard University Press, 2008).

52 Ibid., 861–862.

53 Jürgen Joedicke, *Architekturgeschichte des 20. Jahrhunderts: Von 1950 bis zur Gegenwart* (Stuttgart: Karl Krämer, 1979), 143.

54 Jürgen Joedicke, "Introductory Remark." In "Stadtplanung: Experimente und Utopien / Town-Planning: Experiments and Utopias." *Bauen + Wohnen* 21 (May 1967), 165.

55 Ibid.

56 Ibid.

57 Jürgen Joedicke, "Phantasie und Phantastik in der modernen Architektur," in *Für eine lebendige Baukunst: Notizen und Kommentare* (Stuttgart: Karl Krämer, 1965), 109.

58 Wiener, *The Human Use of Human Beings*, 16.

59 Sigfried Giedion, *Architektur und Gemeinschaft* (Hamburg: Rororo, 1956); English edition: *Architecture, You and Me*, ed. and trans. Jacqueline Tyrwhitt (Cambridge, MA: Harvard University Press, 1958). The German word *Gemeinschaft* means "community" in English.

60 Giedion, "The Tragic Conflict," in *Architecture, You and Me*, 12.

61 Giedion, "Art as the Key to Reality," in *Architecture, You and Me*, 6.

62 Tange, "The Expo '70 Master Plan and Master Design," in Kultermann, 282–299.

63 Tange, "Function, Structure and Symbol," in Kultermann, 245.

64 Ibid., 246–255.

65 Tange, "Tokaido-Megalopolis," in Kultermann, 150–167.

66 Tange, "A Plan for Tokyo, 1960," in Kultermann, 114–149.

67 Max Bense, "Urbanismus und Semiotik," *Arch+* 3 (1968): 23–25.

68 Michael Grüning, *Der Wachsmann-Report: Auskünfte eines Architekten* (Berlin: Verlag der Nation, 1988), 547.

1 "Pläne von Inge Scholl und Otl Aicher," in *Hochschule für Gestaltung Ulm: Die Moral der Gegenstände*, ed. Herbert Lindinger (Berlin: Ernst & Sohn, 1987), 15.

2 "Exposé: Unterlagen für die Besprechung von Inge Scholl mit McCloy," in Lindinger, 16.

3 Max Bill, letter to Walter Gropius, May 2, 1950, Walter Gropius Archive, Houghton Library, Harvard University, Cambridge, MA.

4 Otl Aicher, "Bauhaus und Ulm," in Lindinger, 125.

5 "Automation schafft Raum für Kultur: Max Bill sprach im Haus Industrieform," *Industriekurier*, March 9, 1957.

6 Ibid.

7 Max Bense, "Kybernetik oder die Metatechnik einer Maschine"" (1951), in *Max Bense. Ausgewählte Schriften*, vol. 2: *Philosophie der Mathematik, Naturwissenschaft und Technik*, ed. Elisabeth Walther (Stuttgart: J.B. Metzler, 1998), 429–449.

8 Reyner Banham, quoted in Lindinger, 82.

9 Bense, "Kybernetik oder die Metatechnik einer Maschine," 436.

10 See Michael Hagner, "Intellektuelle Wissenschaft, Hyperprofessionalismus und das Allgemeine," in *Wandel oder Niedergang? Die Rolle der Intellektuellen in der Wissensgesellschaft*, ed. Martin Carrier und Johannes Roggenhofer (Bielefeld: transcript, 2007), 65–81.

11 Tomás Maldonado, "Norbert Wiener heute in Ulm," newspaper article (no title, no date), HfG-Archiv Ulm.

12 Tomás Maldonado, "Neue Entwicklungen in der Industrie und die Ausbildung des Produktgestalters," *Ulm: Quarterly Bulletin of the Hochschule für Gestaltung Ulm* 2 (October 1958): 31, HfG-Archiv Ulm.

13 Tomás Maldonado, quoted in Martin Krampen and Günther Hörmann, *Die Hochschule für Gestaltung Ulm: Anfänge eines Projekts der radikalen Moderne / The Ulm School of Design: Beginnings of a Project of Unyielding Modernity* (Berlin: Ernst & Sohn, 2003), 83–84.

14 Wachsmann repeatedly emphasized that he had "nothing to say about a current building project" and that he was also "not interested in building a house." See Konrad Wachsmann, "Modular Coordination and Planning," Hochschule für Gestaltung Ulm, August 12, 1955, unpublished lecture, Konrad-Wachsmann-Archiv, Akademie der Künste Berlin.

15 See Michael Grüning, *Der Wachsmann-Report: Auskünfte eines Architekten* (Berlin: Verlag der Nation, 1986), 486 ff.

16 See Herbert Gilbert, *The Dream of the Factorymade House: Walter Gropius and Konrad Wachsmann* (Cambridge, MA: The MIT Press, 1984).

17 See Edward Alden Jewell, "Modern Museum opens 4 Displays," *New York Times*, February 6, 1946, 31.

18 See Gerhard Curdes, *Die Abteilung Bauen an der HfG Ulm: Eine Reflexion zur Entwicklung, Lehre und Programmatik* (Ulm: Club Off ULM e.V., 2001).

19 Konrad Wachsmann, "Zur Industrialisierung des Bauens," Technische Hochschule Stuttgart, June 28, 1956, unpublished lecture, Konrad-Wachsmann-Archiv, Akademie der Künste Berlin.

20 Konrad Wachsmann, *Wendepunkt im Bauen* (Wiesbaden: Otto Krauskopf, 1959; Reprint Dresden: Verlag der Kunst, 1989). English edition: *The Turning Point of Building: Structure and Design*, trans. Thomas E. Burton (New York, NY: Reinhold, 1961). While the English title is used in this book, the translations by A. Kotmair were based on the original German text.

21 Konrad Wachsmann, lecture at the press conference for his book *Wendepunkt im Bauen*, Frankfurter Hof, Frankfurt am Main, October 13, 1959, unpublished lecture, Konrad-Wachsmann-Archiv, Akademie der Künste Berlin.

22 Konrad Wachsmann, "The Electrical Energy and the Machine as the Tool of Our Time," Hochschule für Gestaltung Ulm, August 19, 1955, unpublished lecture, Konrad-Wachsmann-Archiv, Akademie der Künste Berlin, 4.

23 See Kurt Auckenthaler, *Architektur, Automation, Atom* (Wels: Oberösterreichischer Landesverlag, 1959).

24 Konrad Wachsmann, *Wendepunkt im Bauen* (1959), reprint (Dresden: Verlag der Kunst, 1989), 107 ff.

25 Ibid., 208.

26 Ibid., 104.

27 Ibid., 66.

28 Ibid., 66.

29 Ibid., 66.

30 Konrad Wachsmann, "The Pedagogic Impact of Automation" (no date, c. 1959), unpublished lecture, Konrad-Wachsmann-Archiv, Akademie der Künste Berlin, 8.

31 Wachsmann, *Wendepunkt im Bauen*, 208.

32 The Institute of Design in Chicago was founded in 1937 by former Bauhaus master László Moholy-Nagy as the "New Bauhaus." Former Bauhaus director Ludwig Mies van der Rohe later became the head of its architecture department.

33 Wachsmann, *Wendepunkt im Bauen*, 207.

34 See Peter Rodemeier, "Konrad Wachsmann – oder die Liebe zur Geometrie," in *Vom Sinn des Details: Zum Gesamtwerk von Konrad Wachsmann*, ed. J. Martina Schneider (Cologne: Rudolf Müller, 1988), especially the section "Das Studium im Team," 60 ff.

35 Wachsmann, *Wendepunkt im Bauen*, 207.

Aesthetics, Revolts, Calculations

1   Herman Grégoire and Abraham Moles, "Das Bild des modernen Menschen,"
    in *Enzyklopädie des technischen Jahrhunderts: Epoche Atom und Automation*, vol. 10
    (Geneva: Kister, 1959), 75 ff.

2   Ibid., 76.

3   Ibid.

4   Ibid., 82.

5   Ibid.

6   Ibid.

7   Max Bense, *Brazilian Mind* [*Brasilianische Intelligenz* (1965)], ed. Georg Vrach-
    liotis, trans. Simon Cowper (Berlin: Spector Books, 2022 forthcoming).

8   Max Bense, *Ungehorsam der Ideen: Abschliessender Traktat über Intelligenz und
    technische Welt* (1965), 2nd edition (Cologne: Kiepenheuer & Witsch, 1966), 95.

9   Ibid. "It must be added that art does not necessarily exclude technology, nor
    does technology necessarily exclude art, and it is precisely this connection that
    indicates that the idea of rationality present in the reality they each produce is
    identical: it is a creative rationality."

10 Max Bense, "Thesen über die Notwendigkeit der Ästhetik in der Architektur,"
    Deutsche Architekten- und Ingenieur-Zeitschrift, 1977.

11 Bense, *Ungehorsam,* 94 ff.

12 Abraham Moles, "Arbeitsgruppe 4 (2. und 3. Studienjahr Bauen) – Gliederung
    der Aufgabenbereiche von Wohnung und Stadt," unpublished document, 1965,
    HfG-Archiv Ulm.

13 Manfred Kiemle, *Ästhetische Probleme der Architektur unter dem Aspekt der
    Informationsästhetik* (Quickborn: Schnelle, 1967).

14 See Kiemle, introduction to *Ästhetische Probleme der Architektur* (no page number).

15 Max Bense, *Einführung in die informationstheoretische Ästhetik* (Reinbek:
    Rowohlt, 1969), 7.

16 See George David Birkhoff, *Aesthetic Measure* (Cambridge, MA: Harvard
    University Press, 1933).

17 Max Bense, "Ästhetische Kommunikation," in *Semiotik: Allgemeine Theorie der
    Zeichen* (Baden-Baden: Agis, 1967), 18.

18 Ibid., 7–8.

19 Sokratis Georgiadis in conversation with the author, Stuttgart, December 12, 2008.

20 See *Die Abendzeitung*, Berlin, special issue, June 7, 1967.

21 See Jesko Fezer, "Polit-Kybernetik," *Arch+* 186/187 (2008): 96–106.

22 See "Kritische Universität, Freie Studienorganisation der Studenten in Hoch-
    und Fachschulen von Westberlin, Programm und Verzeichnis der Studienveran-
    staltung im WS 1967/68," 44 ff, http://infopartisan.net/archive/1967/266750. html.

23 See "Mit dem Latein am Ende: Spiegel-Serie über Krise und Zukunft der deutschen Hochschulen (Architekten)," *Der Spiegel* (September 8, 1969).

24 Sokratis Georgiadis in conversation with the author, Stuttgart, April 7, 2009.

25 Wolfgang Pehnt, *Deutsche Architektur seit 1900* (Munich: Deutsche Verlags-Anstalt, 2005), 375.

26 Kiemle, *Ästhetische Probleme der Architektur*, 11–53.

27 Ibid., 11–23.

28 See Elisabeth Walther, *Allgemeine Zeichenlehre: Einführung in die Grundlagen der Semiotik* (Stuttgart: Deutsche Verlags-Anstalt, 1974).

29 See Claude E. Shannon and Warren Weaver, *The Mathematical Theory of Communication* (Urbana, IL: University of Illinois Press, 1949).

30 See Max Bense, *Aesthetica: Einführung in die neue Aesthetik* (Baden-Baden: Agis, 1965).

31 See Helmar Frank, "Informationspsychologie," in *Kybernetik: Brücke zwischen den Wissenschaften* (Frankfurt am Main: Umschau, 1965), 5; expanded edition, 259–273.

32 Abraham A. Moles, *Informationstheorie und ästhetische Wahrnehmung* (1958), trans. H., B. & P. Ronge (Cologne: DuMont, 1971).

33 Helmar Frank, *Kybernetische Analysen subjektiver Sachverhalte* (Quickborn: Schnelle, 1964).

34 Kiemle, "Anwendung der Informationsästhetik auf die Architektur," in *Ästhetische Probleme der Architektur*, 53–131.

35 Ibid., 55.

36 Ibid., 99–129.

37 Ibid., 54.

38 Ibid., introduction (no page number).

39 Ibid., 33.

40 See Reyner Banham, *The New Brutalism: Ethic or Aesthetic?* (London: The Architectural Press, 1966).

41 Kiemle, 118.

42 Ibid.

43 Wolfgang Pehnt, quoted in Kiemle, ibid.; see also Wolfgang Pehnt, "Was ist Brutalismus?," *Das Kunstwerk* 3 (1960): 14–27.

44 Kiemle, 118.

45 Ibid.

46 See Henry-Russell Hitchcock and Philip Johnson, *The International Style: Architecture since 1922* (New York, NY: W.W. Norton & Co., 1932); see also Charles Jencks, *Late-Modern Architecture* (New York, NY: Rizzoli, 1980.

47 Kiemle, 119.

48 Ibid., 120.

49 Ibid., 122.

50 Ibid., 121.

51 Eberhard Schnelle and Alfons Wankum, *Architekt und Organisator: Methoden und Probleme der Bürohausplanung* (Quickborn: Schnelle, 1964).

52 Ottomar Gottschalk, *Flexible Verwaltungsbauten: Planung, Funktionen, Flächen, Ausbau, Einrichtung, Kosten, Beispiele* (Quickborn: Schnelle, 1968).

53 Johannes Holschneider, *Schlüsselbegriffe der Architektur und Stadtbaukunst: Eine Bedeutungsanalyse* (Quickborn: Schnelle, 1968).

54 Curt Siegel, *Strukturformen der modernen Architektur* (Munich: Callwey, 1960). Schnelle published two books by Siegel: *Bürohaus als Großraum: Büroneubau der C. F. Boehringer & Soehne GmbH, Mannheim: Zielsetzung, Planung und Erfahrung*, with Kurd Alsleben, Erhard Büttner, Claus W. Hess, Wolfgang Schnelle, Curt Siegel, Rudolf Wonneberg (Quickborn: Schnelle, 1961); and *Bürobaukosten: Untersuchung über die Wirtschaftlichkeit von Büro und Verwaltungskosten*, with Curt Solf (Quickborn: Schnelle, 1967).

55 Helmar Frank, "Die Etablierung der Informationsästhetik, in *Ästhetische Information: Eine Einführung in die kybernetische Ästhetik*, ed. Helmar Frank and Herbert W. Franke (Berlin: Institut für Kybernetik, 1997), 14.

56 The *Arch+* founders were Ulrich Bäte, Peter Dietze, Dieter Hezel, Wolfram Koblin, Peter Lammert, Gernot Minke, Aylâ Neusel, and Stephan Waldraff.

57 See Hans Ronge, ed., *Kunst und Kybernetik: Ein Bericht über drei Kunsterziehertagungen – Recklinghausen 1965, 1966, 1967* (Cologne: DuMont Schauberg, 1968).

58 The aim of creating a scientific form of architectural criticism with the help of information aesthetics is evident in a debate between Max Bense and Günter Pfeiffer, printed in *Frankfurter Allgemeine Zeitung* in 1968. See Günter Pfeiffer, "Ist Kunst berechenbar? Max Bense und der Computer," *Frankfurter Allgemeine Zeitung*, February 17, 1968.

59 Kiemle, 52.

60 "Ende offen: Kunst und Antikunst," panel discussion with Max Bense, Max Bill, Arnold Gehlen, and Joseph Beuys, broadcast live for the television show *Wochenendforum* on February 6, 1970, Westdeutscher Rundfunk Köln; see also Claus Pias, "Hollerith 'Feathered Crystal': Art, Science, and Computing in the Era of Cybernetics," trans. Peter Krapp, *Grey Room* 29 (Winter 2008): 110–134.

61 The author owes this term to a conversation with Peter Bexte.

62 Hagner and Hörl, *Die Transformation des Humanen*, 75.

63 See Clara Bodenmann-Ritter, ed., *Joseph Beuys. Jeder Mensch ein Künstler: Gespräche auf der documenta 5, 1972* (Frankfurt am Main: Ullstein, 1975).

64 Frieder Nake, "Werk, Kunstwerk, Information, Zeichen: Achtzig Sätze für Elisabeth Walther," in *Kontinuum der Zeichen: Elisabeth Walther-Bense und die Semiotik*, ed. Karl Gfesser and Udo Bayer (Stuttgart: J.B. Metzler, 2002), 9–13.

Swinging Cybernetics

1 Gordon Pask, "The Architectural Relevance of Cybernetics," *Thinking about Architecture and Planning—A Question of Ways and Means*, ed. Royston Landau, special issue, *Architectural Design*, September 1969: 494–496.

2 See Stafford Beer, *Cybernetics and Management* (London: English Universities Press, 1959).

3 See Andrew Pickering, "Cybernetics and the Mangle: Ashby, Beer and Pask," *Social Studies of Science* 32 (2002): 413–437.

4 In an interview, artist Nicolas Schöffer related an exchange of letters he had with Norbert Wiener. In 1956, he had told Wiener about his plan to design cybernetic sculptures. Wiener's reply in 1957 was "the greatest disappointment." Wiener wrote: "Monsieur, art is one thing, science is another." Quoted in "Das wird ein unglaubliches Fest – Nicolas Schöffer über die programmierte Kunst der Zukunft," *Der Spiegel*, February 8, 1970, 156.

5 See Gordon Pask, *An Approach to Cybernetics* (London: Hutchison, 1961); Gordon Pask, *Conversation Theory: Applications in Education and Epistemology* (Amsterdam: Elsevier, 1976).

6 See the cover of *Time* magazine from April 15, 1966; see also David Gilbert, "The Youngest Legend in History: Cultures of Consumption and the Mythologies of Swinging London," *The London Journal* 31, no. 1 (July 2006): 1–14.

7 Pask, "The Architectural Relevance of Cybernetics," *Architectural Design*, 496.

8 Ibid.

9 Ibid.

10 Ibid., 494.

11 Ibid., 496.

12 Ibid., 495.

13 Ibid., 494.

14 Robin McKinnon-Wood, "Early Machinations," *Systems Research* 10 (1993), 129.

15 See Andrew Pickering, *The Cybernetic Brain: Sketches of Another Future* (Chicago, IL: University of Chicago Press, 2010).

16 Gordon Pask, "A Comment, a Case History and a Plan (1968)," in *Cybernetics, Art and Ideas*, ed. Jasia Reichardt (London: Studio Vista, 1971), 78, 80.

17 See László Moholy-Nagy, "Zur Geschichte der kinetischen Plastik," in *Von Material zu Architektur* (1929), facsimile of the 1st edition (Berlin: Gebr. Mann, 2001), 162–164.

18 László Moholy-Nagy, quoted in "Aus der Vitrine—Digital, Teil 7: László Moholy-Nagy: Licht-Raum-Modulator," http://www.bauhaus.de/bauhaus1919/kunst/kunst_modulator.htm.

19 See Walter Schobert, Angelika Leitner, Uwe Nitschke, *The German Avant-Garde*

Film of the 1920s, exhib. cat., Museum Tinguely, Basel, February 10 to May 16, 2010 (Munich: Goethe-Institut, 1989), 55 ff; see also Roland Wetzel, ed., *Le Mouvement: Vom Kino zur Kinetik,* exhib. cat., Museum Tinguely, February 10 to May 16, 2010. (Heidelberg: Kehrer, 2010).

20 See Isabelle Moffat, "'A Horror of Abstract Thought': Postwar Britain and Hamilton's 1951 'Growth and Form' Exhibition," *October* 94 (Fall 2000): 89–112.

21 See D'Arcy Wentworth Thompson, *On Growth and Form* (1917) (Cambridge: University Press, 1952).

22 Kathleen Lonsdale, review of *Aspects of Form, Acta Crystallographica* 6, part 2 (1953): 224.

23 *Aspects of Form: A Symposium on Form in Nature and Art,* ed. Lancelot Law Whyte (London: Percy Lund Humphries, 1951).

24 W. Grey Walter, "Activity Patterns in the Human Brain," in *Aspects of Form,* 179–196.

25 See Andrew Pickering, "Mit der Schildkröte gegen die Moderne: Gehirn, Technologie und Unterhaltung bei Grey Walter, in *Kultur im Experiment,* ed. Henning Schmidgen, Peter Geimer (Berlin: Kadmos, 2004), 102–123; see also Rolf Pfeiffer, *Understanding Intelligence* (Cambridge, MA: The MIT Press, 2001); see also Rodney Brooks, *Cambrian Intelligence: The Early History of the New AI* (Cambridge, MA: The MIT Press, 1999).

26 See Andrew Pickering, "Raum: die letzte Grenze," in *Kunstkammer – Laboratorium – Bühne. Schauplätze des Wissens im 17. Jahrhundert,* ed. Helmar Schramm, Ludger Schwarte, and Jan Lazardzig (Berlin: De Gruyter, 2003), 1–9.

27 Jasia Reichardt, ed., *Cybernetic Serendipity: The Computer and the Arts,* exhib. catalogue, Institute of Contemporary Arts, London, August 2 to October 20, 1968 (London: Studio International, 1968).

28 A letter from Jasia Reichardt to Max Bense clearly shows that the focus of the exhibition was to be on cybernetics from the start: "We have been following in the footsteps of your original suggestions, and quite clearly cybernetics and computers are taking over." Letter from Jasia Reichardt to Max Bense, January 4, 1967, unpublished document, Max Bense Handschriften-Nachlass, Deutsches Literaturarchiv Marbach.

29 John Weeks, "Interdeterminate Dimensons in Architecture," in Reichardt, *Cybernetic Serendipity,* 69.

30 Ibid.

31 John Cage, "Composition as Process II: Indeterminacy," lecture on September 8, 1958, Darmstadt, in John Cage, in *Silence: Lectures and Writings* (Middletown, CT: Wesleyan University Press, 1961), 35–40.

32 Charles Jencks, *Architecture 2000: Predictions and Methods* (New York, NY: Praeger, 1971), 44.

33 Weeks, 69.

34 See Theodore G. Remer, ed., *Serendipity and the Three Princes* (Norman: University of Oklahoma Press, 1965); see also Royston M. Roberts, *Serendipity: Accidental Discoveries in Science* (New York, NY: Wiley, 1989).

35 "Exhibitions: Cybernetic Serendipity," *Time*, October 4, 1968, http://content. time.com/time/subscriber/article/0,33009,838821,00.html.

36 Gordon Pask, "The Colloquy of Mobiles," in Reichardt, *Cybernetic Serendipity*, 34–35.

37 Ibid., 35.

38 Ibid., 34.

39 Ibid.

40 Gordon Pask, "Fun Palace Project. Cybernetics Committee, Introductory Document, Circulation List and Basic Plans," unpublished manuscript, Gordon-Pask-Archiv, Institut für Zeitgeschichte, University of Vienna.

41 "Draft of Fun Palace Booklet," reprinted in Stanley Matthews, *From Agit-Prop to Free Space: The Architecture of Cedric Price* (London: Black Dog Publishing, 2007), 275.

42 Ibid.

43 Joan Littlewood, "A Laboratory of Fun," in *New Scientist*, no. 391 (May 14, 1964): 432.

44 Erika Fischer-Lichte, *Ästhetik des Performativen* (Frankfurt am Main: Suhrkamp, 2004), 29.

45 Ibid., 19 ff.

46 See *Theater seit den 60er Jahren: Grenzgänge der NeoAvantgarde*, ed. Erika Fischer-Lichte, Friedmann Kreuder, and Isabel Pflug (Tübingen: UTB, 1998).

47 Pask, "Fun Palace Project. Cybernetics Committee, Introductory Document."

48 Pask, "The Architectural Relevance of Cybernetics," 496.

49 The architect John Frazer, a student of Pask, went on to develop Pask's idea of evolutionary architecture. See John Frazer, *An Evolutionary Architecture* (London: Architectural Association, 1995); see also Georg Vrachliotis, "Der Sprung vom linearen ins kalkulatorische Bewusstsein: Evolutionäre Denkmodelle und Architektur," in *Precisions: Architektur zwischen Kunst und Wissenschaft*, ed. Ákos Moravánszky and Ole W. Fischer (Berlin: Jovis, 2008), 232–261.

50 Gordon Pask, "Organisational Plan as Programme," from the minutes of the Fun Palace Cybernetics Committee meeting, January 27, 1965, reprinted in Stanley Matthews, *From Agit-Prop to Free Space: The Architecture of Cedric Price*, 120.

51 Ibid.

52 Ibid.

53 Pask, "Fun Palace Project. Cybernetics Committee, Introductory Document."

Drawing Machines, Machine Drawings

1 Oswald Mathias Ungers and Peter Neitzke, "Das kann man nicht einem Maschinenprozess überlassen!," in *CAD: Architektur automatisch?*, ed. Walter Ehlers, Gernot Feldhusen, Carl Steckeweh (Braunschweig: Friedr. Vieweg & Sohn, 1986), 249.

2 Ibid., 251.

3 See Jasper Cepl, *Oswald Mathias Ungers: Eine intellektuelle Biographie* (Cologne: Walther König, 2007), particularly the chapters "1968. Zwischen Berlin und Cornell," 229–253 and "1969–1973. In Cornell," 253–299.

4 Horst Albach and Oswald Mathias Ungers, *Optimale Wohngebietsplanung*, vol. 1: *Analyse, Optimierung und Vergleich der Kostenstädtischer Wohngebiete* (Wiesbaden: Gabler, 1969). No further volumes were published.

5 Oswald Mathias Ungers, Tilman Heyde, and Tom Dimock, "Eine Serie von interaktiven Planungsprogrammen – SIPP," *Werk* 6 (1972): 347– 352.

6 Werner Oechslin, "Geometrie und Linie: Die Vitruvianische 'Wissenschaft' von der Architekturzeichnung," *Daidalos* 1 (1981): 20 ff.

7 See Vilém Flusser, "The Gesture of Writing," in *Gestures*, trans. Nancy Ann Roth (Minneapolis, MN: University of Minnesota Press, 2014), 19–25.

8 See Walter Koschatzky, *Die Kunst der Zeichnung: Technik, Geschichte, Meister-werke* (Munich: DTV, 1999); see also *Die Architekturzeichnung: Vom barocken Idealplan zur Axonometrie*, ed. Winfried Nerdinger and Florian Zimmermann (Munich: Prestel, 1985).

9 Ungers and Neitzke, 253.

10 See Theo Lutz, "Stochastische Texte," *Augenblick: Zeitschrift für Tendenz und Experiment* 4, no. 1 (1959): 3–9; see also *Konkrete Poesie International*, ed. Max Bense and Elisabeth Walther, Edition Rot, no. 21 (Stuttgart: Hansjörg Mayer, 1965).

11 "Computer Graphics and Architecture. Program Statement: On the Relevance of Computer Processes, Especially Computer Graphics, to Architecture," unpublished document, no author, no date, Warren McCulloch Archive, American Philosophical Society, Philadelphia, PA.

12 Walter Gropius, "Computers for Architectural Design," in *Architecture and the Computer: Proceedings of the First Boston Architectural Center Conference, Boston, Massachusetts, December 5, 1964 (Boston, MA: Boston Architectural College, 1964).*

13 The residential district Gropiusstadt [literally: Gropius City] was built in Berlin from 1962 to 1975. See *Gropiusstadt: Soziale Verhältnisse am Stadtrand. Soziolo-gische Untersuchung einer Berliner Grosssiedlung*, ed. Heidede Becker, Karl-Dieter Keim (Stuttgart: Kohlhammer, 1977).

14 H. Morse Payne, "Welcome," in *Architecture and the Computer,* 1.

15 Ibid.

16 Ibid.

17 Natalie Jaffe, "Architects Weigh Computers' Uses; 500 Conferees Receive Both Criticism and Comfort," *New York Times,* December 6, 1964.

18 Ibid.

19 Christopher Alexander, *Notes on the Synthesis of Form* (Cambridge, MA: Harvard University Press, 1964).

20 Christopher Alexander, "A Much Asked Question About Computers and Design," in *Architecture and the Computer,* 52.

21 Ibid.

22 Ibid., 53.

23 Ibid., 55.

24 Steven A. Coons, "Computer Aided Design," in *Computer Graphics in Architecture and Design: Proceedings of the Yale Conference on Graphics in Architecture held in New Haven, Connecticut, April 1968,* ed. Murray Milne (New Haven, CT: Yale School of Art and Architecture, 1969), 9, 26.

25 Ivan E. Sutherland, "Sketchpad: A Man–Machine Graphical Communication System," (1963) Technical Report No. 574, University of Cambridge Department of Computer Science and Technology, 2003, https://www.cl.cam.ac.uk/techreports/UCAM-CL-TR-574.pdf.

26 Ibid., 9.

27 Ibid., 18.

28 Douglas C. Engelbart, *Augmenting Human Intellect: A Conceptual Framework,* Summary Report AFOSR-3223 for Air Force Office of Scientific Research, Stanford Research Institute, Menlo Park, California, October 1962, http://www.dougengelbart.org/pubs/augment-3906.html.

29 Ibid.

30 Ibid.

31 Ibid.

32 Ibid.

33 Ibid.

34 See Marshall McLuhan and Quentin Fiore, *The Medium Is the Massage: An Inventory of Effects* (New York, NY: Bantam Books, 1967).

35 See Frieder Nake, "Informatik als Gestaltungswissenschaft: Eine Herausforderung an das Design," in *Algorithmik, Kunst, Semiotik: Hommage für Frieder Nake,* ed. Karl-Heinz Rödiger (Heidelberg: Synchron, 2003), 142–165.

36 See Christoph Klütsch, *Computergrafik: Ästhetische Experimente zwischen zwei Kulturen. Die Anfänge der Computerkunst in den 1960er Jahren* (Vienna: Springer, 2007); see also *Ex Machina – Frühe Computergrafik bis 1979,* ed. Wulf Herzo-

genrath and Barbara Nierhoff-Wielk, exhib. cat., Kunsthalle Bremen, June 17 to August 26, 2007 (Berlin: Deutscher Kunstverlag, 2007).

37 "Computer-Grafik: Weltpremiere der 'schöpferischen' Rechenmaschine in Stuttgart," *Stuttgarter Nachrichten*, November 20, 1965.

38 See Hans Dieter Heilige, "Zur Genese des informatischen Programmbegriffs: Begriffbildung, metaphorische Prozesse, Leitbilder und professionelle Kulturen," in Rödiger, *Algorithmik, Kunst, Semiotik*, 42–75.

39 Letter from Georg Nees to Max Bense, December 20, 1964, unpublished document, Max Bense Handschriften-Nachlass, Deutsches Literaturarchiv Marbach.

40 Lutz, 3.

41 "Computer-Grafik: Weltpremiere der 'schöpferischen' Rechenmaschine in Stuttgart."

42 Konrad Wachsmann, "Reason and Anti-Reason," Diogenes Forum University of Southern California, School of Philosophy, Los Angeles, April 26, 1965, unpublished lecture, Konrad-Wachsmann-Archiv, Akademie der Künste Berlin, 3 ff.

43 See Frieder Nake, "Nachahmung von Bildern Paul Klees," in *Ästhetik als Informationsverarbeitung. Grundlagen und Anwendungen der Informatik im Bereich ästhetischer Produktion und Kritik* (Vienna: Springer, 1974), 214–220.

44 Grüning, 159.

45 See Frieder Nake, "Künstliche Kunst: Zur Produktion von Computer-Grafiken," lecture held in Recklinghausen, 1966, in Ronge, *Kunst und Kybernetik*, 136.

46 Georg Trogemann, "Code und Maschine," *Code: Zwischen Operation und Narration*, ed. Andrea Gleiniger and Georg Vrachliotis (Basel: Birkhäuser, 2010), 41.

47 See Wolfgang Coy, "Aus der Vorgeschichte des Computers als Medium," in *Computer als Medium*, ed. Norbert Bolz, Friedrich A. Kittler, and Christoph Tholen (Munich: Wilhelm Fink, 1994), 19.

48 Trogemann, "Code und Maschine," 41.

49 Frieder Nake, letter to the author, May 5, 2008.

50 See Georg Trogemann and Jochen Viehoff, *CodeArt: Eine elementare Einführung in die Programmierung als künstlerische Praktik* (Vienna: Springer, 2004).

51 Bense, "Projekte generativer Ästhetik," in *Aesthetica*, 338.

52 Weeks, 69.

53 Döring, 84–85.

54 See Karl Gerstner, *Kalte Kunst: Zum Standort der heutigen Malerei* (Teufen: Niggli, 1957).

55 Karl Gerstner, *Programme entwerfen: Statt Lösungen für Aufgaben Programme für Lösungen* (1964), (Baden: Lars Müller, 2007).

56 Ibid., 8.

57 Ibid.

58 Ibid., 28.

59 Ibid.

60 See Eckhard Schulze-Fielitz, "Stadtbausysteme/Urban Systems," in *Eckhard Schulze-Fielitz, Metasprache des Raums/Metalanguage of Space*, ed. Wolfgang Fiel, trans. Peter Blakeney and Christine Scheffler (Vienna: Springer, 2010), 120–131.

61 In the second edition of his book *Programme entwerfen* (1968) Gerstner added a new chapter, "Programm as Computer-Graphik" [Program as computer graphic], which addressed four images from Frieder Nake's *Serie 20I*, which Nake created in 1966 at the Technical University of Stuttgart computer center. It is interesting to note how Gerstner introduced Nake: "The designer is per se a programmer." in Gerstner, *Programme entwerfen*, 21.

62 Gerstner, *Programme entwerfen*, 26–27.

63 See Peter Weibel and Margit Rosen, eds., *bit international. [Nove] tendencije – Computer und visuelle Forschung. Zagreb 1961–1973*, exhib. cat., Zentrum für Kunst und Medientechnologie Karlsruhe, February 23, 2008 to February 22, 2009 (Karlsruhe: ZKM | Zentrum für Kunst und Medientechnologie, 2007).

64 Margit Rosen, ed., *Bit International: A Little-Known Story About a Movement, a Magazine, and the Computer's Arrival in Art: New Tendencies and Bit International, 1961–1973* (Cambridge, MA: The MIT Press, 2010).

65 Weeks, 65.

66 See Rosen, 427–431; see also Leonardo Mosso, *Programmierte Architektur*, ed. Umbro Apollonio and Carlo Belloni (Milan: Studio di informazione estetica and Vanni Scheiwiller, 1969).

67 Rosen, 429.

68 "4004 entwirft Messestand: Computer als Mitarbeiter des Architekten," *Siemens Data Report* 4/70 (July 1970): 2–7; see also Ingeborg Rocker, "Berechneter Zufall: Max Benses Informationsästhetik," in *Kulturtechnik Entwerfen: Praktiken, Konzepte und Medien in Architektur und Design Science*, ed. Daniel Gethmann and Susanne Hauser (Bielefeld: transcript, 2009), 245–269.

69 Gropius, "Computers for Architectural Design?," 41–42.

70 Bense, "Projekte generativer Ästhetik," 338.

71 Frieder Nake, letter to the author, May 5, 2008.

Individualization Systems

1 "Panel Discussion: The Past and Future of Design by Computer," in Milne, *Computer Graphics in Architecture and Design*, 98.

2 Ibid.

3   Lewis Mumford, *The Myth of the Machine: Technics and Human Development* (New York, NY: Harcourt, 1967).

4   Lewis Mumford, *The Myth of the Machine: The Pentagon of Power* (New York, NY: Harcourt, 1970), 191.

5   "Panel Discussion," in Milne, *Computer Graphics in Architecture and Design,"* 100.

6   Ibid.

7   Frieder Nake, letter to the author, May 5, 2008.

8   Nicholas Negroponte, *Architecture Machine* (Cambridge, MA: The MIT Press, 1970); *Soft Architecture Machines* (Cambridge, MA: The MIT Press, 1975).

9   See Steve J. Heims, *John von Neumann and Norbert Wiener: From Mathematics to the Technologies of Life and Death* (Cambridge, MA: The MIT Press, 1980).

10 H.H. Goldstine and A. Goldstine (1946), "The Electronic Numerical Integrator and Computer (ENIAC)," in *The Origins of Digital Computers: Selected Papers,* 3rd edition, ed. B. Randell (Berlin: Springer, 1982), 359–375.

11 "The Research Laboratory of Electronics was probably the most exciting place in the world for anyone interested in communications. We were doing research on neurophysiology, we were studying electrical noise problems, we were doing coding, we were following Shannon's work on information theory […]. Out of this I acquired the idea from Norbert Wiener that we would understand both living system communications and machines better if we worked on them not necessarily together but in the same environment." Stewart Brand in conversation with Jerome Wiesner, "The Golden Age of Communication Science," in Stewart Brand, *The Media Lab: Inventing the Future at MIT* (New York, NY: Viking, 1987), 134.

12 See Lily E. Kay, "Von logischen Neuronen zu poetischen Verkörperungen des Geistes," trans. Andrea Stumpf, in Pias, *Cybernetics/Kybernetik,* vol. 2, 169–191; English original: "From Logical Neurons to Poetic Embodiments of Mind," *Science in Context* 14, no. 4 (2001): 591–614.

13 See Ute Bernhardt and Ingo Ruhmann, "Computer im Krieg: die elektronische Potenzmaschine," in Bolz et al., *Computer als Medium,* 183–209.

14 Lily E. Kay, *Who Wrote the Book of Life? A History of the Genetic Code* (Stanford, CA: Stanford University Press, 2002), 102.

15 Friedrich Kittler, "Rock Music: ein Missbrauch von Heeresgerät," in *Medien und Maschinen,* ed. Theo Elm and Hans H. Hiebel (Freiburg: Rombach, 1991), 253 f.

16 Alan Turing, "Computing Machinery and Intelligence," in *Mind* 59 (1950): 433–460.

17 John McCarthy, Marvin Minsky, Nathaniel Rochester, and Claude E. Shannon, "Proposal for Dartmouth Summer Research Project on Artificial Intelligence," August 13, 1955, reprinted in *AI Magazine,* 27/4 (2006), 12–14. For an influential

criticism see Joseph Weizenbaum, *Computer Power and Human Reason: From Judgment to Calculation* (New York, NY: W.H. Freeman and Company, 1976).

18 Nicholas Negroponte, *The Architecture Machine*, 11 ff.

19 Nicholas Negroponte, "URBAN5," in *The Architecture Machine*, 70–93.

20 Negroponte, *The Architecture Machine*, 119–121.

21 Ibid., 13.

22 Warren S. McCulloch, "Toward Some Circuitry of Ethical Robots or an Observational Science of Genesis of Social Evaluation in the Mind-Like Behavior of Artifacts" (1956), in Warren S. McCulloch, *Embodiments of Mind* (Cambridge, MA: The MIT Press, 2016), 217–226.

23 Nicholas Negroponte, "A Preface to a Preface," *The Architecture Machine* (no page number).

24 McCulloch, "Toward Some Circuitry of Ethical Robots," 218.

25 *Laboratory of Lighting Design. Progress Report No. 2,* internal report of the Massachusetts Institute of Technology Department of Architecture, July 15, 1954, unpublished document, Warren McCulloch Archive, American Philosophical Society, Philadelphia, PA.

26 Gordon Pask, "Aspects of Machine Intelligence," in Nicholas Negroponte, *Soft Architecture Machines*, 7–31.

27 Nicholas Negroponte, "A Preface to a Preface," *The Architecture Machine* (no page number).

28 Joseph C.R. Licklider, "Man-Computer Symbiosis," *IRE Transactions on Human Factors in Electronics* 1 (March 1960): 4–11.

29 Stewart Brand, review of *The Architecture Machine* by Nicholas Negroponte, in *The Last Whole Earth Catalog: Access to Tools*, 1971, 321. See also Georg Vrachliotis, "Whole Earth Catalog. Die Katalogisierung der Welt," in *Versuche das Glück im Garten zu finden*, ed. Franziska Bark-Hagen (Baden: Lars Mueller Publishers, 2011), 120–138.

30 The first issue had less than 100 pages and a print run of around a thousand copies. Just five years later, it had over 700 pages and a circulation of over a half a million. See Fred Turner, *From Counterculture to Cyberculture: Stewart Brand, the Whole Earth Network, and the Rise of Digital Utopianism* (Chicago, IL: University of Chicago Press, 2008).

31 Reyner Banham, "Alternative Network for the Alternative culture?," in *Design Participation Conference: Proceedings of the Design Research Society's Conference, Manchester, September 1971*, ed. Nigel Cross (London: Academy Editions, 1972), 15–18; see also Nicholas Negroponte, "Aspects of Living in an Architecture Machine," in ibid., 63–67; Yona Friedman, "Information Processes for Participatory Design," in ibid., 45–50.

32 See Dieter Schulz, *Amerikanischer Transzendentalismus: Ralph Waldo Emerson, Henry David Thoreau, Margaret Fuller* (Darmstadt: Wissenschaftliche Buchgesellschaft, 1997).

33 Banham, "Alternative Network," 18.

34 Stewart Brand, "We owe it all to the Hippies," in "*Welcome to Cyberspace*," special issue, *Time*, March 1, 1995, 54–56, http://content.time.com/time/subscriber/article/0,33009,982602,00.html.

35 Yona Friedman, "Ein Architektur-Versuch," in *Bauwelt* 48 (April 1957): 361.

36 See *Yona Friedman: Structures Serving the Unpredictable*, ed. Sabine Lebesque und Helene Fentener van Vlissingen, exhib. cat., Netherlands Architecture Institute Rotterdam, 1999 (Rotterdam: NAi Publishers, 1999).

37 See John Habraken, J.T. Boekholt, A.P. Thyssen, and P.J.M. Dinjens, *Variations: The Systematic Design of Supports* (Cambridge, MA: The MIT Press, 1976).

38 Ingo Bohning, *Autonome Architektur und partizipatorisches Bauen: Zwei Architekturkonzepte* (Zurich: Birkhäuser, 1980).

39 Max Bense, "Urbanismus und Semiotik," *Arch+* 3 (1968): 23–25.

40 Yona Friedman, "Computer-Aided Participatory Design," in Negroponte, *Soft Architecture Machines*, 93.

41 Yona Friedman, *Toward a Scientific Architecture* (Cambridge, MA: The MIT Press, 1975), 4.

42 Ibid., 6.

43 Ibid., 53.

44 Ibid., 57.

45 Nicholas Negroponte, foreword to Friedman, *Toward a Scientific Architecture* (no page number).

46 Nicholas Negroponte and Guy Weinzapfel, "Architecture-by-Yourself: An Experiment with Computer Graphics for House Design," *in SIGGRAPH '76. Proceedings of the 3rd Annual Conference on Computer Graphics and Interactive Techniques* (New York, NY: ACM Press, 1976), 74–78.

47 Ibid., 74.

48 Friedman, *Toward a Scientific Architecture*, 9.

49 Negroponte, *Soft Architecture Machines*, 1.

50 Ibid., 157.

51 Negroponte and Weinzapfel, "Architecture-by-Yourself," 78.

52 Yona Friedman, "About the Flatwriter" (1971) in *Pro Domo* (Barcelona: Actar, 2006), 137.

53 See Lucien Kroll, "Paysage," in *Lucien Kroll: Bauten und Projekte* (Stuttgart: Hatje, 1987), 138–141; see also Lucien Kroll, *CAD-Architektur: Vielfalt durch Partizipation* (Karlsruhe: C.F. Müller, 1985).

54 Abraham Moles, "Kybernetik, eine Revolution in der Stille," in *Enzyklopädie des technischen Jahrhunderts: Epoche Atom und Automation*, vol. 10 (Geneva: Kister, 1959), 7.

55 Ibid., 8.

56 Sybille Krämer, Operative Bildlichkeit: Von der 'Grammatologie' zu einer 'Diagrammatologie'? Reflexionen über erkennendes 'Sehen'," in *Logik des Bildlichen: Zur Kritik der ikonischen Vernunft*, ed. Martina Hessler and Dieter Mersch (Bielefeld: transcript, 2009), 94–123.

Epilogue: Return of the Material

1   Manfred Fassler, *Cyber-Moderne: Medienrevolution, globale Netzwerke und die Künste der Kommunikation* (Vienna: Springer, 1999).

2   Moles, "Die Kybernetik, eine Revolution in der Stille," 9.

3   Wolfgang Coy, "Zum Streit der Fakultäten: Kybernetik und Informatik als wissenschaftliche Disziplinen." In Pias, *Cybernetics/Kybernetik* vol. 2, 253–263.

4   Ibid., 258.

5   See Daniel Gethmann and Susanne Hauser, eds., *Kulturtechnik Entwerfen: Praktiken, Konzepte und Medien in Architektur und Design Science* (Bielefeld: transcript, 2009). See also the research group on Tools of Design/ *Werkzeuge des Entwerfen* at the International Research Institute for Cultural Technologies and Media Philosophy (IKKM) at Bauhaus University Weimar.

6   Lutz Dammbeck's exhibition *Re-reeducation* was at Galerie COMA in Berlin from May 29 to July 7, 2007.

7   See Jack Burnham, ed., *Software – Information Technology: Its New Meaning for Art*, exhib. cat., Jewish Museum, New York, New York, September 16 to November 8, 1970 (New York, NY: Jewish Museum, 1970)

8   Fabio Gramazio and Matthias Kohler, "Digital Materiality in Architecture: Bridging the Realms of the Virtual and Physical," in *Explorations in Architecture: Teaching, Design, Research*, ed. Reto Geiser (Basel: Birkhäuser, 2008), 179–199.

9   Nikolaus Kuhnert and Anh-Ling Ngo, "Entwerfen im digitalen Zeitalter," *Arch+* 189 (October 2008): 7.

10 Urs Leonard Hirschberg, Daniel Gethmann, Ingrid Böck, and Harald Kloft, eds. "GAM.06: Nonstandard Structures," *Graz Architecture Magazine* 6 (2010): 172–179.

11 Charles Jencks, *The Architecture of the Jumping Universe: A Polemic. How Complexity Science is Changing Architecture and Culture*. London: Academy Editions, 1995. German edition: "Eine Polemik: wie die Komplexitätstheorie Architektur und Kultur verändert," *Arch+* 141 (April 1998). See also Andrea Gleiniger and Georg Vrachliotis, eds., *Komplexität: Entwurfsstrategie und Weltbild* (Basel: Birkhäuser, 2008).

12 Winfried Nerdinger and Rainer Barthel, eds., *Wendepunkt(e) im Bauen: Von der seriellen zur digitalen Architektur*, exhib. cat., Architekturmuseum der Technischen Universität München, Pinakothek der Moderne, March 18 to June 13, 2010 (Munich: Detail, 2010), 176–179.

13 See Georg Vrachliotis and Fabian Scheurer, "Was die wollen sind Kathedralen zum Nulltarif: Ein Blick hinter die Kulissen der digitalen Architekturproduktion – Georg Vrachliotis im Gespräch mit Fabian Scheurer," in Hirschberg et al., "GAM.06: Nonstandard Structures," 206–216.

14 See Achim Menges and Jan Knippers, *Architecture Research Building: ICD/ITKE 2010–2020* (Basel: Birkhäuser, 2021).

15 Tobias Bonwetsch, Fabio Gramazio, and Matthias Kohler, "Digitales Handwerk," in Hirschberg et al., "GAM.06: Nonstandard Structures," 172–179.

16 Fabio Gramazio and Matthias Kohler, "Die digitale Materialität der Architektur," *Arch+* 198/199 (May 2010): 42–43.

17 See https://www.unglobalpulse.org.

18 See Timo Elliott, "7 Definitions of Big Data You Should Know About," July 5, 2013, http://timoelliott.com/blog/2013/07/7-definitions-of-big-data-you-should-know-about.html; see also Kenneth Cukier and Victor Mayer-Schönberger, *Big Data: Die Revolution, die unser Leben ändern wird* (Munich: Redline 2013).

19 Pulse Lab Jakarta, ed., *From Urban Data Collection to Urban Design: A Guide to Participatory Approaches around the Globe*, United Nations Report, 2017.

20 See Lisa Gitelman, ed., *Raw Data is an Oxymoron* (Cambridge, MA: The MIT Press, 2013).

21 See Orit Halpern, *Beautiful Data: A History of Vision and Reason Since 1945* (Durham, NC: Duke University Press, 2014); see also Steffen Mau, *Das Metrische Wir: Über die Quantifizierung des Sozialen* (Frankfurt am Main: Suhrkamp, 2017); see also Alex Pentland, *Social Physics: How Social Networks Can Make Us Smarter* (New York, NY: Penguin Books, 2015).

22 See Roberto Simanowski, *Data Love* (Berlin: Matthes & Seitz, 2014).

23 Trogemann, "Code und Maschine," 41.

24 Benjamin Bratton, *The Stack: On Software and Sovereignty* (Cambridge, MA: The MIT Press, 2016).

25 Ibid., 3.

26 Ibid., xviii.

References

"4004 entwirft Messestand: Computer als Mitarbeiter des Architekten." *Siemens Data Report* 4/70 (July 1970): 2–7.

Albach, Horst and Oswald Mathias Ungers. *Optimale Wohngebietsplanung*, vol. 1: *Analyse, Optimierung und Vergleich der Kostenstädtischer Wohngebiete.* Wiesbaden: Gabler, 1969.

Alexander, Christopher. "A Much Asked Question About Computers and Design." In Boston Architectural Center, *Architecture and the Computer*, 52–57.

Alexander, Christopher. *A Pattern Language: Towns, Buildings, Constructions.* New York, NY: Oxford University Press, 1977.

Alexander, Christopher. *Notes on the Synthesis of Form.* Cambridge, MA: Harvard University Press, 1964.

Allen, Edward, ed. *The Responsive House: Selected Papers and Discussions from the Shirt-Sleeve Session in Responsive Housebuilding Technologies Held at the Department of Architecture, Massachusetts Institute of Technology, Cambridge, Massachusetts, May 3–5, 1972.* Cambridge, MA: MIT Press, 1974.

Anders, Günter. *Die Antiquiertheit des Menschen*, vol. 1: *Über die Seele im Zeitalter der zweiten industriellen Revolution.* Munich: C.H. Beck, 1956.

Anders, Günter. *Die Antiquiertheit des Menschen*, vol. 2: *Über die Zerstörung des Lebens im Zeitalter der dritten industriellen Revolution.* Munich: C.H. Beck, 1980.

Apollonio, Umbro and Carlo Belloni, eds. *Leonardo Mosso: Programmierte Architektur.* Milan: Studio di informazione estetica and Vanni Scheiwiller, 1969.

"Architektur und technisches Denken / Architecture and Technical Thinking" *Daidalos* 18, December 1985.

Arnheim, Rudolf. "Manfred Kiemle: Ästhetische Probleme der Architektur unter dem Aspekt der Informationsästhetik." *Journal of Aesthetics and Art Criticism* 28, no. 4 (1970): 551–552.

Ashby, W. Ross. *An Introduction to Cybernetics.* London: Chapman & Hall, 1956.

Ashby, W. Ross. *Design for a Brain: The Origin of Adaptive Behavior.* New York, NY: Wiley, 1952.

Auckenthaler, Kurt. *Architektur, Automation, Atom.* Wels: Oberösterreichischer Landesverlag, 1959.

Aumann, Philipp. *Mode und Methode: Die Kybernetik in der Bundesrepublik Deutschland.* Göttingen: Wallstein, 2009.

"Aus der Vitrine – Digital, Teil 7: László Moholy-Nagy: Licht-Raum-Modulator." Bauhaus Dessau. http://www.bauhaus.de/bauhaus1919/kunst/kunst_modulator.htm.

"Automation schafft Raum für Kultur: Max Bill sprach im Haus Industrieform." *Industriekurier*, March 9, 1957.

Baecker, Dirk. "Kommunikation." In *Ästhetische Grundbegriffe: Historisches Wörterbuch*, vol. 3, ed. Karlheinz Barck, Martin Fontius, Dieter Schlenstedt, Burkhart Steinwachs, and Friedrich Wolfzettel, 384–423. Stuttgart: J.B. Metzler, 2001.

Banham, Reyner. "A Clip-On Architecture." *Design Quarterly* 63, 1965.

Banham, Reyner. "Alternative Network for the Alternative Culture?" In Cross, *Design Participation Conference*, 15–18.

Banham, Reyner. *Megastructure: Urban Futures of the Past*. London: Thames & Hudson, 1976.

Banham, Reyner. *The New Brutalism: Ethic or Aesthetic?* London: The Architectural Press, 1966.

Becker, Heidede and Karl-Dieter Keim, eds. *Gropiusstadt: Soziale Verhältnisse am Stadtrand. Soziologische Untersuchung einer Berliner Grosssiedlung*. Stuttgart: Kohlhammer, 1977.

Beer, Stafford. *Cybernetics and Management*. London: English Universities Press, 1959.

Bense, Max. *Aesthetica: Einführung in die neue Aesthetik*. Baden-Baden: Agis, 1965.

Bense, Max. "Ästhetische Kommunikation." In *Semiotik: Allgemeine Theorie der Zeichen*. Baden-Baden: Agis, 1967, 18–25.

Bense, Max. *Brasilianische Intelligenz: Eine cartesianische Reflexion*. Wiesbaden: Limes, 1965.

Bense, Max. *Brazilian Mind* (1965). Edited by Georg Vrachliotis. Translated by Simon Cowper. Berlin: Spector Books, 2022 (forthcoming).

Bense, Max. *Einführung in die informationstheoretische Ästhetik*. Reinbek: Rowohlt, 1969.

Bense, Max. Foreword to *Denkmaschinen* by Louis Couffignal. Translated by Elisabeth Walther with Max Bense. Stuttgart: Klipper, 1955.

Bense, Max. "Kybernetik oder die Metatechnik einer Maschine" (1951). In Walther, *Max Bense: Ausgewählte Schriften*, vol. 2, 429–449.

Bense, Max. "Thesen über die Notwendigkeit der Ästhetik in der Architektur." *Deutsche Architekten- und Ingenieur-Zeitschrift* (1977).

Bense, Max. *Ungehorsam der Ideen: Abschliessender Traktat über Intelligenz und technische Welt* (1965). 2nd edition. Cologne: Kiepenheuer & Witsch, 1966.

Bense, Max. "Urbanismus und Semiotik." In "Urbanismus und Semiotik." *Arch+* 3 (1968): 23–25.

Bense, Max and Elisabeth Walther, eds. *Konkrete Poesie International.* Edition rot 21. Stuttgart: Hansjörg Mayer, 1965.

Bernhardt, Ute and Ingo Ruhmann. "Computer im Krieg: die elektronische Potenzmaschine." In Bolz, *Computer als Medium*, 183–209.

Bertaux, Pierre. *Mutation der Menschheit: Diagnosen und Prognosen.* Frankfurt am Main: Fischer, 1963.

Bill, Max. Letter to Walter Gropius, May 2, 1950. Walter Gropius Archive, Houghton Library, Harvard University, Cambridge, MA.

Birkhoff, George David. *Aesthetic Measure.* Cambridge, MA: Harvard University Press, 1933.

Bodenmann-Ritter, Clara. *Joseph Beuys: Jeder Mensch ist ein Künstler. Gespräche auf der documenta 5, 1972.* Frankfurt am Main: Ullstein, 1975.

Bohning, Ingo. *Autonome Architektur und partizipatorisches Bauen.* Zurich: Birkhäuser, 1980.

Bolz, Norbert, Friedrich A. Kittler, and Christoph Tholen, eds. *Computer als Medium.* Munich: Wilhelm Fink, 1994.

Bonwetsch, Tobias, Fabio Gramazio, and Matthias Kohler. "Digitales Handwerk." *GAM: Graz Architecture Magazine 6: Nonstandard Structures* (2010): 172–179.

Boston Architectural Center. *Architecture and the Computer: Proceedings of the First Boston Architectural Center Conference, Boston, Massachusetts, December 5, 1964.* Boston, MA: Boston Architectural College, 1964.

"Brainy Man Builds Better Brains," feature on Gordon Pask and his Musicolour machine. *Electronics Illustrated*, February 1960, 102–103.

Burnham, Jack, ed. *Software – Information Technology: Its New Meaning for Art.* Exhibition catalogue, Jewish Museum, New York, New York, September 16 to November 8, 1970. New York, NY: Jewish Museum, 1970.

Brake, Klaus. "Hochschuldidaktik und politische Realität in der Ausbildungs-reform der Architekten und Planer." In *Hochschuldidaktik und politische Realität*, seminar at ETH Zurich Department of Architecture, November 7 to 11, 1971, 162. Zurich: Architektura Publikationsladen, 1971.

Brand, Stewart. Review of *The Architecture Machine* by Nicholas Negroponte. *The Last Whole Earth Catalog: Access to Tools*, 1971, 321.

Brand, Stewart. *The Media Lab: Inventing the Future at MIT.* New York, NY: Viking, 1987.

Brand, Stewart. "We Owe It All to the Hippies." In "Welcome to Cyberspace." Special issue, *Time*, March 1, 1995, 54–56, http://content.time.com/time/subscriber/article/0,33009,982602,00.html.

Bratton, Benjamin. *The Stack: On Software and Sovereignty.* Cambridge, MA: MIT Press, 2016.

Brooks, Rodney. *Cambrian Intelligence: The Early History of the New AI.* Cambridge, MA: MIT Press, 1999.

"Bürolandschaften." In *Lexikon der Planung und Organisation,* edited by Hans Niewerth and Jürgen Schröder, 26. Quickborn: Schnelle, 1968.

Cage, John. "Composition as Process II: Indeterminacy." Lecture on September 8, 1958, Darmstadt. In *Silence: Lectures and Writings,* 35–40. Middletown, CT: Wesleyan University Press, 1961.

Cepl, Jasper. *Oswald Mathias Ungers: Eine intellektuelle Biographie.* Cologne: Walther König, 2007.

Chernikhov, Yakov – see Tschernichow, Jakow.

Cherry, Colin. *On Human Communication: A Review, a Survey, and a Criticism* (1957). 2nd edition. Cambridge, MA: MIT Press, 1966.

Claus, Jürgen. *Expansion der Kunst: Action, Environment, Kybernetik, Technik, Urbanistik.* Reinbek: Rowohlt, 1970.

"Computer-Grafik: Weltpremiere der 'schöpferischen' Rechenmaschine in Stuttgart," *Stuttgarter Nachrichten,* November 20, 1965.

"Computer Graphics and Architecture. Program Statement: On the Relevance of Computer Processes, Especially Computer Graphics, to Architecture." Unpublished document. Warren McCulloch Archive, American Philosophical Society, Philadelphia, PA.

Coons, Steven A. "Computer Aided Design," in Milne, *Computer Graphics in Architecture and Design,* 10–16.

Coy, Wolfgang. "Aus der Vorgeschichte des Computers als Medium." In Bolz, *Computer als Medium,* 19–39.

Coy, Wolfgang. "Zum Streit der Fakultäten: Kybernetik und Informatik als wissenschaftliche Disziplinen." In Pias, *Cybernetics / Kybernetik,* vol. 2, 253–263.

Cross, Nigel, ed. *Design Participation Conference: Proceedings of the Design Research Society's Conference, Manchester, September 1971.* London: Academy Editions, 1972.

Cukier, Kenneth and Victor Mayer-Schönberger. *Big Data: Die Revolution, die unser Leben ändern wird.* Munich: Redline 2013.

Curdes, Gerhard. *Die Abteilung Bauen an der HfG Ulm: Eine Reflexion zur Entwicklung, Lehre und Programmatik.* Ulm: Club Off ULM e.V., 2001.

Custer, W. and H. Imesch, eds. *Systemdenken: Dokumentation einer Vorlesungsreihe: Kurs ORL 1, 1972/1973.* Zurich: ETH Zurich Department of Architecture, 1974.

"Das wird ein unglaubliches Fest: Nicholas Schöffer über die programmierte Kunst der Zukunft." *Der Spiegel,* February 8, 1970, 152–159.

Die Abendzeitung. Berlin, special issue, June 7, 1967.

Döring, Wolfgang. *Perspektiven einer Architektur.* Frankfurt am Main: Suhrkamp, 1970.

Dotzler, Bernd, ed. *Futurum Exactum: Ausgewählte Schriften zur Kybernetik und Kommunikationstheorie.* Vienna: Springer, 2002.

Elliott, Timo. "7 Definitions of Big Data You Should Know About," July 5, 2013. http://timoelliott.com/blog/2013/07/7-definitions-of-big-data-you-should-know-about.html.

"Ende offen: Kunst und Antikunst." Panel discussion with Max Bense, Max Bill, Arnold Gehlen, and Joseph Beuys, Werner-von-Siemens School, Dusseldorf, February 6, 1970. Live broadcast for the television show *Wochenendforum* on Westdeutscher Rundfunk Köln.

Engelbart, Douglas C. *Augmenting Human Intellect: A Conceptual Framework.* Summary Report AFOSR-3223 for Air Force Office of Scientific Research, Stanford Research Institute, Menlo Park, California, October 1962. http://www.dougengelbart.org/pubs/augment-3906.html.

"Exhibitions: Cybernetic Serendipity," *Time,* October 4, 1968. http://content.time.com/time/subscriber/article/0,33009,838821,00.html.

Fassler, Manfred. *Cyber-Moderne: Medienrevolution, globale Netzwerke und die Künste der Kommunikation.* Vienna: Springer, 1999.

Fehl, Gerhard, Mark Fester, and Nikolaus Kuhnert, eds. *Planung und Information: Materialien zur Planungsforschung.* Gütersloh: Bertelsmann, 1972.

Feldhusen, Gernot. *Soziologie für Architekten: Wissenschaft in der Planungspraxis,* Stuttgart: Deutsche Verlags-Anstalt, 1975.

Fezer, Jesko. "Polit-Kybernetik." In "Radikale Architektur." *Arch+* 186/187 (2008): 96–106.

Fischer-Lichte, Erika, Friedemann Kreuder, and Isabel Pflug, eds. *Theater seit den 6oer Jahren: Grenzgänge der Neo-Avantgarde.* Tubingen: UTB, 1998.

Fischer-Lichte, Erika. *Ästhetik des Performativen.* Frankfurt am Main: Suhrkamp, 2004.

Flechtner, Hans-Joachim. *Grundbegriffe der Kybernetik: Eine Einführung.* 4th edition. Stuttgart: Wissenschaftliche Verlagsgesellschaft, 1969.

Flusser, Vilém. *Gesten: Versuch einer Phänomenologie.* Frankfurt am Main: Fischer, 1997.

Flusser, Vilém. *Gestures.* Translated by Nancy Ann Roth. Minneapolis, MN: University of Minnesota Press, 2014.

Forrester, Jay Wright. *Urban Dynamic.* Cambridge, MA: MIT Press, 1969.

Frank, Helmar. *Kybernetische Analysen subjektiver Sachverhalte.* Quickborn: Schnelle, 1964.

Frank, Helmar. "Informationspsychologie." In *Kybernetik: Brücke zwischen den Wissenschaften.* 5th and expanded edition, 259–273. Frankfurt am Main: Umschau, 1965.

Frank, Helmar and Herbert W. Franke, eds. *Ästhetische Information: Eine Einführung in die kybernetische Ästhetik.* Berlin: Institut für Kybernetik, 1997.

Frazer, John. *An Evolutionary Architecture*. London: Architectural Association, 1995.

Friedman, Yona. "Ein Architektur-Versuch." *Bauwelt* 48 (April 1957), 361–363.

Friedman, Yona. "Information Process for Participatory Design." In Cross, *Design Participation Conference*, 45–51.

Friedman, Yona. Introduction to "Computer-Aided Participatory Design." In Negroponte, *Soft Architecture Machines*, 92–97.

Friedman, Yona. *Pro Domo*. Barcelona: Actar, 2006.

Friedman, Yona. *Toward a Scientific Architecture*. Translated by Cynthia Lang. Cambridge, MA: MIT Press, 1975.

Galison, Peter. "War against the Center." *Grey Room* 4 (Summer 2001): 7–33.

Gerovitch, Slava. *From Newspeak to Cyberspeak: A History of Soviet Cybernetics*. Cambridge, MA: MIT Press, 2002.

Gerstner, Karl. *Kalte Kunst: Zum Standort der heutigen Malerei*. Teufen: Niggli, 1957.

Gerstner, Karl. *Programme entwerfen: Statt Lösungen für Aufgaben Programme für Lösungen* (1964). Baden: Lars Müller, 2007.

Gethman, Daniel and Susanne Hauser, eds. *Kulturtechnik Entwerfen: Praktiken, Konzepte und Medien in Architektur und Design Science*. Bielefeld: Transcript, 2009.

Giedion, Sigfried: *Architecture, You and Me: The Diary of a Development* (1956). Edited and translated by Jacqueline Tyrwhitt. Cambridge, MA: Harvard University Press, 1958.

Giedion, Sigfried: *Architektur und Gemeinschaft*. Hamburg: Rororo, 1956.

Giedion, Sigfried: *Mechanization Takes Command: A Contribution to Anonymous History*. New York, NY: Oxford University Press, 1948.

Giedion, Sigfried: *Space, Time and Architecture: The Growth of a New Tradition* (1967). 5th revised and enlarged edition. Cambridge, MA: Harvard University Press, 2008.

Gilbert, David. "The Youngest Legend in History: Cultures of Consumption and the Mythologies of Swinging London." *The London Journal* 31, no. 1 (July 2006): 1–14.

Gilbert, Herbert: *The Dream of the Factorymade House: Walter Gropius and Konrad Wachsmann*. Cambridge, MA: MIT Press, 1984.

Gitelman, Lisa, ed. *Raw Data is an Oxymoron*. Cambridge, MA: MIT Press, 2013.

Gleiniger, Andrea and Georg Vrachliotis, eds. *Komplexität: Entwurfsstrategie und Weltbild*. Basel: Birkhäuser, 2008.

Gnädi, Thomas. "Die Stadt als Verkehrs- und Kommunikationssystem." In *Anthologie zum Städtebau*, vol. 1.2, edited by Vittorio Magnago Lampugnani, Katia Frey, and Eliana Perotti, 1081–1161. Berlin: Gebr. Mann, 2008.

Goldstine H.H. and A Goldstine. "The Electronic Numerical Integrator and Computer (ENIAC)" (1946). In *The Origins of Digital Computers: Selected Papers*, 3rd edition, edited by B. Randell, 359–375. Berlin: Springer, 1982.

Gottschalk, Ottomar. *Flexible Verwaltungsbauten. Planung, Funktionen, Flächen, Ausbau, Einrichtung, Kosten, Beispiele.* Quickborn: Schnelle, 1968.

Gramazio, Fabio and Matthias Kohler. "Digital Materiality in Architecture: Bridging the Realms of the Virtual and Physical." In *Explorations in Architecture*, edited by Reto Geiser, 179–199. Basel: Birkhäuser, 2008.

Gramazio, Fabio and Matthias Kohler. "Die digitale Materialität der Architektur." In "Haus der Zukunft." *Arch+* 198/199 (May 2010): 42–43.

Grégoire, Herman and Abraham Moles. "Das Bild des modernen Menschen." In *Enzyklopädie des technischen Jahrhunderts: Epoche Atom und Automation*, vol. 10, 75–95. Geneva: Kister, 1959.

Grey, W. Walter. "Activity Patterns in the Human Brain." In Whyte, *Aspects of Form*, 179–196.

Grüning, Michael. *Der Wachsmann-Report: Auskünfte eines Architekten.* Berlin: Verlag der Nation, 1988.

Gugerli, David. "Kybernetisierung der Hochschule: Zur Genese des universitären Managements." In Hagner and Hörl, *Die Transformation des Humanen*, 414–439.

Habraken, John, J.T. Boekholt, A.P. Thyssen, and P.J.M. Dinjens. *Variations: The Systematic Design of Supports.* Cambridge, MA: MIT Press, 1976.

Hagner, Michael. "Bilder der Kybernetik: Diagramm und Anthropologie, Schaltung und Nervensystem." In *Konstruierte Sichtbarkeiten: Wissenschafts- und Technikbilder seit der frühen Neuzeit*, edited by Martina Hessler, 383–405. Munich: Wilhelm Fink, 2006.

Hagner, Michael. "Intellektuelle Wissenschaft, Hyperprofessionalismus und das Allgemeine." In *Wandel oder Niedergang? Die Rolle der Intellektuellen in der Wissensgesellschaft*, edited by Martin Carrier and Johannes Roggenhofer, 65–81. Bielefeld: Transcript, 2007.

Hagner, Michael. "Vom Aufstieg und Fall der Kybernetik als Universalwissenschaft." In Hagner and Hörl, *Die Transformation des Humanen*, 38–71.

Hagner, Michael and Erich Hörl, eds. *Die Transformation des Humanen: Beiträge zur Kulturgeschichte der Kybernetik.* Frankfurt am Main: Suhrkamp, 2008.

Hagner, Michael and Georg Vrachliotis. "Die Stadt als kybernetische Kommunikationsmaschine." In *Text & Stadt: Eine ideeengeschichtliche Analyse der Quellentexte zur Stadt und Städtebau des 18. bis frühen 20. Jahrhunderts*, edited by Vittorio Magnago Lampugnani, Katia Frey, and Eliana Perotti, 127–137. Berlin: Gebr. Mann, 2011.

Haller, Fritz. *Totale Stadt: ein Modell.* Olten: Walter, 1968.

Haller, Fritz. *Totale Stadt: ein globales Modell/Integral Urban: A Global Model.* Olten: Walter, 1975.

Halpern, Orit. *Beautiful Data: A History of Vision and Reason since 1945.* Durham, NC: Duke University Press, 2014.

Hamilton, Blair. "Pneumatic Structures, Cybernetics and Ecology." In Allen, *The Responsive House,* 236–247.

Haseloff, Otto Walter. *Kybernetik als soziale Tatsche: Anwendungsbereiche, Leistungsformen und Folgen für die industrielle Gesellschaft.* Hamburg: Decker, 1963.

Hecker, Michael: *Structurel – Structural: Einfluss "strukturalistischer" Theorien auf die Entwicklung architektonischer und städtebaulicher Ordnungs und Gestaltungssprinzipien in WestDeutschland im Zeitraum von 1959–1975.* PhD dissertation, University of Stuttgart Department of Architecture and Urban Planning, 2007.

Heilige, Hans Dieter. "Zur Genese des informatischen Programmbegriffs: Begriffsbildung, metaphorische Prozesse, Leitbilder und professionelle Kulturen." In Rödiger, *Algorithmik, Kunst, Semiotik,* 42–75.

Heims, Steve J. *John von Neumann and Norbert Wiener: From Mathematics to the Technologies of Life and Death.* Cambridge, MA: MIT Press, 1980.

Hein, Carola. "Trauma und Stadtplanung: Der Wiederaufbau von Tokio und Hiroshima nach dem Zweiten Weltkrieg." In *Stadt und Trauma: Annäherungen, Konzepte, Analysen,* edited by Bettina Fraisl and Monika Stromberger, 105–122. Würzburg: Königshausen & Neumann, 2004.

Herzogenrath, Wulf and Barbara Nierhoff-Wielk, eds. *Ex Machina: Frühe Computergrafik bis 1979.* Exhibition catalogue, Kunsthalle Bremen, June 17 to August 26, 2007. Berlin: Deutscher Kunstverlag, 2007.

Hilberseimer, Ludwig. *The Nature of Cities: Origin, Growth, and Decline, Pattern and Form, Planning Problems.* Chicago, IL: Paul Theobold & Co., 1955.

Hitchcock, Henry-Russell and Philip Johnson. *The International Style: Architecture since 1922.* New York, NY: W.W. Norton & Co, 1932.

Holschneider, Johannes. *Schlüsselbegriffe der Architektur und Stadtbaukunst: Eine Bedeutungsanalyse.* Quickborn: Schnelle, 1968.

Hörl, Erich. *Sacred Channels: The Archaic Illusion of Communication.* Translated by Nils F. Schott. Amsterdam: Amsterdam University Press, 2018.

"How U.S. Cities Can Prepare for Atomic War: MIT Professors Suggest a Bold Plan to Prevent Panic and Limit Destruction." *Life,* December 18, 1950, 77–86.

"Ideale Stadtkonzepte." In *Anthologie zum Städtebau,* vol. 1.1, edited by Vittorio Magnago Lampugnani, Katia Frey, and Eliana Perotti, 7–205. (Berlin: Gebr. Mann, 2008).

Isozaki, Arata. "Computer-Aided City." *Kenchiku Bunka* 310 (August 1972), 138–149.

Jaffe, Natalie. "Architects Weigh Computers' Uses; 500 Conferees Receive Both Criticism and Comfort." *New York Times,* December 6, 1964, 69.

Jencks, Charles. *Architecture 2000: Predictions and Methods*. New York, NY: Praeger, 1971.

Jencks, Charles. "Eine Polemik: wie die Komplexitätstheorie Architektur und Kultur verändert." In "Die Architektur des springenden Universums." *Arch+* 141 (April 1998).

Jencks, Charles. *Late-Modern Architecture*. New York, NY: Rizzoli, 1980.

Jencks, Charles. *The Architecture of the Jumping Universe: A Polemic. How Complexity Science is Changing Architecture and Culture*. London: Academy Editions, 1995.

Jewell, Edward Alden. "Modern Museum Opens 4 Displays." *New York Times*, February 6, 1946, 31.

Joedicke, Jürgen. *Architekturgeschichte des 20. Jahrhunderts: Von 1950 bis zur Gegenwart*. Stuttgart: Karl Krämer, 1979.

Joedicke, Jürgen. "Introductory Remark." In "Stadtplanung: Experimente und Utopien/Town-Planning: Experiments and Utopias." *Bauen + Wohnen* 21 (May 1967), 165.

Joedicke, Jürgen. "Phantasie und Phantastik in der modernen Architektur." In *Für eine lebendige Baukunst: Notizen und Kommentare*, 109–112. Stuttgart: Karl Krämer, 1965.

Kargon, Robert and Arthur P. Molella. "The City as Communications Net: Norbert Wiener, the Atomic Bomb, and Urban Dispersal." *Technology and Culture* 45, no. 4 (October 2004): 764–777.

Kawazoe, Noboru. "Material and Man" (1960). In *Anthologie zum Städtebau*, vol. 3, edited by Vittorio Magnago Lampugnani, Katia Frey, and Eliana Perotti, 230–232. Berlin: Gebr. Mann, 2005.

Kay, Lily E. *Das Buch des Lebens: Wer schrieb den genetischen Code?*. Translated by Gustav Rossler. Frankfurt am Main: Suhrkamp, 2005.

Kay, Lily E. *Who Wrote the Book of Life? A History of the Genetic Code*. Stanford, CA: Stanford University Press, 2002

Kay, Lily E. "Von logischen Neuronen zu poetischen Verkörperungen des Geistes." Translated by Andrea Stumpf. In Pias, *Cybernetics/Kybernetik*, vol. 2, 169–191.

Kay, Lily E. "From Logical Neurons to Poetic Embodiments of Mind: Warren S. McCulloch's Project in Neuroscience." *Science in Context* 14, no. 4 (2001): 591–614. doi: 10.1017/S0269889701000266.

Kiemle, Manfred. *Ästhetische Probleme der Architektur unter dem Aspekt der Informationsästhetik*. Quickborn: Schnelle, 1967.

Kittler, Friedrich. "Rock Music: ein Missbrauch von Heeresgerät." In *Medien und Maschinen: Literatur im technischen Zeitalter*, edited by Theo Elm and Hans H. Hiebel, 245–257. Freiburg: Rombach, 1991.

Klütsch, Christoph. *Computergrafik: Ästhetische Experimente zwischen zwei Kulturen. Die Anfänge der Computerkunst in den 1960er Jahren*. Vienna: Springer, 2007.

261

Koschatzky, Walter. *Die Kunst der Zeichnung: Technik, Geschichte, Meisterwerke.* Munich: DTV, 1999.

Krampen, Martin and Günther Hörmann. *Die Hochschule für Gestaltung Ulm: Anfänge eines Projekts der radikalen Moderne/The Ulm School of Design: Beginnings of a Project of Unyielding Modernity.* Berlin: Ernst & Sohn, 2003.

Krämer, Sybille. "Operative Bildlichkeit: Von der 'Grammatologie' zu einer 'Diagrammatologie'? Reflexionen über erkennendes 'Sehen'." In *Logik des Bildlichen: Zur Kritik der ikonischen Vernunft,* edited by Martina Hessler and Dieter Mersch, 94–123. Bielefeld: Transcript, 2009.

Kritische Universität, "Ziele und Organisation der kritischen Universität, in *Kritische Universität, Freie Studienorganisation der Studenten in Hoch- und Fachschulen von Westberlin, Programm und Verzeichnis der Studienveranstaltung im WS 1967/68,* 44 ff. http://infopartisan.net/archive/1967/266750.html.

Kroll, Lucien. *CAD-Architektur: Vielfalt durch Partizipation.* Karlsruhe: C.F. Müller, 1985.

Kroll, Lucien. *Lucien Kroll: Bauten und Projekte.* Stuttgart: Hatje, 1987.

Kuhnert, Nikolaus and Anh-Linh Ngo. "Entwerfen im digitalen Zeitalter." In "Entwurfsmuster: Raster, Typus, Pattern, Script, Algorithmus, Ornament." *Arch+* 189 (October 2008): 6–9.

Kultermann, Udo., ed. *Kenzo Tange 1946–1969: Architecture and Urban Design/ Architektur und Städtebau/Architecture et Urbanisme.* Zurich: Artemis, 1970.

Kurokawa, Kisho. "Capsule Declaration." *Space Design,* no. 3 (March 1969): 18.

Kurokawa, Kisho. *Metabolism in Architecture.* London: Studio Vista, 1977.

Laboratory of Lighting Design. Progress Report No. 2, internal report of the Massachusetts Institute of Technology Department of Architecture, July 15, 1954, unpublished document, Warren McCulloch Archive, American Philosophical Society, Philadelphia, PA.

Lang, Eberhard. *Zur Geschichte des Wortes Kybernetik: Beiheft zu Band 9 der Reihe Grundlagenstudien aus Kybernetik und Geisteswissenschaften.* Quickborn: Schnelle, 1968.

Lange, Barbara. "Soziale Plastik." In *Begriffslexikon zur zeitgenössischen Kunst,* edited by Hubertus Butin, 276. Cologne: Snoeck, 2002.

Lauritzen, Lauritz, ed. *Städtebau der Zukunft: Tendenzen, Prognosen, Utopien.* Dusseldorf: Econ, 1969.

Lebesque, Sabine and Helene Fentener van Vlissingen, eds. *Yona Friedman: Structures Serving the Unpredictable.* Exhibition catalogue, Netherlands Architecture Institute Rotterdam, 1999. Rotterdam: NAi Publishers, 1999.

Leitner, Angelika and Uwe Nitschke, eds. *The German Avant-Garde Film of the 1920s/Der Deutsche Avant-Garde Film der 20er Jahre,* 55 ff. Munich: Goethe-Institut, 1989.

Lévi-Strauss, Claude. *Structural Anthropology* (1958). Translated by Claire Jacobson and Brooke Grundfest Schoepf. New York, NY: Basic Books, 1963.

Licklider, Joseph C. R. "Man–Computer Symbiosis." *IRE Transactions on Human Factors in Electronics* 1 (March 1960): 4–11.

Lindinger, Herbert, ed. *Hochschule für Gestaltung Ulm: Die Moral der Gegenstände.* Berlin: Ernst & Sohn, 1987.

Littlewood, Joan. "A Laboratory of Fun." *New Scientist*, May 14, 1964, 432.

Lonsdale, Kathleen. Review of *Aspects of Form. Acta Crystallographica* 6, part 2 (1953): 224.

Lüchinger, Arnulf. *Strukturalismus in Architektur und Städtebau.* Stuttgart: Krämer, 1981.

Luhmann, Niklas. "Kybernetische Regelung." in *Zweckbegriff und Systemrationalität*, 107–114. Frankfurt am Main: Suhrkamp, 1977.

Lutz, Theo. "Stochastische Texte." *Augenblick: Zeitschrift für Tendenz und Experiment* 4, no. 1 (1959): 3–9.

Maldonado, Tomás. "Neue Entwicklungen in der Industrie und die Ausbildung des Produktgestalters." in *Ulm: Quarterly Bulletin of the Hochschule für Gestaltung Ulm* 2, (October 1958): 31.

Maldonado, Tomás. "Norbert Wiener heute in Ulm." Newspaper article, no title, no date. HfG-Archiv Ulm.

Martin, Reinhold. *The Organizational Complex. Architecture, Media, and Corporate Space.* Cambridge, MA: MIT Press, 2003.

Martin, Reinhold. "The Organizational Complex: Cybernetics, Space, Discourse." *Assemblage* 37 (December 1998): 102–127.

Matthews, Stanley. *From Agit-Prop to Free Space: The Architecture of Cedric Price.* London: Black Dog Publishing, 2007.

Mau, Steffen. *Das Metrische Wir: Über die Quantifizierung des Sozialen.* Frankfurt am Main: Suhrkamp, 2017.

McCarthy, John, Marvin Minsky, Nathaniel Rochester, and Claude E. Shannon. "Proposal for Dartmouth Summer Research Project on Artificial Intelligence, August 13, 1955." Reprint. *AI Magazine* 27, no. 4 (Winter 2006): 12–14.

McCulloch, Warren S. "Toward Some Circuitry of Ethical Robots or an Observational Science of Genesis of Social Evaluation in the MindLike Behavior of Artifacts." *Acta Bioetheoretica* 11 (1956), 147–156. Reprinted in Warren S. McCulloch, *Embodiments of Mind.* Cambridge, MA: MIT Press, 2016, 217–226.

McKinnon-Wood, Robin. "Early Machinations." *Systems Research* 10, no. 3 (1993): 129–132.

McLuhan, Marshall and Quentin Fiore. *The Medium Is the Massage: An Inventory of Effects.* New York, NY: Bantam Books, 1967.

Medina, Eden. "Designing Freedom, Regulating a Nation: Socialist Cybernetics in Allende's Chile." *Journal of Latin American Studies* 38, no. 3 (2006): 571–606.

Menges, Achim and Jan Knippers, *Architecture Research Building: ICD/ITKE 2010–2020*. Basel: Birkhäuser, 2021.

Milne, Murray, ed. *Computer Graphics in Architecture and Design: Proceedings of the Yale Conference on Graphics in Architecture Held in New Haven, Connecticut, April 1968*. New Haven, CT: Yale School of Art and Architecture, 1969.

Mindell, David. *Between Human and Machine: Feedback, Control, and Computing Before Cybernetics*. Baltimore, MD: Johns Hopkins University Press, 2002.

"Mit dem Latein am Ende: Spiegel-Serie über Krise und Zukunft der deutschen Hochschulen (Architekten)." *Der Spiegel,* September 8, 1969, 74–80.

Moffat, Isabelle. "A Horror of Abstract Thought: Postwar Britain and Hamilton's 1951, 'Growth and Form' Exhibition." *October* 94 (Fall 2000): 89–112.

Moholy-Nagy, László: "Zur Geschichte der kinetischen Plastik." In *Von Material zu Architektur*. facsimile of the 1st edition, 162–164. Berlin: Gebr. Mann, 2001.

Moles, Abraham. "Arbeitsgruppe 4 (2. und 3. Studienjahr Bauen): Gliederung der Aufgabenbereiche von Wohnung und Stadt." Unpublished document, 1965. HfG-Archiv Ulm.

Moles, Abraham. *Informationstheorie und ästhetische Wahrnehmung* (1958). Translated by H., B., & P. Ronge. Cologne: DuMont, 1971.

Moles, Abraham. "Kybernetik, eine Revolution in der Stille." In *Enzyklopädie des technischen Jahrhunderts: Epoche Atom und Automation,* vol. 10, 7–9. Geneva: Kister, 1959.

Mumford, Lewis. *The Myth of the Machine: Technics and Human Development*. New York, NY: Harcourt, 1967.

Mumford, Lewis. *The Myth of the Machine: The Pentagon of Power*. New York, NY: Harcourt, 1970.

Nake, Frieder: "Informatik als Gestaltungswissenschaft: Eine Herausforderung an das Design." In Rödiger, *Algorithmik, Kunst, Semiotik,* 142–165.

Nake, Frieder. "Künstliche Kunst: Zur Produktion von Computer-Grafiken." Lecture held in Recklinghausen, 1966. In Ronge, *Kunst und Kybernetik,* 128–139.

Nake, Frieder. "Nachahmung von Bildern Paul Klees." In *Ästhetik als Informationsverarbeitung. Grundlagen und Anwendungen der Informatik im Bereich ästhetischer Produktion und Kritik,* 214–220. Vienna: Springer, 1974.

Nake, Frieder. "Werk, Kunstwerk, Information, Zeichen: Achtzig Sätze für Elisabeth Walther." In *Kontinuum der Zeichen: Elisabeth Walther-Bense und die Semiotik,* edited by Karl Gfesser and Udo Bayer, 9–13. Stuttgart: J.B. Metzler, 2002.

Negroponte, Nicholas. "Aspects of Living in an Architecture Machine." In Cross, *Design Participation Conference,* 63–68.

Negroponte, Nicholas. "Concerning Responsive Architecture." In Allen, *The Responsive House,* 302–306.

Negroponte, Nicholas. Foreword to *Towards a Scientific Architecture* by Yona Friedman. Cambridge, MA: MIT Press, 1975.

Negroponte, Nicholas. *Soft Architecture Machine.* Cambridge, MA: MIT Press, 1975.

Negroponte, Nicholas. *The Architecture Machine: Toward a More Human Environment.* Cambridge, MA: MIT Press, 1970.

Negroponte, Nicholas and Guy Weinzapfel. "Architecture-by-Yourself: An Experiment with Computer Graphics for House Design," in *SIGGRAPH '76. Proceedings of the 3rd Annual Conference on Computer Graphics and Interactive Techniques,* 74–78. New York, NY: ACM Press, 1976.

Nerdinger, Winfried and Florian Zimmermann, eds. *Die Architekturzeichnung: Vom barocken Idealplan zur Axonometrie.* Munich: Prestel, 1985.

Nerdinger, Winfried and Rainer Barthel, eds. *Wendepunkt(e) im Bauen: Von der seriellen zur digitalen Architektur.* Exhibition catalogue, Architekturmuseum der Technischen Universität München, Pinakothek der Moderne, March 18 to June 13, 2010. Munich: Detail, 2010.

Oechslin, Werner. "Geometrie und Linie: Die Vitruvianische 'Wissenschaft' von der Architekturzeichnung." *Daidalos* 1 (1981): 20–35.

"Panel Discussion: The Past and Future of Design by Computer." In Milne, *Computer Graphics in Architecture and Design,* 98–106.

Pask, Gordon. "A Comment, a Case History and a Plan (1968)." In Reichardt, *Cybernetics, Art and Ideas,* 76–99.

Pask, Gordon. *An Approach to Cybernetics.* London: Hutchinson, 1961.

Pask, Gordon. "Aspects of Machine Intelligence." In Negroponte, *Soft Architecture Machines,* 7–31.

Pask, Gordon. *Conversation Theory: Applications in Education and Epistemology.* Amsterdam: Elsevier, 1976.

Pask, Gordon. "Fun Palace Project. Cybernetics Committee, Introductory Document, Circulation List and Basic Plans." Unpublished manuscript. Gordon-Pask-Archiv, Institut für Zeitgeschichte, University of Vienna.

Pask, Gordon. "Organisational Plan as Programme," from the minutes of the Fun Palace Cybernetics Committee meeting, January 27, 1965. Reprint. In Matthews, *From Agit-Prop to Free Space,* 120.

Pask, Gordon. "The Architectural Relevance of Cybernetics." In "Thinking About Architecture and Planning – A Question of Ways and Means," edited by Royston Landau, 494–496. Special issue, *Architectural Design,* September 1969.

Pask, Gordon. "The Colloquy of Mobiles." In Reichardt, *Cybernetic Serendipity: The Computer and the Arts,* 34–35.

Pehnt, Wolfgang. *Deutsche Architektur seit 1900*. Munich: Deutsche Verlags-Anstalt, 2005.

Pehnt, Wolfgang. "Was ist Brutalismus?" *Das Kunstwerk* 3 (1960): 19–27.

Pentland, Alex. *Social Physics: How Social Networks Can Make Us Smarter*. New York, NY: Penguin Books, 2015.

Pfeiffer, Günter. "Ist Kunst berechenbar? Max Bense und der Computer." *Frankfurter Allgemeine Zeitung*, February 17, 1968.

Pfeiffer, Rolf. *Understanding Intelligence*. Cambridge, MA: MIT Press, 2001.

Phol, Walfried: "Wie Architektur langweilig wird: Eine kritische Auseinandersetzung mit Manfred Kiemle, Ästhetische Probleme der Architektur unter dem Aspekt der Informationsästhetik." In *Architektur und Städtebau im 20. Jahrhundert*, vol. 1: *Kapitalistischer Städtebau. Architektur und Informationsästhetik*, edited by Joachim Petch, 201– 247. Berlin: Verlag für das Studium der Arbeiterbewegung, 1974.

Pias, Claus, ed. *Cybernetics: The MacyConferences 1946–1953, The Complete Transactions*. Zurich: Diaphanes, 2003.

Pias, Claus, ed. *Cybernetics / Kybernetik: The MacyConferences 1946–1953*, vol. 2: *Essays und Dokumente*. Zurich: Diaphanes, 2004.

Pias, Claus. "Hollerith 'Feathered Crystal': Art, Science, and Computing in the Era of Cybernetics." Translated by Peter Krapp. *Grey Room* 29 (Winter 2008): 110–134.

Pias, Claus. "Jenseits des Werkzeugs: Kybernetische Option der Architektur zwischen Informationsästhetik und Design Amplifier." In *Kulturtechnik Entwerfen: Praktiken, Konzepte und Medien in Architektur und Design Science*, edited by Daniel Gethmann and Susanne Hauser, 269–287. Bielefeld: Transcript, 2009.

Pias, Claus. "The Age of Cybernetics." In Pias, *Cybernetics*, 9–43.

Pias, Claus. "Unruhe und Steuerung: Zum utopischen Potential der Kybernetik." In *Die Unruhe der Kultur: Potentiale des Utopischen*, edited by Jörn Rüsen and Michael Fehr, 301–325. Weilerswist: Velbrück, 2004.

Pickering, Andrew. "Cybernetics and the Mangle: Ashby, Beer and Pask." *Social Studies of Science* 32 (2002): 413–437.

Pickering, Andrew. "Mit der Schildkröte gegen die Moderne: Gehirn, Technologie und Unterhaltung bei Grey Walter." In *Kultur im Experiment*, edited by Henning Schmidgen and Peter Geimer, 102–123. Berlin: Kadmos, 2004.

Pickering, Andrew. "Raum: die letzte Grenze." In *Kunstkammer – Laboratorium – Bühne: Schauplätze des Wissens im 17. Jahrhundert*, edited by Helmar Schramm, Ludger Schwarte, and Jan Lazardzig, 1–9. Berlin: De Gruyter, 2003.

Pickering, Andrew. *The Cybernetic Brain: Sketches of Another Future*. Chicago, IL: University of Chicago Press, 2010.

Picon, Antoine. "Architektur und Wissenschaft: Wissenschaftliche Exaktheit oder produktives Missverständnis?" In *Precisions: Architektur zwischen Wissenschaft und Kunst*, edited by Ákos Morávanszky and Ole W. Fischer, 48–81. Berlin: Jovis, 2008.

Rabinowitch, Eugen. "Civil Defense: The Long-Range View." In "Civil Defense Against Atomic Attack." Special issue, *Bulletin of the Atomic* 6, no. 8–9 (August/September 1950): 226–230.

Reichardt, Jasia, ed. *Cybernetic Serendipity: The Computer and the Arts*. Exhibition catalogue, Institute of Contemporary Arts, London, August 2 to October 20, 1968. London: Studio International, 1968.

Reichardt, Jasia. Letter from Jasia Reichardt to Max Bense, January 4, 1967. Unpublished document Max Bense Handschriften-Nachlass, Deutsches Literaturarchiv Marbach.

Remer, Theodore G., ed. *Serendipity and the Three Princes*. Norman, OK: University of Oklahoma Press, 1965.

Roberts, Royston M. *Serendipity: Accidental Discoveries in Science*. New York, NY: Wiley, 1989.

Rocker, Ingeborg. "Berechneter Zufall: Max Benses Informationsästhetik." In *Kulturtechnik Entwerfen: Praktiken, Konzepte und Medien in Architektur und Design Science*, edited by Daniel Gethmann and Susanne Hauser, 245–269. Bielefeld: Transcript, 2009.

Rodemeier, Peter. "Konrad Wachsmann – oder die Liebe zur Geometrie." In *Vom Sinn des Details: Zum Gesamtwerk von Konrad Wachsmann*, edited by Martina Schneider, 53–64. Cologne: Rudolf Müller, 1988.

Rödiger, Karl-Heinz, ed. *Algorithmik, Kunst, Semiotik: Hommage für Frieder Nake*. Heidelberg: Synchron, 2003.

Ronge, Hans, ed. *Kunst und Kybernetik: Ein Bericht über drei Kunsterziehertagungen – Recklinghausen 1965, 1966, 1967*. Cologne: DuMont Schauberg, 1968.

Rosen, Margit, ed. *Bit International: A Little-Known Story About a Movement, a Magazine, and the Computer's Arrival in Art: New Tendencies and Bit International, 1961–1973*. Cambridge, MA: MIT Press, 2010.

Schnelle, Eberhard. Foreword to *Flexible Verwaltungsbauten* by Ottomar Gottschalk, 14. Quickborn: Schnelle, 1963.

Schnelle, Eberhard and Alfons Wankum. *Architekt und Organisator: Methoden und Probleme der Bürohausplanung*. Quickborn: Schnelle, 1964.

Schulz, Dieter. *Amerikanischer Transzendentalismus: Ralph Waldo Emerson, Henry David Thoreau, Margaret Fuller*. Darmstadt: Wissenschaftliche Buchgesellschaft, 1997.

Schulze-Fielitz, Eckhard. "Stadtbausysteme / Urban Systems." In *Eckhard Schulze-Fielitz, Metasprache des Raums / Metalanguage of Space*. Edited by

Wolfgang Fiel, translated by Peter Blakeney & Christine Scheffler, 120–131. Vienna: Springer, 2010.

Schwarz, Hans-Peter. "Die Mythologie des Konstruktiven: Zerstreute Gedanken zur Naturgeschichte der Maschine." In *Vision der Moderne: Das Prinzip Konstruktion*, edited by Heinrich Klotz, 46–56. Exhibition catalogue, German Architecture Museum, Frankfurt am Main, June 6 to September 17, 1986. Munich: Prestel, 1986.

Segal, Jérome. "Kybernetik in der DDR: Dialektische Beziehungen." In Pias, *Cybernetics/Kybernetik*, vol. 2, 227–253.

Shanken, Edward. "Cybernetics and Art: Convergence in the 1960s." In *From Energy to Information: Representation in Science and Technology, Art, and Literature*, edited by Bruce Clarce and Linda Dalrymple Henderson, 255–279. Stanford, CA: Stanford University Press, 2002.

Siegel, Curt. *Strukturformen der modernen Architektur*. Munich: Callwey, 1960.

Simanowski, Roberto. *Data Love*. Berlin: Matthes & Seitz, 2014.

Spitz, René. *HfG Ulm: Der Blick hinter den Vordergrund. Die politische Geschichte der Hochschule für Gestaltung (1953–1968)*. Stuttgart: Edition Axel Menges, 2002.

Sutherland, Ivan E. *Sketchpad: A Man–Machine Graphical Communication System* (1963), Technical Report No. 574, University of Cambridge Department of Computer Science and Technology, 2003. http://www.cl.cam.ac.uk/techreports/UCAM-CL-TR-574.pdf.

Systemtechnik: Arbeits- und Unterrichtshilfsmittel zur Übung "System." Zurich: ETH Zurich Department of Architecture, 1972.

Tange, Kenzo. "A Plan for Tokyo, 1960." In Kultermann, *Kenzo Tange*, 114–149.

Tange, Kenzo. "Function, Structure and Symbol." In Kultermann, *Kenzo Tange*, 240–246.

Tange, Kenzo. "The Expo '70 Master Plan and Master Design." In Kultermann, *Kenzo Tange*, 282–299.

Taube, Mortimer. *Der Mythos der Denkmaschine: Kritische Betrachtungen zur Kybernetik*. Reinbek: Rowohlt, 1966.

Trogemann, Georg. "Code und Maschine." In *Code: Zwischen Operation und Narration*, edited by Andrea Gleiniger and Georg Vrachliotis, 41–53. Basel: Birkhäuser, 2010.

Trogemann Georg and Viehoff, Jochen: *CodeArt: Eine elementare Einführung in die Programmierung als künstlerische Praktik*. Vienna: Springer, 2004.

Tschernichow, Jakow. *Konstruktion der Architektur und Maschinenformen* (1931). Translated by N. A. Jepantschin. Basel: Birkhäuser, 1991.

Turing, Alan. "Computing Machinery and Intelligence." *Mind* 59, no. 236 (October 1950): 433–460.

Turner, Fred. *From Counterculture to Cyberculture: Stewart Brand, the Whole Earth Network, and the Rise of Digital Utopianism*. Chicago, IL: University of Chicago Press, 2006.

UN Global Pulse and Pulse Lab Jakarta, ed. *From Urban Data Collection to Urban Design: A Guide to Participatory Approaches around the Globe*. United Nations Report, 2017. https://www.unglobalpulse.org/.

Ungers, Oswald Mathias and Peter Neitzke. "Das kann man nicht einem Maschinenprozess überlassen! In *CAD: Architektur automatisch?* Edited by Walter Ehlers, Gernot Feldhusen, Carl Steckeweh, 247–254. Braunschweig: Friedr. Vieweg & Sohn, 1986.

Ungers, Oswald Mathias, Tilman Heyde, and Tom Dimock. "Eine Serie von interaktiven Planungsprogrammen – SIPP." *Werk* 6 (1972): 347–352.

Vrachliotis, Georg. "Der Sprung vom linearen ins kalkulatorische Bewusstsein: Evolutionäre Denkmodelle und Architektur." In *Precisions: Architektur zwischen Kunst und Wissenschaft*, edited by Ákos Moravánszky and Ole W. Fischer, 232–261. Berlin: Jovis, 2008.

Vrachliotis, Georg. "Whole Earth Catalog: Die Katalogisierung der Welt." In *Versuche das Glück im Garten zu finden*, edited by Franziska Bark-Hagen, 120–138. Baden: Lars Mueller Publishers, 2011.

Vrachliotis, Georg and Fabian Scheurer. "Was die wollen sind Kathedralen zum Nulltarif: Ein Blick hinter die Kulissen der digitalen Architekturproduktion." In "Nonstandard Structures." *GAM: Graz Architecture Magazine* 6 (2010): 206–216.

Wachsmann, Konrad. Lecture at the press conference for his book *Wendepunkt im Bauen*, Frankfurter Hof, Frankfurt am Main, October 13, 1959. Unpublished lecture. Konrad- Wachsmann-Archiv, Akademie der Künste Berlin.

Wachsmann, Konrad. "Modular Coordination and Planning." Hochschule für Gestaltung Ulm, August 12, 1955. Unpublished lecture. Konrad-Wachsmann-Archiv, Akademie der Künste Berlin.

Wachsmann, Konrad. "Reason and Anti-Reason." Diogenes Forum, University of Southern California, School of Philosophy, Los Angeles, April 26, 1965. Unpublished lecture. Konrad-Wachsmann- Archiv, Akademie der Künste Berlin.

Wachsmann, Konrad. "The Electrical Energy and the Machine as the Tool of Our Time." Hochschule für Gestaltung Ulm, August 19, 1955. Unpublished lecture. Konrad-Wachsmann-Archiv, Akademie der Künste Berlin.

Wachsmann, Konrad. "The Pedagogic Impact of Automation." No date, c. 1959, unpublished lecture. Konrad-Wachsmann-Archiv, Akademie der Künste Berlin.

Wachsmann, Konrad. *The Turning Point of Building: Structure and Design*. Translated by Thomas E. Burton. New York, NY: Reinhold, 1961.

Wachsmann, Konrad. *Wendepunkt im Bauen*, Wiesbaden 1959 (Reprint Dresden 1989).

Wachsmann, Konrad. "Zur Industrialisierung des Bauens." Technische Hochschule Stuttgart, June 28, 1956. Unpublished lecture. Konrad-Wachsmann-Archiv, Akademie der Künste Berlin.

Walther, Elisabeth. *Allgemeine Zeichenlehre: Einführung in die Grundlagen der Semiotik*. Stuttgart: Deutsche Verlags-Anstalt, 1974.

Walther, Elisabeth, ed. *Max Bense: Ausgewählte Schriften*, vol. 2: *Philosophie der Mathematik, Naturwissenschaft und Technik*. Stuttgart: J.B. Metzler, 1998.

Weaver, Warren and Claude E. Shannon. *The Mathematical Theory of Communication*, Urbana, IL: University of Illinois Press, 1949.

Weeks, John. "Indeterminate Dimensions in Architecture." In Reichardt, *Cybernetic Serendipity: The Computer and the Arts,* 69.

Weibel, Peter and Margit Rosen, eds. *bit international. [Nove] tendencije – Computer und visuelle Forschung. Zagreb 1961–1973*. Exhibition catalogue, Zentrum für Kunst und Medientechnologie Karlsruhe, February 23, 2008 to February 22, 2009. Karlsruhe: ZKM | Zentrum für Kunst und Medientechnologie, 2007.

Weizenbaum, Joseph. *Computer Power and Human Reason: From Judgment to Calculation*. New York, NY: W.H. Freeman and Company, 1976.

Wellesley-Miller, Sean. "Self-Organising Environments." In Cross, *Design Participation Conference*, 58–62.

Wentworth Thompson, D'Arcy. *On Growth and Form* (1917). Cambridge: University Press, 1952.

Wetzel, Roland, ed. *Le Mouvement: Vom Kino zur Kinetik*. Exhibition catalogue, Museum Tinguely, February 10 to May 16, 2010. Heidelberg: Kehrer, 2010.

"What the Scientists are saying." *Bulletin of the Atomic Scientists* 6, no. 3 (March 1950): 71–75.

Whyte, Lancelot, ed. *Aspects of Form: A Symposium on Form in Nature and Art*. London: Percy Lund Humphries, 1951.

Wiener, Norbert. *A Life in Cybernetics: Ex-Prodigy: My Childhood and Youth and I Am a Mathematician: The Later Life of a Prodigy*. Cambridge, MA: MIT Press, 2018.

Wiener, Norbert. "A Scientist Rebels" (1946). In *Norbert Wiener: Collected Works*, vol. 4, edited by Pesi Rustom Masani, 748. Cambridge, MA: MIT Press, 1986.

Wiener, Norbert. "Cybernetics." *Scientific American* 179, no. 5 (November 1948): 14–19.

Wiener, Norbert. *Cybernetics: Or Control and Communication in the Animal and the Machine* (1948). 2nd edition. Cambridge, MA: MIT Press, 1961.

Wiener, Norbert. *I am a Mathematician: The Later Life of a Prodigy*. Garden City, NY: Doubleday, 1956.

Wiener, Norbert. *Kybernetik: Regelung und Nachrichtenübertragung im Lebewesen und in der Maschine*. Dusseldorf: Econ, 1963.

Wiener, Norbert. *The Human Use of Human Beings: Cybernetics and Society* (1950). London: Free Association Books, 1989.